D1627477

MUSTANG
THE UNTOLD STORY
THE ALLISON-ENGINED MUSTANGS IN CONCEPTION, DEVELOPMENT AND COMBAT

MATTHEW WILLIS

With additional research, advice, assistance and editing by
Bob Sikkel

Published by Key Books
An imprint of Key Publishing Ltd
PO Box 100
Stamford
Lincs PE19 1XQ

www.keypublishing.com

ISBN 978 1 913295 88 2

20 21 22 23 24   10 9 8 7 6 5 4 3 2 1

Author's Note
All images are from the author's collection unless otherwise stated.

Typeset by SJmagic DESIGN SERVICES, India.

Contents

Acknowledgements

First, I would like to offer my profound thanks to Bob Sikkel. Any merit this book has is the result in no small part of his tireless efforts. Bob initially volunteered to edit the text of the first three chapters, but ended up providing information, research, documents, direction and support throughout various rewrites of the text. Perhaps more importantly, Bob comprehensively challenged the text and the author, mercilessly skewering errors and questioning the author's assumptions.

Many members of the P-51 Special Interest Group (SIG) helped with information, answering many questions patiently, and the information produced and made available by the SIG has also proved invaluable. Members who helped with the book include Charles Neely, Craig Quattlebaum, Colin Ford (the unofficial historian for No. 268 Squadron RAF), Michael Vorrasi (RIP), Michael Scalingi, Christian Alamy and Lieutenant Colonel Mike Gleichman USAFR (retired).

The P-51 Mustang Group on Facebook similarly provided a valuable resource and sounding board, and members who helped particularly include Tom Griffiths, James William Marshall and Chris Fahey. Others who kindly assisted include Edgar Brookes (RIP) and Graham Boak.

Many individuals and institutions made photographs and illustrations available, including Stephen Fryer of the Harrowbeer Interest Group, Adrian Balch, Richard Howes and the Pye Telecom Historic Collection, Wojtek Matusiak, Warbird Depot, Jim Buckel, Mike Gleichman, Mark Watt, Doug Gordon and Doug Fisher.

I offer my deepest thanks to Second Lieutenant Grahm Nordlund, US Army, who provided wonderful information and photographs from the career of his grandfather, First Lieutenant Maurice Nordlund of the 111th Tactical Reconnaissance Squadron. Lieutenant Nordlund, an Army Boeing Apache pilot, is very much the inheritor of the Allison Mustang pilots' tradition, given the strong association between that aircraft and army support. The Allison Mustang was predominantly used in support of army forces in one way or another, so it is particularly appropriate that Lieutenant Nordlund has provided a heartfelt foreword to the text.

To anyone I have omitted, I apologise profusely.

Foreword

When the young pilots of those magnificent machines donned their flight gear, buckled their harnesses and ran up their engines, no one knew for sure if they were coming back.

Too many times, a lock would have to be broken off the foot-locker belonging to what we would today call a 'fallen angel', their belongings sorted and shipped to their next of kin. A youthful life so vibrant and exciting, full of cherished memories captured in yellow-faded photographs, perfume-soaked love letters and sentiments, all rendered frozen in time in just seconds, with the uncertain news of a fellow airman's passing. No one would truly know how he passed, if he suffered or went quickly; they would only remember his face at breakfast that morning...

Still, these men, many of whom were not yet able to buy a beer or even hold a driver's licence, raised their hand time and again for high-risk missions in which there was no guarantee whatsoever of their own safety. They did it not for decoration or praise; they did it for each other, for the guys on the ground. They did it while in the close presence of a fierce and far more experienced enemy. Most of all, they did it with pride. The pilots of the Air Corps always held a very strict level of integrity and a keen sense of ownership in their duty; a trait that is still visible in army aviation today.

Though the pilots of this incredible generation slowly leave us, we bear in our own hearts the selflessness and sacrifice that they, through their actions, so gallantly displayed to the world. We are still here, strong in heart and tradition, willing, no matter the cost, to protect those boys on the ground.

Second Lieutenant Grahm Nordlund, 1st Battalion of the 227th Aviation Regiment, grandson of First Lieutenant Maurice Nordlund DFC, 111th Tactical Reconnaissance Squadron, 68th Reconnaissance Group

First Lieutenant Maurice Nordlund of the 111th TRS 'Snoopers' with his P-51 in Italy, 1943. (Grahm Nordlund)

Introduction

An Untold Story?

The North American Mustang is one of the most well-known and well-studied of aircraft, the subject of many hundreds, probably thousands, of books and articles. How could there possibly be an untold story left within that vast library?

When the project began, seeking to write an overview of the Allison-engined Mustang variants, it seemed a straightforward matter. Once research began in earnest, however, it became clear that it would not be a simple case of recounting the history of the type. The question arose – which history?

It was quickly found that much of what was commonly understood about the Allison Mustang variants was neither entirely correct, nor entirely complete. The published record was strewn with myths and misconceptions, many arising from the period immediately after the Second World War, or even during it, when primary sources were restricted or unavailable. Some of the oft-repeated suggestions about the type arose out of the agendas of individuals and organisations with one eye on their legacy. Others grew through misconceptions and misunderstandings by those who were there at the time and which they put forward in good faith. Many of these ideas persist, despite valiant efforts by some authors to correct the record.

It is hard to ignore the common perception of the Allison Mustangs (particularly in the UK) as merely a prelude to the 'definitive' Merlin-engined versions. Nor the notion that these early members of the famous fighter family were, to put it bluntly, not very good. For many, the Mustang story starts when Rolls-Royce test pilot Ronald Harker took an RAF Mustang Mk I for a spin while visiting a testing establishment, and his realisation that with a new two-stage supercharged Merlin 60 series, the Mustang could be not just good but superlative. This narrative completely ignores the facts of the Allison Mustangs' contribution in service, and effectively rewrites the debate that was already being held over the Mustang's strengths and weaknesses.

Underlying that perception was a series of smaller-scale but equally significant misperceptions and myths. That the United States Army Air Forces (USAAF) was not interested in the Mustang at first. That the attack-specialist A-36A was developed in that form to get around purchasing limits. A widespread misunderstanding around the specific variants of Allison Mustang and the sequence they appeared in. Even the names applied to the aircraft are the subject of considerable confusion.

In the event, it became necessary to start from first principles, and this began to reap some interesting results. By placing the development, evolution, use and retirement of the aircraft in as full a context as possible, the truth behind many of these commonly accepted ideas began to emerge. The author – aided, guided and encouraged by Bob Sikkel – looked at the history of the aircraft within the orbit of tactical doctrine, strategy, even politics as well as the changing nature of the war as the Mustang crews were fighting it. Only through viewing the early variants of the Mustang through this prism can the story of its creation and evolution be truly understood.

The approach taken was to make an extensive study of primary sources and re-evaluate material in published sources, from both sides of the Atlantic. Contemporary documents relating to the procurement, development and employment of the type were examined, particularly in light of the 'cross pollination' of technical and tactical information between British and American users. It should be stated here clearly that there are occasions when it was felt to be appropriate to apply deduction, or even a degree of speculation to reach a conclusion where the available evidence was unclear. Where this is done, it is only in cases where it benefits the narrative, and is explicitly pointed out. Readers should be free to make up their own minds about our conclusions.

This is not to say that there have not been many fine works of history doing justice to aspects of the Allison Mustang story. New knowledge is emerging all the time, continuing to add to the Mustang story and adjust some of the erroneous thinking that has persisted. Neither is it claimed that this book is in any way a definitive study of the Allison Mustang – it is doubtful that such a thing is possible. There is no doubt that there will be slips and mistakes and even unwitting repetition of myths that have snuck through despite the best efforts of the author and which are solely his responsibility.

It is only hoped that the text that follows will add to the library of Mustang knowledge in a constructive way, restore some of the esteem that the aircraft and the people who made it a reality and a success are due and encourage more study of the Allison-engined Mustangs in their own right.

Chapter 1

The Path to the Mustang

Background and Genesis, 1937–40

It is difficult to state with absolute authority when the first idea that sparked the creation of the Mustang took place. Most new military aircraft come into being through a clean-sheet design in response to a specific requirement. This was not quite how it happened in the case of the Mustang.

In the mid-1930s, the British and French governments had begun to consider how to ensure their countries would have enough aircraft and manufacturing capacity for the major European war that was becoming ever more likely. The British rearmament plans developed through 1936 and 1937 called for a tripling of available first-line aircraft. In 1938, an additional focus was placed on fighter defences, with an increase from the planned 30 'Metropolitan' fighter squadrons to 38, with a further two overseas.[1]

Furthermore, moves were made to develop Canada's aviation industry and also to explore the considerable potential offered by the United States of America. A mission 'to investigate the possibilities of making use of the American aircraft industry' was dispatched to the US by the British government in 1938. A similar mission from France had also made approaches to America. Following discussions between the British and French governments in April 1938, the two missions began to work much more closely together. [2]

In 1938 and at the beginning of 1939, Britain did not consider it desirable to order fighter aircraft from the US. The British government was unimpressed with the quality of American first-line aircraft available at the time and felt that the cost was high.[i]

France, however, needed to supplement its home-grown fighter rearmament with purchases overseas, until its under-developed industry could catch up. During 1938, the French government ordered 100 Curtiss Model 75 fighters[ii] (the export version of the P-36) – it came as something of a surprise to the French government that it had been allowed to do so.[3] This was in fact indicative of changing attitudes in US circles. Indeed, the War Department and Army Air Corps (AAC) were not insensible to both the gathering war clouds in Europe and the need for US aircraft to compete with the best from European industries.

On the outbreak of war, a further British mission was developed into a full 'British Purchasing Commission' (BPC) under Arthur Purvis. The British Air Commission (BAC) under Sir Henry Self was set up within the broader Purchasing Commission to concentrate on aircraft and other aviation-related materiel.

By this time, Britain and France were concerned not just with the purchase of materiel to boost their immediate rearmament, but that the US industrial base would continue to meet their ongoing needs as the war progressed. On 1 August 1939, Lord Riverdale had been informed of the spare capacity in the aircraft industry in America and the extent to which it might be expected to expand in the coming years.[4] There was evidently a great deal of scope for harnessing this excess capacity and turning it to the Allies' needs. The opportunity would not last forever though, especially if America entered the war itself. Placing large orders with US companies would help cement this process and ensure in advance that British and French requirements

---

i 'The Chancellor of the Exchequer recollected that the mission sent to America in 1938 had reported, first, that American machines were not very good and, secondly, that they were expensive. Remarking that the French had a smaller Air Force than ourselves, but more gold, he suggested that it would be more appropriate for them than for us to buy American aircraft.' CAB 65/4/6 '74th Conclusions, Minute 3 Confidential Annex' 7 November, 1939.

ii Its original intention had been to purchase up to 150. The first order was for 100, followed by a second order for 100 finalised the following year.

were not crowded out. Therefore both governments worked hard to secure orders of aircraft and engines that were then only in the planning stages.

The American government had proved unexpectedly amenable to the approaches of the British and French governments, despite the existence of legislation designed to protect US neutrality. Riverdale had remarked during his 1939 mission that his contacts at the War Department were 'anxious to help us in every possible way'. Some within the US government recognised that the country might be drawn into war, and were determined to build the country's air forces up to the most modern, effective standards possible.

A Need for Fighters

The British government's mood with regard to fighters began to change when hostilities began. In particular, the vulnerability of British aircraft manufacturing to aerial bombardment was a cause for concern. Of most concern was the fact that the Rolls-Royce engines used by all the UK's most modern fighters were constructed in only two factories. American aircraft provided some insurance against Britain's fighter or aero-engine construction capability being completely wiped out. While it later proved unrealistic, fears of an overwhelming 'knockout blow' from long-range bombers persisted for some time after the outbreak of war. The British government was therefore keen to secure fighters that could be useful into 1941, though the BPC still regarded American military aircraft then in service as 'obsolete, and unsuitable for European conditions'.[5]

The US government had a policy dictating which aircraft and related items of hardware could be released to the export market[iii] and updated this in March 1940 (by which time embargo concerns had been eased by the allowance of 'cash & carry') – this permitted existing machinery to be exported to Britain and France, on the understanding that the exporting manufacturers' most advanced types under development would be initially reserved for the US air forces. Britain and France would in effect be subsidising development of new types for the USAAF.

---

iii   This document was termed 'Outline of policy of the War and Navy Departments for the release of aircraft, aircraft engines, and items of aircraft equipment and accessories for export and domestic sale and for the release of information and data pertinent to articles on which release is required', originally established on June 13, 1938.

The position with regard to fighters became even more acute for both Britain and France in May 1940, when the 'Blitzkrieg' attack on France began. Suddenly, France was fighting for its life, and Britain faced the very real possibility of its most powerful ally being knocked out of the war within a very short space of time. The defeat of France would put most of the UK's industrial centres within range of German bombers, crucially, with fighter escort. This eventuality had not been seriously planned for at so early a stage in the war. Furthermore, the British and French governments had established collaborative plans regarding the supply of aircraft equipment and weapons that were thrown into disarray following the invasion and rapid German advance.[iv] All of Britain's carefully-constructed pre-war rearmament plans were about to be rendered obsolete.

At this point, the War Cabinet became desperate to secure every last fighter as quickly as it could, even obsolescent designs. On 11 May, the Secretary of State for Foreign Affairs suggested that the British government ask the US authorities to provide aircraft at once from their own existing stock, on the understanding that these would be replaced from the orders which had already been placed with manufacturers in the United States.[v]

The situation remained parlous. It was estimated that an additional 12 fighter squadrons would be needed as soon as possible, while losses in France had proved much higher than anticipated – to maintain serviceability, all salvageable components and instruments had to be reclaimed from crashed aircraft wherever possible.

North American Enters the Frame

Despite British concerns over the quality of US frontline aircraft in 1938 and 1939, with expansion under way, one area where the UK urgently needed more aircraft was for training. Potential obsolescence was less

---

iv These included a joint scheme for purchase and licence-manufacture of the Belgian FN Browning 0.50in machine gun, manufacturing of British aircraft instruments in France, supply of fuel-tank lining material in both directions (French 'Mousse' rubber to the UK and British 'Linatex' to France), and supply of Rolls-Royce Merlin engines for French Amiot bombers – indeed, despite the British government's best efforts to recover them, 130 Merlins were left in France when it was overrun.

v This was discussed at Cabinet on 11 May 1940 (see CAB 65/7/13) and the BPC was approached with the suggestion.

critical with training aircraft than with combat aircraft, so large orders were placed in 1938 and 1939, including one for 200 Harvard Mk Is from the North American Aviation company (NAA) in June 1938. This served as a very useful introduction between the BPC and NAA and was, along with a purchase of Lockheed Hudsons, the first British order for American aircraft in quantity.

As the need for fighters became acute in early 1940, the only existing US fighter that looked like it might be competitive the following year was the Curtiss Model 81, designated the P-40 in US Army service. This was a development of the radial-engined P-36 (Model 75), mating a new liquid-cooled Allison engine to the 1934-vintage airframe with relatively few changes. The prototype XP-40 had first flown in 1938, by which time it had already been ordered by France, but the first production machine did not fly until April 1940.

In addition, Curtiss was known to be planning a promising new fighter, the Model 86, designated the P-46 by the US Army, which had been ordered in prototype form in September 1939. Curtiss had conceived the Model 86 as a successor to the P-40, which was something of a stop-gap in any case. The Model 86 was intended to be a significant, albeit evolutionary, step from the P-40 – smaller, neater and more aerodynamically refined by taking advantage of the smaller frontal area of a liquid-cooled inline engine, a new version of the Allison V-1710, the F-series. Reflecting European practice, self-sealing fuel tanks and armour were designed in from the start.

The F-model Allison (developed in parallel with the E-model for the mid-engined Bell P-39), was a new 1,150hp version of the V-1710 with a spur reduction gear. This feature allowed a more compact installation and slightly lower frontal area, while also reducing weight. The new reduction gear was capable of handling more power than the existing C-model's epicyclic gear. The first large production order for Allison engines was made in late June 1939. This included a 'sea-level' variant, the F2R/L[vi], for pre-production Lockheed YP-38s. Five 'altitude-rated' F3R engines were

---

vi The L or R suffix on Allison engines indicated in which direction they rotated. Most of these for single-engined types were of the 'R' sub-type, but twin-engined aircraft such as the P-38 sometimes had 'handed' engines.

ordered in January 1940 – two each for the XP-46 and Republic's XP-47, and one to perform the model proving-trial.

The BAC expressed interest in orders for the export versions of the Model 81 and the Model 86, which were released for export following negotiations between the various governments. Britain and France had by this time merged their purchasing commissions and in April 1940 placed orders for 1,440 fighters from Curtiss, initially made up of 480 Model 81s (which would become known as Tomahawks in British service) and 960 of the as-yet unflown Model 86s.[vii]

Furthermore, the BAC had made approaches to see if further production of the P-46 could be arranged. One company that this was put to was NAA. The California-based manufacturer had made a name for itself building training aircraft and was in the process of developing a modern bomber; though it had no experience with state-of-the-art fighter aircraft. Britain had, however, a good working relationship with NAA, having already ordered considerable numbers of Harvard trainers as mentioned above.

Shortly after the Air Commission under Self arrived in the US on 4 March 1940, James H. 'Dutch' Kindelberger, the president and general manager of NAA, was approached to see if the company could build Curtiss Model 86 fighters for Britain under licence.[viii]

Kindelberger famously discussed this with NAA's chief designer, Edgar Schmued, and rapidly decided to offer the BAC something different. According to Schmued, NAA 'desperately wanted to build a fighter'.[6] Schmued and Kindelberger were evidently determined that this fighter would not be somebody else's design…[ix]

---

vii   The breakdown of the 1,440 Curtiss fighters was revised in May to 600 Model 81s and 840 Model 86s. Later, Britain took over French orders, and the Model 87 (Kittyhawk) replaced the Model 86, leading to further confusion concerning the April 1940 order.

viii It is not entirely clear when this approach was made, and a number of dates from late 1939 to early March 1940 have been cited. However, the Commission's priorities were not established until 16 February, and it did not arrive in the US until 4 March. The NAA internal specification for the fighter that would become the Mustang had been drawn up by 15 March.

ix   For a detailed account of the genesis and development of the Mustang, see Chapter 3 of Ray Wagner's biography of Edgar Schmued, *Mustang Designer*, Smithsonian Books, 1996.

Edgar Schmued, chief design engineer at North American Aviation and creator of the Mustang, standing (rather awkwardly) on the wing of an early Mustang (NA-73, NA-83 or NA-91) in a photograph dated July 1942 when the type had only been in front-line service for a few months.

A proposal was therefore drawn up for an aircraft that NAA insisted would be at least as good as the P-46. J. Leland Atwood, NAA's chief engineer and executive, recalled that the basic proposal, incorporating certain innovative aerodynamic features, was quickly answered with a letter of intent. The BAC also stipulated that each completed aircraft should cost no more than $40,000.[7]

The British authorities nevertheless required assurance of NAA's ability to make good on its promises. In May 1940, the BAC/BPC noted that the specification and performance schedules of the NAA design would have to be compared with that of the P-46 to ensure that the aircraft was 'in general conformance' with the Curtiss type. North American was in fact persuaded to purchase design, aerodynamic and cooling data from Curtiss, though the company appeared to be amply confident in its own abilities not to need any additional data. (Atwood mentioned the acquisition of this data in a letter to Sir Henry Self on 1 May, indicating that the information relating to a 'similar airplane' to the North American design would be of assistance to NAA.)[x] The sale of data would have represented some consolation for Curtiss, which had lost a potentially lucrative deal for its design to be built under licence, not to mention offsetting some of the cost the company had already incurred.

The transfer of data has sometimes been taken as an indication that the P-46's design provided some inspiration to NAA's designers – something NAA later strenuously denied. It is more likely that the only truly beneficial information in the package, as far as NAA was concerned, was the detailed wind-tunnel results which allowed NAA to refine its own design, but chiefly to satisfy itself that its own machine was fundamentally better. As it turned out, the P-46 does not seem to have offered a particularly great improvement even over the existing Model 81 – indeed, before long, Curtiss proposed dropping the P-46 altogether. The Curtiss company had newer designs on the drawing board, and in the meantime felt that a moderately updated P-40 using the F-series V-1710 would offer comparable performance and could be in production faster than the Model 86. The new type was known by Curtiss as the Model 87 and became the Kittyhawk in RAF service and P-40D/E in US service.

NAA was evidently not impressed by the P-46 and both Schmued and Kindelberger were adamant in later years that their design owed nothing to the P-46 despite some broad similarities in the aircraft's layout, such as the positioning of the radiator in the rear fuselage.

Much later, sources related to Curtiss claimed that the P-46, when it eventually flew (as the XP-46), displayed a similar performance to the NA-73X.[8] This was not the case – the prototype P-46 was around 20mph slower than early production Mustangs, and was even slightly slower than the Model 87.

One potential difficulty remained – that NAA had never designed or built a fighter from scratch before. Could it be trusted with British hopes and money? The only direct experience with fighter aircraft that the company had to draw on was a cheap, simple single-seater labelled the

---

x   Two days later, Self replied to Atwood requesting that the performance schedule of the NAA design be related to that of the P-46, to ensure that the two aircraft were comparable.

NA-50, which NAA sold to Peru in small numbers. The NA-50 was based heavily on the NA-16 trainer design and was hardly at the cutting edge of combat technology.

The existence of the NA-50 was perhaps sufficient as a fig-leaf for ordering an untried aircraft, however. When the head of the BAC, Sir Henry Self, persuaded of the virtues of NAA's clean-sheet design, agreed to purchase 400 aircraft in a letter of intent dated 11 April, the order he placed was for 'NA-50B' fighters. It is unclear what this classification was designed to achieve – certainly the new fighter bore no resemblance to the pedestrian NA-50.[xi]

In fact, NAA was not as green as it appeared when it came to fighter design. Richard Schleicher, NAA Chief Structures Engineer, recalled that Schmued had given the subject a great deal of thought: 'As far back as 1934–35, Ed was designing the various installations that later would be found in NAA aircraft – particularly the P-51,' said Schleicher. 'He had layouts of the 'ideal' cockpit, engine, and gun installations… Once the performance requirements were known, Ed needed only a few days to evolve a new three-view.'[9] Schmued had previous paper projects to draw upon as well. A sketch of a lightweight fighter that Schmued had prepared in the hope of attracting orders from the French Armée de l'Air displayed some similarity to the later Mustang,[xii] especially around the cockpit and the shape of the flying surfaces.

---

xi North American used the system of 'NA numbers' in several different ways. The primary use was both as a charge number and as a model number. Each new contract or project for a definite customer received a new NA charge number, for such purposes as tracking billable hours, drawing and part identification, and so on. However, this new 'NA-XX' might be identical to, or closely related to, an existing model. Thus, the (charge number) NA-68 fighter for 'Siam' was also model number NA-50A – though different in a number of ways, it was closely related to the NA-50s sold to Peru. NAA also used the numbers colloquially, so 'NA-16' could generically refer to any member of the very successful two-seat trainer family, despite there being fixed and retractable-gear branches and a wide variety of engines among them, all with different model numbers. 'NA-50B' may have simply been shorthand for 'the new fighter proposal for Britain'.

xii A number of contemporary and later NAA and Schmued designs, including the Morrow 'Victory' trainer and T-28 Trojan, employed similar shapes to the NA-73. This suggests that designer and company were not averse to recycling ideas, and the practice was both effective and efficient in terms of design time and effort.

The NAA design team was clearly determined that the new aircraft would be at the cutting edge of fighter design. For example, the proposal presented to the BAC suggested an advanced cooling system designed to ensure the greatest possible recovery of losses to radiator drag. In addition to this, NAA strongly considered a paper by the National Advisory Committee on Aeronautics (NACA) which proposed the possibility of wing aerofoil sections with lower drag than had hitherto been thought achievable.[10] Unlike some other manufacturers of fighter aircraft, however, the company was resolute in its desire to produce an aerodynamically efficient design that in no way compromised mass-production practicality – it should be as simple to produce as it was high performance.

Kindelberger had visited German aircraft manufacturers in 1938 to examine mass-production techniques. Two of the factories he visited were Heinkel and Messerschmitt, which at that time were building or developing high performance fighters designed with ease of production in mind. The Messerschmitt Bf 109 and Heinkel He 100 had both held speed records and eclipsed the performance of any aircraft in US service at the time, yet used straightforward shapes and were not labour-intensive to produce.[xiii] This visit may have had some influence on NAA's design priorities. A distinct focus on ease of production in the Mustang's design could have been one legacy of Kindelberger's visit to Germany (see page 24).

With the possibility of a large order, should the British be impressed, NAA immediately set about creating a design that promised a considerable advance over the fighters in production or planning in the US at the time. This could not help but interest the BAC, and this was especially so if the new aircraft could be ready quickly.

---

xiii The ability of some German aircraft manufacturers to develop high performance aircraft that were easy to mass produce, and the US industry's interest in learning from this, can be seen in Vultee Aircraft's exhaustive study of a captured Messerschmitt Bf 110 C in 1941 for circulation to other manufacturers. Vultee noted that 'ingenious design' had ensured that the Bf 110 was suited for '"Blitzkrieg production" as well as blitzkrieg warfare.' (See Report No 260-28: Analysis of the Messerschmitt Me-110 Airplane, December 1941).

Most significantly, the new aircraft had the blessing of the US government's War Department and the US Army Air Corps who were taking a keen interest in the developments proposed by NAA. In May 1940, a release agreement for export of the NA-73 was made by the US government, but with the proviso that two of the production airframes would be passed to the Air Force, and the government would furnish equipment for the fitting-out of these two aircraft.

The development of the NA-73 in fact marked quite a departure for the US government in terms of its attitude to the sharing of military technology. By early 1940, the War Department and the Air Force clearly saw opportunities in the European war for them to develop their own strength at minimal cost, by encouraging innovations for which the cost and risk of development would be borne by foreign governments.

The extent to which North American had the government's blessing can be seen in the fact that it was already working on important bomber contracts for the US Army, which the foreign fighter could potentially have distracted them from. The B-25 was approved in September 1939, and two prototypes of the B-28 bomber had been ordered in February 1940.

With all hurdles having been cleared, the BAC could proceed with the formal contract, which reduced the total to 320 (allocated the serials AG345 to AG664) plus spares, and required that all aircraft be delivered by 1 October 1941, with an option for further production if required. The additional AAC prototypes were allocated the designation XP-51, and were essentially RAF specification Mustangs with some equipment exchanged for US-standard kit. These two aircraft were given the USAAF serials 41-038 and 41-039.

Design and Creation

When NAA received the agreement to proceed from Self, Schmued was given permission to hand-pick his team of engineers and design staff. After a few weeks there were already around 50 people on the project. Schmued was determined that maximising the performance of the aircraft would not in any way compromise the ability to produce it in quantity. Schmued decided on constructing all surfaces apart from the flying ones on the principles of 'conic lofting', otherwise known as 'second-degree curves'. All external surfaces were sections of a cone, which made them easy for airflow to follow and yet largely eliminated the need for complex compound curvature.[xiv]

Famously, Schmued decided to position the radiator in the rear fuselage with the intake scoop beneath the cockpit. The principles set out by F. W. Meredith of the Royal Aircraft Establishment (RAE) Farnborough in 1936[11] were fairly well known at the time if not well implemented; Meredith's work indicated that hot air from engine or radiator exhausts could produce thrust when ejected at higher pressure, and this could help to offset the drag incurred by the radiator. (Aircraft designers had begun to implement Meredith's findings in the late 1930s, but it remained poorly understood – moreover, the 'Meredith Effect' produced most of its potential advantages at speeds higher than 1930s fighter designs were able to reach.)[12] NACA had recently produced a paper on Meredith's workings and issued it as a technical report.[13] The committee concluded: 'The theory indicates that thrust is derived by adding the waste heat to the cooling air at a pressure above that of the external stream, and the theory has been verified in some degree by experiment. The gains are not large but may be sufficient with a well-designed cooling system on a high-speed airplane to compensate for the cooling losses.'[14]

Some disagreement exists on whether Meredith's mathematics were used by NAA. Atwood, NAA's Chief Engineer, has suggested that the Meredith paper and principles were central to the design, while Ed Horkey, the Chief Aerodynamicist, asserted that NAA did not make use of Meredith's calculations and only sited the radiator in the rear fuselage because it was too big to fit under the nose. (It is indeed the case that the radiator planned for the NA-73 was rather larger than the units planned for contemporary Curtiss fighters, which could be sited under the nose). In any event, whatever the reasons for placing the radiator in the rear fuselage, the

---

xiv The use of simple shapes to facilitate straightforward production may have also contributed to a superficial resemblance between the Mustang and the Messerschmitt 109, also characterised by straight lines and simple shapes. The vague similarity led to a number of cases of mistaken identity later in the war. This, possibly in conjunction with Kindelberger's visit to Germany and Schmued's German heritage, contributed to the suggestion that the Mustang design drew from that of the Bf 109. A rumour even circulated at the time that Schmued had once worked for Messerschmitt – he had not, having only worked as a designer for the US division of Fokker, which later became NAA, and, during a very short period, for Bellanca.

NA-73's radiator tunnel was precisely calculated to reduce the pressure and speed of cooling air as it reached the coolant and oil radiators, then increase air speed and pressure as it passed out of the exit duct. It was precisely the 'well designed cooling system on a high-speed airplane' referred to by NACA in their appraisal of Meredith's paper.

The wings followed an even more innovative pattern. NACA at the time had begun developing so-called 'laminar flow' aerofoils. Airflow over a surface like a wing generally starts in a laminar pattern, with air moving in smooth layers, before breaking down into energy-sapping turbulent flow. Previously, conventional sections with the main thickness around a third of the way back from the leading edge had been thought to be the most efficient in terms of lift versus drag. Attempts to delay flow separation by moving the maximum thickness rearward appeared to offer no advantage when wind-tunnel testing had been carried out.

However, in 1939 NACA found that this conclusion was false and resulted from turbulence in wind tunnels masking the efficiency of certain aerofoil shapes. When NACA obtained a wind tunnel with much lower turbulence, it tested a series of wing sections with the point of maximum thickness at various points aft of the conventional position. These new tests found that it was possible to delay the point at which airflow broke down, and therefore dramatically reduce the energy lost to turbulence.

NACA had not produced its prototype aerofoils with fighter aircraft necessarily in mind so much as the general aerodynamic benefits, so considerable additional work was required to create an aerofoil suited to such an aircraft. Undeterred, Schmued and his team, with NACA's support, went ahead and developed its own wing, based on the principles set out by the Advisory Committee.

Horkey and his team of aerodynamicists laboriously created a section on laminar-flow principles that had a 16% thickness-chord ratio at the root and 11% at the tip. This process was far from straightforward, requiring constant re-calculation to obtain the right pressure distribution.[xv] NACA

---

xv The process involved 'performing a series of pressure distribution calculations until, at the design lift coefficient, the negative pressure reached a maximum at or near the 50% chord point with no adverse pressure gradient ahead of this point' (Hansen, James R., *Wind and Beyond: A Documentary Journey into the History of Aerodynamics in America: Volume II: Reinventing the Airplane*, NASA, pp. 887–8).

provided ongoing support to NAA's designers at this stage, helping them produce the best section for the aircraft and myriad other details. This support continued throughout the design process looking at details such as the positioning and design of wing gun apertures to maintain the critical laminar airflow and using a slightly different section at the wing tips to aid stall characteristics.

G.W. Lewis, the Director of Aeronautical Research at NACA wrote to Ed Horkey on 1 November 1940, offering advice on numerous issues that Horkey had earlier raised. Lewis indicated that discontinuities at the leading edge – around rivets, for example – as small as 0.002–3in would compromise the conservation of laminar flow. He also indicated that laminar flow would be hard to maintain behind the machine gun blast-tube unless air was taken in at the opening, and the muzzle was located very close to the front stagnation point. Lewis advised Horkey that the position of the guns in the initial design was problematic – the 0.50in gun was too high and the 0.30in guns were too low. Lewis also provided information on the NACA 65,2-213.5 aerofoil, which he recommended for the wing tip.[15]

By July, wind-tunnel tests on the NA-73 design indicated that the aircraft had highly efficient aerofoils and very low radiator drag.[16] (In fact the underslung duct was later improved further on production models, by way of creating a 'gutter' to divert boundary-layer flow, leading to even higher efficiency.) Nevertheless, it was a nervous time for all concerned. The laminar-flow aerofoil was so new that nobody knew with any certainty that what looked so promising in the wind tunnel would translate into practice. According to NASA's narrative based on contemporary documents, the wing section was 'considered "too revolutionary" by many experts at the time'.[17] In particular, NACA was concerned about the wing's stalling characteristics.

The innovative aerodynamic features of the NAA design offer some clue as to why the US government had changed its stance on export of the latest military hardware so dramatically. In August 1940, George Mead, the Director of the Airplane and Engine Division of the National Defense Council, wrote to the Aeronautical Board demanding to know why aircraft with the laminar-flow wing were to be permitted to leave the US at a time when domestic aircraft would not yet be so equipped. Mead questioned the wisdom of such a move and suggested it was not desirable from the perspective of national security to release the NAA design for export.[18]

Lieutenant Colonel Ira C. Eaker of the US Army Air Corps responded on behalf of the Chief of the Air Corps the following month. Eaker insisted that examples of the NAA aircraft would be passed to the Air Corps for testing, and that 'complete information' on the aircraft's innovations would be furnished. He went on:

> The Air Corps is conversant with this wing development and in accordance with the mutual agreement will receive full benefit of the engineering work being done without additional expense. It is believed to be in the best interest of the Air Corps to encourage the continuation of the research and development work being done by North American in connection with high-speed wing sections for the NA-73-type aeroplane.[19]

Clearly the NA-73 represented a 'win-win' for the US government – it helped to stimulate the domestic aircraft industry and advance the state-of-the-art in military aircraft, which the US authorities could reap considerable benefits from, while incurring minimal cost.

NACA itself shared the desire to benefit from the new American aircraft being funded by the British government. In his November reply to Ed Horkey, G. W. Lewis lobbied for one of the Army's two specimen aircraft to be sent to Langley for aerodynamic testing. Lewis also pressed Horkey to provide any information possible resulting from the flight tests of the new aircraft, particularly with regard to stalling characteristics and how they compared with the wind-tunnel data.[20]

The prototype was completed by 9 September 1940 but had to wait for its Allison engine to be delivered. In fact, the engine in question was one of the first of the new F3R model V-1710s which was not even to begin official testing until February 1941 – the engine in the NA-73X was only the third 'F' series to fly and one of the first five F3Rs to be built.[21] This engine had already created some difficulties. Problems with the spark-plug wiring had led to a revision which meant the engine did not fit NAA's mount when it arrived – Allison had apparently not informed NAA of the alteration. Horkey would later assert that Allison had not been helpful in trying to integrate the engine into the NAA design, and even that the

The NA-73X prototype Mustang as it appeared when it was rolled out ahead of its first flight on 26 October 1940. The airframe had been completed the month before but had to wait for the engine to be delivered.

carefully calculated aerodynamic curves had to be compromised around the nose because of this. These difficulties created bad feeling between the two companies that would crop up again during the Mustang's career.[22]

After the NA-73X rollout, but before it had flown, further orders were placed, totalling 300 additional aircraft. North American gave this batch the charge number NA-83, and RAF serial numbers were in the AL, AM and AP series.

Chapter 2

The Mustang Finds Its Niche

T he NA-73X's first flight was made on 26 October 1940, with consultant engineer and test pilot Vance Breese at the controls. The aircraft showed acceptable control and stalling characteristics, but initially, there were some significant problems to overcome. In particular, the Allison V-1710 F3R installation was proving troublesome, running very roughly at certain throttle settings. Furthermore, the engine could not be operated at more than 60% throttle.[i]

The engine problems came to a head when Paul Balfour took over test flying the new aircraft from Breese, apparently for the aircraft's first high-speed runs.[ii] Balfour had made two passes over Mines Field and was beginning a third when the engine cut out completely. Balfour attempted to put the aircraft down in a farmer's field but the undercarriage dug into the soft earth and the NA-73X tipped onto its back. There is some controversy over what caused the accident. An oft-repeated story is that Balfour failed to switch fuel tanks (after having refused a briefing on the operation of the aircraft from Schmued) leading to fuel starvation. Other accounts cite a design flaw in the carburettor intake, which cut off the air flow and stalled the engine.

The US Army Air Forces' technical report on the XP-51 appears to attribute the engine stoppage to the carburettor scoop design: 'Considerable

---

i On 2 January 1941, G. W. Lewis of NACA wrote to Sir Henry Tizard saying: 'We do not have any indication as to the drag characteristics of the wing or as to the performance of the airplane with all-out power, as the engine was never operated at more than sixty per cent of its rated power before the crash [of 20 November]'. (Doc 4-28b in NASA, *The Wind and Beyond: A documentary journey into the history of aerodynamics*, p. 910).

ii According to Ray Wagner in *Mustang Designer*, the flight scheduled for 20 November was the first high-speed test run, based on the NAA Airplane Flight Report 'NA-73-92-1/2'.

The NA-73X as it appeared after it was rebuilt following its crash on 20 November 1940. The chief visual difference from its pre-crash earlier appearance is the anti-glare panel on the nose, but there are other detail differences such as the small intake ahead of the exhaust stubs and the deletion of the nose-gun fairings. As seen here the rudder is in a plain finish.

trouble was incurred with the Allison engine installation in the early stages of the aircraft's development. At one particular throttle setting the engine was found to be extremely rough and in one particular instance the engine completely cut out resulting in a forced landing in a plowed field… It was during flight testing of the first Army Air Forces airplane that it was discovered that engine difficulties previously encountered could be overcome by extending the length of the ramming air intake scoop.'[1]

The first few NA-73s, up to and including AG348 and the two XP-51s, were essentially handbuilt to production specifications. The short intake scoop seen on these aircraft was lengthened until it slightly overhung the spinner backplate, gaining as much 'ram air' effect from the propeller as physically possible, and locating the mouth of the intake out of the turbulent boundary-layer air on the nose. This scoop became a characteristic visual feature of the Allison-engined Mustangs, and it is interesting to note that the Curtiss Model 87, with the same engine model, had essentially the same change made to its own intake early in production.

This was not to be the only difficulty related to the engine – indeed, when the F-series first entered production, the powerplant was barely able to meet the stipulated tests. Though it later became a superlatively reliable

The NA-73X in flight, following its rebuild. By now the rudder has had USAAC stripes applied to it. (WW2 in Color)

engine, the V-1710 was regarded with suspicion in some quarters while the difficulties were worked through. The engine's entry into production would also prove to be a bottleneck for both the NA-73 and the Curtiss Model 87.

While the NA-73X was undergoing repairs, the aircraft received the name that would attain iconic status. On 9 December 1940, the BPC wrote to NAA to notify them that the NA-73 had been given the official designation 'Mustang'.

Testing Progresses

Contractor's trials resumed early in the New Year when the NA-73X was repaired after its forced landing. In addition, Captain M. J. Lee of the US Army Air Corps carried out seven 'preliminary performance flights' on the aircraft in March 1941, as part of the conditions of NAA's contract.

These flights took place at the NAA plant ahead of the anticipated delivery of the two XP-51 aircraft.

The first production RAF Mustang Mk I, AG345, flew in late April, and, with the agreement of the Ministry of Aircraft Production, immediately joined the contractor's testing programme, helping make up for lost time. In fact, AG345 probably remained in the US for its entire life, assisting NAA with trials and development, while AG347 was kept until towards the end of Mustang Mk I production. RAF test pilots Squadron Leader M. Crossley and Wing Commander C. Clarkson also joined the test programme at NAA to help develop the aircraft for service and create pilots' notes – and presumably to report some advance information on the new type to their employers. The NA-73X itself was relatively lightly used; it had been flown for less than five hours before Balfour's crash. When production-standard aircraft were available it made more sense to use them for most work, and its 45th and last flight was on 15 July 1941.

By the time a third order (for the sub-type NA-91) was placed in late June or early July 1941, the Lend-Lease Act had been passed. Instead of being purchased directly by Britain, 150 Mustangs were to be paid for by

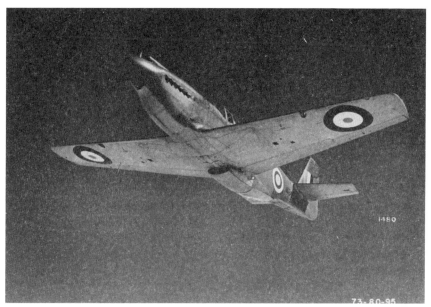

AG345 was the first Mustang for the RAF. It flew in April 1941 and was used extensively for NAA's test programme, as well as being flown by RAF pilots in the US attached to the BPC. It appeared in numerous press photos issued by NAA like this one.

the US and 'lent' to the RAF, bringing the total on order to 770. Under the conditions of the Act, the aircraft covered by the new order were effectively USAAF aircraft, so they were given an Army designation, P-51 (no suffix), and Army serials alongside their RAF identification: 41-37320 to 37469 and FD418 to FD567 respectively.

By 1940, the desired armament for new British fighters was four Hispano 20mm cannon, and NAA's initial design specification (SC-1050) of 15 Mar 1940 had called for just that, according to Schmued.[2] At that time, however, the first examples of a familiarisation order of 33 guns had only just arrived in the US from France, and the Army and Navy would not even begin to negotiate a licence production agreement until the following month. While British Hispano production had begun, there were as yet no aircraft equipped with this armament in regular service there either.

The port side wing gun bay of a Mustang Mk I, the 0.50in gun to the right and the two 0.30in guns left and centre, demonstrating the extent to which the guns had to be canted over to allow them to fit within the wing along with their feed chutes.

The initial armament package of the Mustang was instead eight machine guns, in an unusual layout for RAF fighters – four of these were Colt 0.30in guns mounted in the wings (retaining the American 0.30in calibre gun, rather than the British 0.303in version), and four Colt 0.50in, with two fitted in the wings and two in the nose chin cowling, firing through the airscrew arc. Atwood described this as '... the most practical possible at this time, consistent with the general instructions we have received', in a response dated 1 May to Sir Henry Self's letter of intent.[3]

The Mustang Mk I was finally ready for release in August 1941 – little over a month before delivery of all 320 was to have been accomplished, according to the terms of the first contract! Aircraft AG346 was released in the US for shipment in that month, and the first XP-51 was delivered to Wright Field, though it was not tested properly until October.

The US Army had until that point appeared to be anxious to get its hands on the new fighter, to the extent that the two earmarked airframes, the fourth and tenth, were taken out of their position on the production line and finished ahead of schedule. In fact, the first XP-51 was the second

The second RAF Mustang, and the first to go to the UK, was AG346, arriving on 21 October 1941. It was assembled by Lockheed at Speke. AG346 eventually served with five operational squadrons – 225, 63, 26, 16 and 168, in addition to time at a Mustang OTU. As seen here it has been fitted with a long carburettor intake.

production Mustang to fly (on 20 May), although it was subsequently used to assist with contractor's testing until NAA was satisfied enough to release the aircraft. By the time the aircraft were delivered, the Army's test centres had their hands full with other types.

The delay in testing the XP-51s has been interpreted as a sign that the Army took little interest in the Mustang at this early stage. In reality, delays to the testing of the first aircraft were caused by the still-maturing engine, troublesome oil cooler and issues around the retraction of the undercarriage, which had to be resolved before testing could commence in earnest.[4] Wright Field also requested that the second XP-51 be fitted with an experimental type of automatic-hydraulic gun charger. This apparatus appears to have been delayed, and the aircraft was not handed over to Wright Field until 16 December. According to the official acceptance document, 'The second airplane was thoroughly inspected by the Flying Branch after delivery and then turned over to the Armament Laboratory for firing tests'. While it is true that the Army was focused on other types for future equipment of

The first of two XP-51s, 41-038, in the colour scheme it wore when it was first delivered to the USAAC in August 1941 – bare aluminium apart from USAAC wing and tail markings, an anti-glare panel and silver-painted wing leading edge. It was the fourth aircraft on the NA-73 production line.

the Army Air Force (AAF), there was undoubtedly still much interest in the Mustang's innovative features.

The British maintained pressure on NAA to equip the Mustang with Hispano cannon. NAA apparently first promised that this would happen with the NA-83 order, but in September 1941 this looked doubtful and in early November it was confirmed that the cannon armament would not be incorporated until a later batch, which would be designated NA-91. The NA-73 AG347 performed drag tests with a mock-up cannon installation in October, indicating that this armament was on its way. However, US production of the gun, and the necessary belt feed, was still only getting under way as production was about to move on to the NA-83 series. (In addition to the trials on AG347, NACA tested a mock-up of the cannon wing for stall characteristics during a series of aerodynamic tests on one of the XP-51 aircraft between March and May 1942.[5] The first set of NA-91 wings was fitted to the NA-83 AM190 for further trials in May 1942.)

The NA-83 therefore retained the mixed machine-gun armament. After some discussion, the Air Ministry would elect to retain the Mustang Mk I designation for the NA-83, due to the relatively minor modifications from the NA-73. This would not, however, be formally decided until after the first NA-83s were received by ACC, and some earlier correspondence refers to NA-83s as the Mk II.

Testing in Britain

On 24 October 1941, AG346 became the first Mustang to reach Britain. More followed, though 21 were lost when cargo ships were sunk by U-Boats in December and February, and arrivals remained at a trickle until the latter month. The still-crated aircraft were transported to Speke, where they were to be assembled and any modifications for British service applied by subcontractor Lockheed.

The Aeroplane and Armament Experimental Establishment (A&AEE) at Boscombe Down and the Air-Fighting Development Unit (AFDU) at Duxford both received several Mustang Mk Is by the end of January 1942. This was necessary to establish performance parameters, work out faults and defects, and develop the most appropriate tactical use of the aircraft. As had been the case with the Harvard, engineers from NAA came to the UK to assist with development and to report back to the design team with

NA-73 Mustang Mk I from the first batch AG550 in flight. This aircraft, coded XV-U went to II (AC) Squadron RAF, based at Sawbridgeworth. Here it is piloted by Wing Commander A. J. W. Geddes, the squadron's CO.

any problems that needed rectifying as well as ideas for improvements that arose from testing and operations.[iii]

The A&AEE immediately set about assessing the new fighter's abilities; performance and handling trials were held between January and July 1942. The establishment's test pilots found that the Mustang was easy to handle and performed very well, at least at lower altitudes.

Taxiing was found to be easy (especially as the Mustang Mk I had a steerable tailwheel, which could be engaged or left to castor freely) and the pilots found the view forward to be good due to the narrow nose. Take-off was similarly straightforward, and any tendency to swing could easily be held with the rudder.

In flight, the A&AEE pilots found the controls to be effective in all respects, even in dives up to 500mph. The Mustang was stable at all speeds, and all aerobatic manoeuvres could be carried out satisfactorily.

Interestingly, special attention was paid to rate of roll. During 1940, the RAF had found that this characteristic was of considerable importance in air combat. This was compounded when RAF fighter squadrons began to encounter the Focke-Wulf Fw 190 over France in the second half of 1941. The German fighter's rate of roll was considerably better than that of the Spitfire Mk V, which was the main RAF fighter at the time, despite a change to metal-covered ailerons in Spring 1941 to improve this area. Tests on the Mustang Mk I's roll rate were carried out at 200mph, 300mph and 400mph, and at all speeds the pilots concluded: 'the force on the control column is light enough for full aileron to be applied without undue effort… The rate of roll for full aileron is definitely much faster than on any other present day fighter tested at this establishment.'[6]

The AFDU found that 'the controls are well balanced and can be made light or heavy as required by adjustment of the servo-tabs fitted to ailerons and elevators[iv]. There is little tendency to heavy-up at high speeds… the

---

iii   A relatively large number of NA-73s, at least seven, went to British testing establishments towards the end of 1941 and into 1942. These included AG351, AG357, AG359, AG360, AG365, AG383 and AG422. In addition, at least eight NA-83s, one NA-91, one NA-97 and two NA-99s were trialled at British establishments in 1942–43.

iv   The servo-tabs fitted to the Mustang's control surfaces are well understood, but the AFDU's suggestion that these tabs could be adjusted to assist control 'feel' is apparently unique.

Mustang is as light [on the controls] as the Spitfire but far smoother in all manoeuvres. The aircraft handles extremely well in aerobatics and gives ample warning of the stall.[7]

Landing was also straightforward, and possible in crosswinds of up to 25mph. The landing run was longer than other RAF fighters, partly because of the greater weight of the Mustang. However, the British testing establishments felt that aileron response was bordering on insufficient in that condition. In fact, while aileron response was found to be good at high speeds, this was less the case at lower speeds.[v]

In terms of performance, the AFDU compared the Mustang to a Spitfire Vb, both with full war load. At lower altitudes the Mustang was found to be the faster, with a maximum true airspeed of 375–380mph developed at around 15,000ft. Up to this height, the Mustang was consistently around 30–35mph faster than the Spitfire, but by 25,000ft the advantage had degraded to only 1–2mph.

The Mustang was even better in a dive. 'The Mustang dives very fast, its initial acceleration being particularly good, and in comparative trials was always able to dive away from the Spitfire,' reported the AFDU. 'When diving, recovery was found to be easy even at an indicated speed of 500mph.'

The Spitfire could turn more tightly than the Mustang, although using flap improved the Mustang's rate of turn. The Mustang's advantage over the Spitfire at low and medium altitude was all the more remarkable considering that the Spitfire Mk V had a moderate power advantage,[vi] and was around 2,000lb lighter.[vii] The Mustang's high aerodynamic efficiency overcame these disadvantages and left a great deal of potential for future development.

---

v   Interestingly, in light of the AFDU's satisfaction with the Mustang's controls, and in particular aileron response, the USAAF was concerned that aileron control and roll rate needed to be improved. Tests focusing on this feature were performed on the XP-51 aircraft in late 1942. See the section on 'Eglin Field Trials: P-51' in Chapter 4.

vi   At the peak of the development offered by both these engines, the Merlin produced around 75hp more than the V-1710. The Spitfire's Merlin 45 offered 1,515hp at 11,375ft and 16lb boost, while according to a memo of 2 March 1943 reproduced in Birch, 1987, the Allison V-1710 with overboost could produce 1,440hp at 11,000ft.

vii   Around 400lb of the Mustang's additional weight is accounted for by the greater amount of fuel it could carry.

A great advantage of the Mustang Mk I over other fighters was its range. The Mustang carried more fuel than most comparable aircraft, and on early Mustang Is this was 130 (imperial) gallons (both of AG351's fuel tanks were marked 70gal, but the starboard tank was found to contain 10 gallons less than this). In still air, flights with AG351 at the A&AEE confirmed that a range of 960 miles would be possible, double that of the Spitfire Mk V. The AFDU ascertained that the Mustang's endurance was four hours at maximum economical cruise.

It was not all good news – as with any new type, there were numerous minor problems to deal with. The cockpit was excessively hot at all times, due to the radiator casing emerging into the space behind the pilot's seat. The oil cooler was liable to 'coring', when the oil cooled too much in parts of the matrix and congealed.

The view from the cockpit, when armour plate was fitted behind the seat, was considered very poor. Opening the clear view panels in the side of the hood helped, but these were sucked shut by aerodynamic forces above 250mph. The rear-view mirror, on the other hand, was rated 'especially good'.

The NA-73's climb was perhaps cause for some disappointment as well – at low altitudes it was only slightly worse than the Spitfire, but above 25,000ft the climb became 'very slow and uncomfortable, and controls sloppy'.

Air-firing trials under positive and negative 'G' were carried out at low altitude. In general, the armament worked well but sometimes at negative 'G' the 0.30in guns would misfire resulting in a stoppage. 'The absence of vibration during the firing was remarked on by all pilots', according to the AFDU. The only other problem experienced was when one of AG365's wing guns jumped out of its mounting and shot through the skin. Luckily, this took place when the aircraft was undertaking ground firing tests. It highlighted a problem with the locking pins, which was rectified when the pins were redesigned.

Much to the chagrin of NAA engineers, the specially designed semi-fishtail exhaust stubs, which they believed had excellent flame-damping properties, were found to emit visible blue flames at night to distances well over 100 yards during trials in January 1942. (In US practice, the exhaust stubs tended to be the responsibility of the airframe manufacturer, in contrast to British practice where the exhaust stubs were generally provided by the engine manufacturer unless a design specific to the aircraft was required.)

Mustang Mk I NA-73 model AG351, which was used extensively for testing in the UK, displaying its NAA-designed fishtail exhaust stubs. These were demonstrated to have inadequate flame-damping properties and were subsequently modified or replaced.

Fishtail exhaust stubs from a Curtiss Kittyhawk fitted to Mustang Mk I NA-83 model AL997 – these were judged to have much better flame-damping properties than the NAA version. AL997 was tested at the A&AEE between July and October 1942.

Curtiss Kittyhawk exhausts were tried and found to be much better and the design was changed accordingly. However, there weren't enough of the replacement stubs to go around, so some NA-73 Mk Is either had their original exhaust stubs flattened by hand, or simply stuck with the items as fitted at the factory.

Overall, the AFDU considered the Mustang Mk I 'an excellent medium-altitude fighter. It is pleasant to fly, being very stable, and compares extremely well with the Spitfire'. The pilots concluded it was 'certainly the best American fighter that has yet reached this country'.

By July 1942, the first of the 300, slightly improved, NA-83 model had begun to arrive at testing facilities. The specification of the NA-83 had been amended with possible service in overseas theatres in mind, given that by late 1941 the pressing need for fighters for home defence had been replaced by a need for modern fighters in North Africa and the Middle and Far East. The NA-83 had a different radiator (Harrison instead of Air Research, although the design was similar) and provision for an air filter to be installed in the carburettor scoop trunking.[viii]

General improvements included a new type of gun camera, which was relocated to the nose, and a baffle to reduce cockpit heat. In service, the NA-83 continued to be referred to simply as 'Mustang Mk I', though not until after a debate at the Ministry of Aircraft Production (MAP). Initially it had been understood that the aircraft would continue to be known as Mustang Mk Is, though due to the number of changes, some correspondence had informally referred to NA-83s as the Mustang Mk II. ACC asked for clarification in July 1942, as squadrons began to receive the aircraft, only to be told that the matter was under investigation. By 28 July, the MAP had decided that the differences were not sufficiently important to warrant a new mark number, or to refer to them separately in squadron returns. (In any case, by this time it had already been decided to designate the succeeding NA-91 as the Mk IA).

Production of the NA-91 progressed from May 1942. The only major change from the NA-83 was, at last, the revision of the wing to fit four cannon, and the deletion of nose guns; this was sufficient difference to warrant a new designation, though not an entirely new mark number.

---

viii This feature has generally been attributed to a later model in Mustang development, but there is ample evidence that it was a feature of the NA-83.

AM190 was an NA-83 model Mustang Mk I modified with the armament that would be standard on the next model, the NA-91 (Mustang Mk IA or P-51). The aircraft was fitted with a NA-91-specification wing in May 1942 to trial the 20mm cannon installation. It was evaluated in the US and was then transferred to the UK.

(British testing establishments did not trial the Mk IA extensively; brief firing tests were carried out, as late as 26 April 1943, with Mustang FD446.[ix] These appeared to give satisfactory results.)

The A&AEE evaluated NA-83 AL997 between July and October 1942, and concluded that it was 'simple to fly and has very pleasant handling qualities, the controls at high speed being especially pleasant. Both take-off and landing are easy. In normal flight the view is sufficiently good for reconnaissance work and the high speed at ground level is a considerable advantage for surprise tactics. Altogether the Mustang I should prove extremely efficient for its purpose.'

It was clear, however, that by now the purpose spoken of above was not that of a conventional day fighter, at least not in Europe. Air combat had been tending to become higher than in 1940 – by 1942 it was generally taking place between 22,000ft and 27,000ft. While the Mustang had superlative performance below 18,000ft, above that height it could not compete as the engine lost too much power. There were plenty of circumstances where good low-altitude performance was beneficial though, and the fighter fell almost perfectly into the lap of the specialist RAF organisation developed for working with the Army – Army Co-operation Command (ACC). Indeed, the first 100 had been allocated for ACC before NAA had finished working the bugs out of the initial production aircraft.

A Dire Need for Army Co-operation

Even before the British Expeditionary Force (BEF) arrived in France in 1939, the very great want of a capable army support force, with suitable aircraft, was felt. This had its roots in the nature of the British Army between the wars, which was largely a colonial police force that had little likelihood of fighting a well-equipped, modern army and little need of dedicated air support on the battlefield. The colonial RAF likewise evolved into a general-purpose service, with limited requirement to co-operate with army units beyond reconnaissance and communication needs.

Even when rearmament began in earnest, the Army's priority came a distant third behind the RAF and Royal Navy. It was not until shortly

---

ix   Although the last Mustang Mk IA rolled off the production line in July 1942, the aircraft did not enter squadron service until June 1943.

before the war that a continental-scale army had begun to be formed again, by which time the ability of the Army and RAF to work closely together on the battlefield had effectively been lost. Furthermore, there were few aircraft available – small numbers of Battles and Blenheims of the expeditionary air forces, when they could be spared – for close air support of ground forces, and fewer crews properly trained to carry it out.

The British Secretary of State for War, Leslie Hore-Belisha, pointed out in a Cabinet meeting in November 1939 that army co-operation (AC) consisted of five tasks – reconnaissance, artillery spotting, inter-communication, 'low-flying attack', and transportation of medical supplies and injured personnel. In late 1939, only the first three of these were able to be covered by the existing AC squadrons.[8] Tactical reconnaissance had been less neglected than some of the other elements, and the Army did at least have use of a specialist aircraft, the Westland Lysander. The slow-flying Lysander's ability to carry out its role in the presence of the enemy had, however, been wildly overestimated.

The situation was somewhat similar in the United States. With a Depression budget, a generally isolationist attitude, and little likelihood of a direct attack by ground forces, the US Army's chief 'enemy' was seen as the US Navy. Furthermore, despite being the *Army* Air Corps, the air arm's leaders tended to believe in and aspire to the sort of independent and distinct role for aviation championed in the UK by the RAF.

The doctrine of strategic air power and the primacy of the bomber thus dominated pre-war thinking in both air forces. The bomber might be regarded as a deterrent, a first line of defence (along with the Navy), or even, among the more devout, as rendering a large ground army obsolete. The end result in any case was estrangement between Air and Ground.

Even among tactical thinkers, the battlefield was seen as a dangerous place for friendly aircraft, and there were also fears that the aircraft might pose a bigger risk to the soldiers below than the benefits of their presence warranted. This, with the general trend of aircraft development toward 'bigger, faster, and farther', led Air Force leaders to favour the interdiction role – attacking supply chains and forces on their way to the battlefield rather than on it. The single-engined 'attack' or light bomber therefore began to give way to twin-engined types in both Britain and the US.

The British Army and the War Office had had little say in the aircraft that were developed for the purposes of army support, having been reduced to the level of 'petitioning' the Air Staff with their needs – 'and indeed had to argue with the Air Ministry regarding their tactical requirements' as Secretary of State for War, Leslie Hore-Belisha put it.[9] The Air Staff had, for years, resisted the introduction of close-support aircraft in favour of building up the strategic bombing force. While there were several specifications issued for close-support aircraft in the 1930s, only one, Specification P.4/34 for a light day bomber capable of tactical support, reached the stage of production orders before cancellation.[x] Even this requirement did not lead to an operational dive-bomber – while the Hawker Henley won the competition and went into production, the aircraft was relegated from the outset to target towing. Even single-engined bombers like the Fairey Battle were primarily intended for strategic bombing.

Fighter Reconnaissance

During the Battle of France, the aircrews had discovered to their cost that the Westland Lysander was too slow and vulnerable. The Lysander had been purpose-designed for AC flying, focusing on excellent all-round visibility and slow-flying characteristics when these were thought to be the primary characteristics required for this kind of flying.

While this was the only dedicated AC aircraft available to the BEF, there were other assets. Battles and Blenheims of the Air Component and the Advanced Air Striking Force could address tactical and strategic reconnaissance needs when circumstances permitted. Unfortunately, all proved inadequate to the task in the face of German air superiority.

According to Robert F. Futrell of the United States Air Force Historical Division, 'the British were forced to suspend observation patrols on 30 September, when four out of five Battles were shot down by Me 109s. During the winter of 1939–40, Lysander squadrons perfected tactics based upon the exceptional maneuvrability of this plane, its ability to slow up quickly, to make tight turns and to skid. These tactics brought many

---

x Specification P.4/34 required a high-performance (circa 300mph) aircraft, stressed for dive recovery, which would be capable of tactical support, though this was not necessarily its main role.

Lysanders home safely, but usually well shot up. During the Battle of France (May–June 1940) the best the Lysanders could manage were quick trips over the German lines to examine some particular point of interest, and even these spot reconnaissance missions usually had to be combined with RAF dawn and dusk sweeps.[10] As Sholto-Douglas observed at the time, 'We appear to have forgotten more completely than I would have believed possible one of the plainest lessons of the last war. During the brief periods where the Germans enjoyed air superiority we found ourselves unable to carry out normal Army Co-operation work.'[11]

AC squadrons needed an aircraft that could perform the necessary tactical reconnaissance, artillery spotting and low-level sweeps while being able to go toe-to-toe with the best enemy fighters. According to Futrell: 'In 1940 when the Air Corps put the question to the RAF regarding the suitability of the Lysander for its duties, the British replied that a tactical reconnaissance aircraft was required with higher speed and greater armament protection. In the face of enemy air superiority the British thought it necessary to employ fighter types for observation and to carry out "tip and run reconnaissance", so as to be gone before the enemy could react.[12]

The questions of command and equipment were addressed seriously, but only concluded after France had fallen. For most of 1940, the question of battlefield support or tactical reconnaissance aircraft was moot – fighters were what was needed, urgently and in volume (see previous chapter).

Finally, ACC was formed on 1 December 1940 under Air Marshal Sir Arthur Barratt, taking over responsibility for AC flying, and the 14 existing AC squadrons, from Fighter Command. The new command was established to develop effective interaction with the Army, in fact with direct Army participation, the chief duties being close air support, tactical reconnaissance and artillery spotting. The Air Staff also offered the day bombers of No. 2 Group, Bomber Command, for work with the Army, and a core of 15 squadrons of Fighter Command to be trained in ground attack, but neither would be available yet, and they would still have their existing operational duties to fulfil.

The make-up of ACC was fluid when the organisation was formed, and discussions on structure and equipment would continue into 1942, though the Air Staff's intention, which the Army took as a promise, was to provide ten squadrons each of fighter- and bomber-reconnaissance aircraft. The notion of a single type earmarked specifically for army support was by now evolving into these two overlapping requirements:

Fighter reconnaissance was to undertake reconnaissance missions primarily by day and over comparatively short distances, and to attack (with gunfire) ground targets such as armoured fighting vehicles, in close co-operation with army formations. The Army's guiding specification desired a speed of 350–400mph at under 10,000ft, an endurance of 3 ½ to 4 hours, a heavy armament of both cannon and .303s, plus substantial armour protection.[13]

Bomber reconnaissance was intended to perform recon missions in bad weather or night, for longer distances, and also to attack ground targets, preferably with the ability to perform true dive-bombing, though not at a serious cost to performance. It was hoped that this type would be 'fast, manoeuvrable, and able to operate low', with a normal range of about 1,000 miles, while able to carry a minimum 1,000lb bomb load and defend itself both front and rear.[14]

In early 1941 it was decided as a first step to re-equip three AC squadrons with the Curtiss Tomahawk. In May that year, the Air Ministry decided that 11 squadrons would re-equip with the Tomahawk, but even then only the first three units (26, 268 and 400 squadrons) had been identified. Furthermore, it was already apparent by this time that the Tomahawk was not a viable long-term solution to ACC needs, and squadrons equipped with the Curtiss fighter were to receive Mustangs in due course. (Two other squadrons would receive Blenheims in August, as a stand-in for the bomber-reconnaissance aircraft that were yet to arrive – see Chapter 3.)

The Tomahawks had to be modified to AC standards, including camera and radio fit, which took time and formed bottlenecks in the supply of aircraft. It was also necessary to obtain enough aircraft to equip an operational training unit and to form a reserve pool to replace losses. The force would also be required to share the type with fighter squadrons in the Middle East. In reality, there were not enough Tomahawks to equip the front line squadrons, and not enough spares to keep the aircraft flying when they got there. Pilots were hardly able to fly, and the position with regard to training and morale was 'serious in the extreme', wrote Air Marshal A. S. Barratt to Sir Archibald Sinclair, the Secretary of State for Air, in August 1941.

The Model 81 Tomahawk was also superseded in production by the Model 87 Kittyhawk (P-40D/E to the US) in August. At the same time, promises to Britain's new ally, Russia, represented yet another drain on Britain's overall fighter resources, starting with an immediate 200 Hurricanes and a similar number of Tomahawks. The pressure on Allied forces in North Africa and the Mediterranean was also increasing.

The Bell Airacobra had just begun to arrive in England (initially known as the Caribou during its brief RAF career), and the Kittyhawk and Mustang were expected imminently, though the Kittyhawk was to become the standard fighter for North Africa, and would not be available to the Metropolitan Air Force. The first 100 Mustangs had been allocated for ACC, but there was still some doubt as to how best to share out the rest, and even aircraft from the first batch faced being poached.

ACC was aware that some Mustangs were now arriving in the last months of 1941, and Barratt was reduced to begging the Air Ministry to let him have one aircraft for assessment at a front-line unit, the veteran 26 Squadron. The release of the aircraft would become cause for a great deal more frustration, however. Barratt was informed that 26 Squadron could not have a Mustang for evaluation and acclimatisation until four aircraft had been prepared and sent to the Soviet Union! His response to this setback is not recorded but can perhaps be imagined.

The Mustang could quite possibly have found itself banished to India, or supplanting the Bell Airacobra in the Soviet Air Force. However, the timing of the Mustang's appearance coincided perfectly with the desperate need for new equipment in the RAF's AC squadrons.

In October 1941, Air Vice Marshal P. C. Maltby wrote an impatient letter to the BAC in America, reporting his impressions and urging delivery of the more modern aircraft required from the US, specifically the Brewster Bermuda or Vultee Vengeance for the 'bomber reconnaissance' squadrons (see Chapter 3). 'The Lysander is out of date and in urgent need of replacement,' he insisted.

The equipment of ACC with Tomahawks was proving almost impossible in practice. The RAF only managed to equip eight squadrons despite, for the time being, working up with only eight Tomahawks (plus two reserve) per squadron, each retaining four Lysanders. At the beginning of 1942 more than half the Tomahawks in ACC were unflyable through a lack of spares.

Some squadrons had only one or two serviceable aircraft, and one had none at all. Furthermore two of the squadrons were using the unsuitable Tomahawk Mk I, which had been taken over from French orders and had no armour or self-sealing fuel tanks.

It made perfect sense, therefore, to earmark the Mustang entirely for AC use. On 9 January 1942 (appropriately enough, the same day 26 Squadron received its first Mustang), the decision to replace the Tomahawks with Mustangs as fully as possible was agreed by the Air Ministry. It was not a moment too soon as Mustangs were just beginning to arrive in moderate numbers – 32 had reached the UK by the end of 1941, of which eight had been issued 'to service'.

On 28 January 1942, the priorities for equipping fighter reconnaissance and bomber reconnaissance units were finally established. Seven fighter reconnaissance squadrons, plus the operational training unit, would re-equip with Mustangs as the aircraft became available. (Three more fighter reconnaissance squadrons would remain on Tomahawks until further notice, while it was hoped that a further two would receive Hurricanes for a special operation then being planned. Three squadrons were earmarked to re-equip with Brewster Bermudas, thereby becoming bomber reconnaissance units, although the bomber reconnaissance arm of ACC would ultimately fail to work out as planned).

Measures were then taken to enable the earmarked squadrons to familiarise themselves with the new equipment. Pilots and groundcrew from several AC squadrons would be temporarily attached to the AFDU (which was about to receive some examples of the aircraft).

ACC eagerly awaited its new mount. It appeared that the Army would finally have what it had been asking for since 1939 – a dedicated, capable tactical reconnaissance aircraft. It would in fact receive much more than that.

The Mustang Arrives

On 9 January 1942, 26 Squadron received the first Mustang to reach an operational unit, though it was only one aircraft and only to help the unit familiarise themselves with the type. Agonisingly for the squadron, the weather was so poor the next day that all aircraft were grounded. Finally, on 11 January, a 50-minute test flight was carried out. This was the only flying the squadron was able to do, as all its other aircraft were unserviceable. The situation highlighted the desperate need for Mustangs to reach

AC squadrons. Unfortunately for ACC, Lockheed's initial estimates for getting aircraft to squadrons proved wildly optimistic.

The necessary modifications would now include Modifications 318, 319, 320 and 321 – the addition of an army liaison radio, an F.24 camera, two 12-volt accumulators to power the additional equipment, and seat-back armour. Less substantial modifications included new gunsight reflector glass, a new compass, and replacement aerial. ACC was keen to get on with the work of training pilots and working up with the Army in combined exercises, and for that it would need fully modified aircraft. Initially, an offer to supply squadrons with 'factory stock' Mustangs was refused.

By the end of January, there were 40 Mustangs in the UK and 59 in transit from the US. ACC had expressed a desire to take on 400 Mustang Mk Is, but was still struggling to get those already in the country through to squadrons. Early in February, ACC sanctioned 12 unmodified Mustangs to be delivered to 41 OTU, the operational training unit for AC flying. At the same time, radio installation trials were moved to the RAE to save time and reduce the burden on the AFDU and A&AEE.

Meanwhile, operational squadrons were beginning to receive Mustangs for crew training, or their personnel were gaining experience with the aircraft elsewhere. This would not be trouble free – on 9 February, 26 Squadron's Flight Lieutenant Dawson swerved on landing and ran into a Tiger Moth, damaging the Mustang's propeller. January's appalling weather had extended into February, hampering training further. Pilots grabbed odd hours of flying training when the weather allowed, carrying out other duties such as Army exercises and reconnaissance demands in Tomahawks and Lysanders. On 20 February, Squadron Leader Eyres and Flight Lieutenant Houseman of II (AC) Squadron[xi] paid a visit to the AFDU at Duxford to inspect a Mustang, and arranged a series of crew visits to the unit to build up experience.

However, it became clear that the supply of fully prepared Mustangs to squadrons would slip from February 1942 to the end of April (the early losses in transit cannot have helped). Reluctantly, ACC conceded that some squadrons would have to rearm with unmodified Mustangs so they

---

xi   While the RAF convention is to use Arabic numerals for squadron 'number plates', and role suffixes had generally fallen out of favour by the Second World War, II (AC) Squadron continues to style itself with Roman numeral and suffix to this day, for historical reasons, and as such this style will be used throughout.

could get back into the air and do at least some of the necessary training. Towards the end of February, the Air Ministry directed that Nos. 26, 241 and 613 should be re-equipped with unmodified Mustangs, as long as sufficient aircraft were left at the contractor's to ensure modifications could progress with the minimum of delay.

The difficulty in getting the Mustang into service was not helped by the fact that by the end of February, the Mustang had still not been cleared for gun firing. At this point, without being able to undertake live firing exercises, liaise with the Army over radio or practise photographic reconnaissance, training was severely limited. Early in March, permission was given to use the guns in training, even though armament trials were not yet complete.

The flow of Mustangs was increasing though. By 20 March, there were 93 in the UK, with a further 178 on the way. The main difficulty now was in the modification of the aircraft to AC requirements. Aircraft were sitting at Speke and Abbotsinch awaiting the parts Lockheed needed to complete the modification.

By this time, Air Marshal Barratt had a sinking feeling that the same scenario ACC experienced with the Tomahawk would recur. In April, he wrote to the Air Ministry that, 'the supply of spares required for the modification of the Mustang aircraft is in exactly the same parlous state as that experienced during the modification of the Tomahawk... not one has been modified through lack of spares, in spite of MAP promise that six would be completed by the first week of April'.

An important feature of the Mustang Mk I's adaptation for AC service was the camera fit for tactical reconnaissance. An oblique attachment for an F.24 camera had been designed which fitted onto a tray behind the pilot's head. The camera pointed down and to the side through an aperture in the canopy glazing sealed by a rubber gland.

The camera modification ('Mod 319') caused some difficulties initially, particularly with regard to the hole cut in the glazing to allow the camera an unobstructed view. The first time this was tried in flight, air pressure was reported to have blown part of the canopy off.[xii] The mounting was reworked with more attention given to achieving a good seal.

---

xii On 9 February 1942, Barratt wrote to Air Marshal F. G. Linnell and remarked that, 'they have already had trouble with this as the hood blew off when the last test was carried out' – 36A 'Mustang' from AIR 39/110, 'Re-arming of squadrons, Mustang aircraft'.

The F.24 (24 in focal length) camera that was the main 'weapon' of the Allison Mustang in RAF service. The camera was fitted on this custom mount behind the pilot's head, angled for oblique photography. This installation was tested on AL997.

The F.24's lens pointing through the custom cowl installed in the port (left) glazing behind the pilot. In early aircraft this was opaque (possibly being metal rather than the original glazing) but was left clear in later aircraft. The cowl was supposed to form a seal around the camera lens, but as seen here on the test installation the edge had a tendency to fracture, compromising the seal.

Further air tests were carried out between 27 April and 10 August 1942, at speeds ranging from 150mph to 330mph. This time the canopy remained in place, but under all conditions vibration transmitted to the camera, while the A&AEE remarked that the camera did not fit on the custom seat properly. This was clearly unacceptable – further amendments had to be made to improve vibration damping and make the mounting manufacturing more accurate. However, on the positive side, the camera was accessible and changing of the film magazine was easy.

Nevertheless, several squadrons were now building up their complement of unmodified Mustangs. On 16 April, numbers 2, 4, 16, 26, 241, 268, 613 Squadrons and 41 OTU received instructions to begin the planned disposal of all but a few Tomahawks and Lysanders, as they would soon have enough Mustangs to do most of the necessary squadron flying.

At this time, 26 Squadron, based at Gatwick, only needed one more Mustang to reach its full establishment. No. 241 Squadron at Bottisham was already up to strength, while 613 Squadron at Doncaster had received its first Mustangs the previous day when they had been ferried from Speke. No. 268 Squadron at Snailwell would receive its Mustangs in two days, while II (AC) Squadron at Sawbridgeworth was to begin receiving its Mustangs on 21 April, 16 Squadron at Weston Zoyland on 24 April, and 4 Squadron at York on 28 April.

The operational training unit (41 OTU at Old Sarum), crucial for training ACC pilots on the Mustang, had 12 of the fighters on strength. In the meantime, the squadrons that had not yet received their Mustangs had been allowed to detach crews to those that had, for practice.

ACC ruled that 400 and 414 Royal Canadian Air Force (RCAF) Squadrons would begin re-equipment when the squadrons previously identified were up to strength. Two further squadrons, numbers 225 and 239, would also become Mustang units after ACC's request to equip them with Hurricane Mk IIs or Spitfire Mk Vs for an unspecified 'special operation' was turned down. In fact, these squadrons would be the first to receive a full complement of AC-modified aircraft. The other squadrons were required to gradually exchange their basic models for AC-specification Mustangs when the latter became available.

What's in a Name?

The BPC notified NAA that the NA-73 had been given the official designation 'Mustang' by letter dated 9 December 1940, before the first production example had been completed.

The designation P-51 was already in place, allocated when the two NA-73s were contracted for the United States Army Air Corps (later USAAF) as XP-51s and, in spring 1941, reinforced when the Lend-Lease Act introduced the convention that aircraft for supply to Britain would be allocated to the USAAF first. At this time the American military had no convention for naming aircraft; official references were in alphanumerical designation only. Where aircraft did have names, they were those applied by the manufacturer, often for marketing purposes, and used informally. For example, Curtiss used 'Hawk' with a number of different designs, over many years.

At some point in late 1940 or early 1941, NAA decided to name the NA-73 'Apache'. It is not clear whether or not the company suggested this name to the British, but it seems unlikely as there is no mention of it in the known correspondence between Kindelberger and Self et al. before or after the British selected 'Mustang'.

This term was used in advertising in 1941 once the company was permitted to promote the aircraft publicly, mostly using images based on the original NA-73X. In April 1941, NAA's magazine *Flight Line* included a retouched image of the NA-73X in USAAC markings with the caption 'XP-51 Apache Pursuit.' Images of the 'Apache' began to appear on media such as cigarette cards (such as Leaf-O card C-28) and promotional playing cards (e.g. by Whitman), and in advertising for other companies. For example, an Allison advertisement seen in magazines during 1941 listed a number of aircraft using the V-1710 engine, including the 'North American Apache (US) – The British call it "The Mustang".'

The name 'P-51 Apache' was also colloquially used by some media. The October 1941 issue of *Popular Science* suggested various types that might be taken on by the 'newly formed Air Corps Interceptor Command,' including the 'North American P-51 "Apache."' Just after the USAAF had staked its claim for 55 NA-91s (but months before the first one arrived), the January 1942 issue of *Flying Aces* magazine carried an illustration clearly based on the NA-73X on the cover with the caption 'North American P-51 Apache Latest Air Forces

Pursuit'. A model kit produced in 1942 by Capitol Models of Brooklyn representing one of the earliest Mustang Mk Is (identifiable because of the short carburettor intake scoop) was labelled 'North American "Mustang"' with the subtitle 'US Army designation P-51 "Apache"'.

This has led to suggestions that for a period of time the correct name for P-51s in US service was Apache, but none of this means that the USAAF had adopted the name 'officially' (indeed it had no process by which it could do so until mid-1942). There is no evidence that the name Apache was used in Air Force circles, and available USAAF sources of the time simply refer to the 'P-51'.

With the attack on Pearl Harbor and the entry of the US into the war, the USAAF had acquired some of the NAA aircraft from British orders. *Mustang: The Story of the P-51 Fighter* by Robert Gruenhagen, who had been NAA's official historian, makes this claim:

'At this time the Air Force accepted the Mustang and in an effort to establish its new mission and identity, the name "Apache" was assigned to the P-51. By the time the "Apache" was received by flying units, the

NAA used this edited photograph of the NA-73X, retouched with USAAC markings, to publicise the acquisition of two Mustangs which had been designated XP-51. As a result, the photograph is often erroneously stated to depict an XP-51 and has contributed to confusion between the NA-73X and XP-51, which are entirely different aircraft! (US Library of Congress)

designation had been changed to F-6A indicating a photo recon ship and the name was accepted as Mustang to conform to the standards being established by British use of the airplane.' Other Mustang historians such as Tom Griffiths have also asserted that for a period of time, there was such a thing as a P-51 Apache in the USAAF inventory.

This adds further confusion, as it is not clear when the F-6A designation was first applied, and whether it was ever used in service – though with the eventual appearance of other F-6 models, the designation occasionally resurfaced retroactively. (The modified aircraft were also referred to as P-51s with the new 'dash number' -2, which was consistent with the policy of reserving multiples of five for factory modifications and intervening numbers for modifications that were carried out in the field.)

It was evident even across the Atlantic that Apache was a name applied chiefly by the manufacturer. *Flight* magazine wrote in the 23 July 1942 issue that the NA-73 'was christened the Apache by its makers, and in the US Army Air Forces the type is known as the P-51 pursuit.' The following January, the same publication reaffirmed that the aircraft was 'with the US Army Air Force as the P-51; the makers themselves call it the Apache.'

By this time, the information was out of date. On 13 July 1942, Kindelberger sent a wire to Colonel Arthur Ennis, in charge of the AAF's public relations branch, noting 'Understand from Aeronautical Chamber of Commerce that Air Forces contemplating officially naming all Army aircraft in near future. Accordingly we submit the following as our preference for North American aircraft: for all fighters of P-51 type we suggest name "Mustang", which has long been used by the British and widely publicized through news and advertising.'

Soon after this, references in press releases and press photographs were unanimous in referencing the 'P-51 Mustang'. If there had ever been a time when the type had been referred to as the 'P-51 Apache' it had surely been fleeting, and had passed before the Air Force received the first examples of the type. 'Mustang' was therefore the only name that the P-51 was 'assigned' by the USAAF.

And yet, that wasn't the end! Another interpretation (or assumption) is that the A-36 was called 'Apache' to indicate the significantly different nature of this aircraft from its fighter brethren. This is incorrect – see Chapter 10.

Chapter 3

Challenges and Opportunities

In December 1941 and the first few months of 1942, before the first Mustangs had gone into operational service with the RAF, a number of factors combined to dramatically change the direction of its development. Rather than the pure fighter it was conceived as, the next version would be a specialised dive-bomber. There were many reasons for this, which require some discussion of the context at the beginning of 1942.

The event with the greatest impact on the Mustang's future was the opening of the Japanese war in December 1941. In pre-war planning, the British had considered the prospect of fighting three enemies simultaneously – Germany, Italy, and Japan – and concluded that the Empire could not raise the resources to do so. There was little that the British authorities felt could be done to prepare, other than attempting to avoid such a conflict. However, that eventuality had now come to pass, with the attacks on Pearl Harbour, the Philippines, Malaya, Hong Kong and Singapore. This introduced a vast new theatre and seemed to confirm the planners' worst fears. With it, however, came the USA as a fully fledged fellow combatant at last.

While US participation promised many benefits for the Allies in the long run, in the short term it caused much change and uncertainty. No longer could the lion's share of war production be channelled to the British; no more could US forces defer their own needs.

Discussions between Sir Charles Portal, Chief of Britain's Air Staff, and Chief of the US Army Air Forces, General Henry 'Hap' Arnold, about the division of aircraft between Britain and the US resulted in the 'Arnold-Portal Agreement', signed on 13 January. Naturally this meant some reduction of the number of aircraft due to come to the RAF in 1942. For the moment, however, all of the Mustangs on order remained allocated to Britain. The real question was what would happen after that.

In early January, Roosevelt had announced his aircraft production goals for the next two years: 45,000 combat aircraft to be produced in 1942, plus 15,000 trainers, and for 1943, 100,000 combat aircraft and another large order of trainers! Nevertheless, setting a goal did not necessarily translate to aircraft available to equip squadrons, and both the US and Britain needed to be able to plan the makeup of their forces around the aircraft that would be available. At the same time, the nature of the types of aircraft needed depended on the Allies' strategic plan. There were also supply promises to Russia to keep.

In the preceding months there had been an emphasis on increasing production of heavy bombers. Now, with the expansion of the war, came a renewed demand on both sides of the Atlantic for more air support for ground forces, as well as re-examination of the strategic possibilities and immediate priorities. British (and now American) troops were beleaguered in yet another theatre, and the resources of the North African theatre were handicapped in an attempt to meet the new crisis.

The efficacy of Bomber Command's strategic bombing campaign was, by early 1942, increasingly being called into question by Parliament, and the British and American air forces had very different ideas about how such a campaign should be waged. Despite the emergency in the Pacific, the pressure for a true second front in Europe was also growing. The USSR was hard-pressed and there were fears that the Soviets could be knocked out of the war before the western Allies could bring their full efforts to bear on Nazi Germany.

A Growing Need for Close Support

Between February and April 1942, the US Army drew up plans for a spring 1943 invasion of North-West Europe, codenamed *Roundup*. There was also a contingency plan for a late-1942 invasion (*Sledgehammer*) to be launched if the USSR appeared to be on the brink of defeat by then, though there were serious doubts about the Allies' ability to undertake the operation. The strong drive towards an early invasion was to exercise a rapid and considerable influence on air power doctrine. By extension this was to affect both the kinds of aircraft required by the Army and the nature of their employment. According to the Office of Air Force History's exhaustive history of the AAF during the war:

'To the [US] Air Staff, as to RAF Bomber Command, the bomber offensive had figured as a most vital part of the over-all strategy: an operation which by the destruction of well-chosen targets might suffice to bring Germany to her knees or, more probably, would weaken her war potential to the degree that the success of an invasion would be assured. In the new plans... those opinions were submerged in the new strategy; air plans must be built around the alternative schemes for invasion. This meant, for one thing, a reappraisal of target objectives. General Spaatz explained this necessity to Mr. [Secretary of War Henry L.] Stimson by pointing out that whereas the European strategy had originally been conceived as involving the use of air power *supported by ground forces,* it was now a matter of air power *supporting ground forces.* The new strategy demanded also a re-examination of the needs of the Army air force in Britain in terms of trained units and equipment.'[1]

Casting a long shadow on the battle over tactical doctrine was the success of the Junkers Ju 87 'Stuka' dive-bomber during the German forces' sweep across Europe in 1940. The Ju 87 had been employed in a similar way to artillery, punching holes in defending lines of ground forces through which attacking forces could pour and 'roll up' the defending troops. Public and political demands for a similar capability in Allied air arms spurred a rush to develop the US Army's and the RAF's dive-bombing capability, whether or not the respective Air Staffs were enthusiastic about the idea. This pressure was maintained from 1940 into 1942.

During the aircraft buying frenzy of mid-1940 the British ended up with orders for the Brewster 340 Bermuda/Buccaneer (also on order to the US Navy as the SB2A) and the Vultee V-72 'Vengeance' (initiated for France and not at that time under consideration by US forces), which both made their first flights during 1941. The US Army Air Corps had conducted a trial with some borrowed Marine Corps Douglas SBDs during 1940 summer manoeuvres, and as a result ordered a modest number of de-navalised SBDs, which they designated A-24. At the end of the year the Army added an order for 100 A-25 aircraft; a land-based version of the Curtiss SB2C, an aircraft designed to the same requirement as the Brewster 340. The Curtiss was the first prototype of the new generation of dive-bombers to fly.

The Brewster Model 340 Buccaneer, one of the two dive-bombers rejected by the USAAF in early 1943 in favour of 'obtaining a suitable dive-bomber, low-attack fighter' in their place – the aircraft that would become the A-36A.

In mid-1941, the Brewster had fallen so far behind schedule that there seemed little point in the British placing an additional order under Lend-Lease (though for book-keeping purposes the US Army designation 'A-34' had been reserved against the possibility), so instead more Vengeances (designated A-31 by the Air Corps) were ordered for the RAF. These aircraft were meant to fill the 'bomber reconnaissance' role that had been shaped to incorporate close support of ground forces, as a complement to the 'fighter reconnaissance' role being pursued by the RAF in ACC.

For themselves, the US Army ordered another small batch of A-24s and two XA-32 prototypes from Brewster. The latter was a powerful, heavily armed single-seat dive-bomber, the kind of aircraft that the Air Corps felt might prove the ultimate answer for close support.

The *Roundup/Sledgehammer* plan meant that the AAF, as the Air Corps had by then been renamed, would need more close-support aircraft, and quickly. Arnold noted in mid-February that units for direct army support were 'still wallowing around looking for someone who takes an interest in them and in their activities'.[2] This may have been largely true, but there certainly were activities – the AAF's premier dive-bomber unit, the

27th Bombardment Group (Light), was even then hurrying to reach Java in time to assist in its defence with its A-24 Banshees.

Back in the US, the Materiel Division deferred hundreds of heavy bombers from the 1942 fiscal year plan, at the same time as it added several thousand fighters, dive-bombers and trainers. While a higher number of these relatively small aircraft could be built (and paid for) compared to heavy bombers, thereby helping to meet the Commander in Chief's lofty production goal, there were other compelling justifications for this change. Trainers of all kinds were needed to prepare the personnel required by a vastly expanding force; fighters were at that time receiving more recognition than they had pre-war, and represented a greater priority while the Allies were still on the defensive.

The interest in dive-bombers referred to above also affected the procurement figures, for it was at this time that the AAF placed their first large orders for them: 1,200 A-24s to be built at the new B-24 plant under Douglas management in Tulsa, and 3,000 A-25s, to which the Curtiss-Wright plant in St Louis would be dedicated. The AAF also took over some Vengeance aircraft from British orders and placed a modest order of their own – the Vengeance built to US specification would be designated A-35.

However, in light of initial experience in the Pacific, the A-24 'was considered by Army airmen to be too slow, too limited in range, and too vulnerable to enemy fighters',[3] while the Vengeance was experiencing significant development problems (as would the SB2C/A-25). Bringing the Vengeances built for the RAF to US Army standards was proving to be difficult. Some in the Air Force wanted to cancel the aircraft, but it continued, albeit with low priority for equipment and material. (The following February, Major General Davenport Johnson, Director of Military Requirements, lambasted the decision to go ahead with the A-31, describing it as of 'little or no use to the AAF' and a 'waste of material, manpower, and time'.)[4]

There was already little hope of bringing these new aircraft into service in time for the proposed 1943 invasion. On 4 February 1942, Colonel K. B. Wolfe, Chief of the Production Engineering Section, suggested that in light of the difficulties in modifying the Army's A-31s to acceptable standards, it was 'apparent that we [would] not be able to obtain a useful dive-bomber of any type before March or April 1943'. He went on, 'it is recommended that all contracts on A-31 airplanes be cancelled and concentration be given to obtaining a suitable dive-bomber, low-attack fighter in its place.'[5] A different solution was needed, and quickly.

North American was well placed to assist the Air Force with its new-found desire for a 'low-attack fighter'. NAA was keen for a decision to be reached on the Mustang's future, as without further orders, elements of production would start to be wound down at the beginning of May, and the production run would be completed in August. The Inglewood plant could then focus on the B-25, but if Mustang production was to continue, NAA needed to know soon in order to avoid disruption. On 2 February, 'Dutch' Kindelberger wrote to Materiel Division at Wright Field to raise the subject of 'Production of P-51 Mustang Fighter Airplanes' in this context.

Kindelberger reminded Materiel Division of the type's history and current production progress, and indicated a number of potential improvements that could be made if production continued; he stated that the Mustang had been 'tested with a new blower raising the engine rating from 1,150hp at 12,000 feet to 1,125hp at 15,000 feet', and indicated that Allison was working on a two-speed engine that would increase speed to 'substantially more than 400mph at at least 21,000 feet'.

Kindelberger then went on to suggest that bomb racks could be provided and 'dive flaps' installed, and that extra fuel tanks could be fitted to extend maximum range. (While he did not give any specific details, there was at that time a push for overload tanks to allow delivery by air, not necessarily for operational use, so the tanks suggested were not necessarily 'combat tanks'.)

Furthermore, Kindelberger reiterated that two examples had been turned over to the Air Corps, and concluded that:

> This Company believes that this airplane is the best combat fighter *and ground support plane* [author's emphasis] currently in production in this country, all points considered. It is certainly the most adaptable to production and easiest to maintain in service... Consequently it is felt that within a few months there will be a great demand for additional quantities of these airplanes, particularly after actual combat experience is obtained.
>
> If additional airplanes are ordered at once, the new features can be engineered and incorporated and comparatively little loss of production will result... Your immediate comment is urgently requested.

It is evident that, along with company pride in their design, at this point NAA was considering any elements that might appeal to the prospective customer. 1942 would turn out to be a busy year indeed for the Mustang.

Allison did not pursue the two-speed engine for long, despite NAA's enthusiasm for the idea. The other engine development Kindelberger mentioned (the developed 'F' series engine with higher rated altitude) would come to fruition, though this would not be realised for some time. Allison had indeed been working on a higher supercharger drive ratio, which would raise the engine's critical altitude, mainly to provide the P-39 and P-40 with a much-needed boost at higher altitudes. Engine testing and service trials in the P-39J, however, revealed problems with excessive wear, so this engine went back to the drawing board for improvement, and with it, seemingly, the most immediate means of improving the Mustang as a pure fighter.

It was, then, the developments Kindelberger offered toward the Mustang's potential for close support that would initially have the more significant influence on its future.

You Take the Low Road...

While the US was grappling with its need for close-support aircraft, the RAF's ACC was busy re-equipping with the Mustang. The new type was perfect for the fighter-reconnaissance task and its abilities would later reinforce the idea of a more directly offensive role for the aircraft. By the beginning of 1942, the performance of the Mustang at low level was becoming widely recognised, even though the aircraft had yet to go into action. It is likely that British pilots' evaluations while at North American had been seen by the AAF, and first impressions of the aircraft now beginning to arrive in England were available in the US. AAF pilots had been allowed to fly some Mustangs in California and had passed their impressions up the chain, while at Wright Field, the XP-51 was found to outperform the P-40E (which used the same model of Allison), and, up to about 15,000ft, the Merlin-powered P-40F as well.[6]

In the last week of February, a meeting took place in the office of Col H. A. Craig, head of the AAF's Air War Plans Division, during which

After its testing by the USAAC, XP-51 41-039 went to the NACA at Langley, Virginia, in December 1941 for aerodynamic testing. It is seen here at Langley in November 1943, having gained a coat of Olive Drab paint.

a ground-attack version of the Mustang was proposed.[i] It is not entirely clear who had first planted the seed – it is possible that the British had had some influence in one way or another, given the current preoccupation with close-support aircraft. It is apparent, however, that both the Army and NAA were keen to make it work. The 'close support' Mustang would not simply be a fighter-bomber of the kind then beginning to find favour, such as the contemporary 'Hurribomber' variants of the Hawker Hurricane. Neither would it be a tactical reconnaissance aircraft with light potential for strafing, as the Mustang Mk Is of AC Command were.

The proposal for the next Mustang was that it be equipped with dive brakes to convert it into a bona fide dive-bomber. This rapidly found favour with the AAF due to the factors described above – the inadequacy

---

i   A memo from Kindelberger dated 5 March 1942 refers to the meeting 'in [Craig's] office last week', quoted in Ludwig, Paul A. *P-51 Mustang: Development of the Long Range Escort Fighter*, p. 74.

of existing dive-bombers, the delays in newer dive-bomber programmes, set against the urgent need for large numbers of this class of aircraft.

It was not quite as simple as signing on the dotted line. Materiel Division raised the following objections to an order for an attack variant of the Mustang on 5 March:

a. An immediate lack of engines (due to a planned increase in the rate of P-39 production).
b. Impact on B-25 production rate.
c. The development project required to turn the P-51 into a dive-bomber: dive brake design, bomb racks, and cannon installation.

Materiel Division felt that production at Inglewood should conclude with the end of the initial British orders, though also mentioning that it was studying the possibility of setting up P-51 production at NAA's Kansas City plant 'when engines and GFE [Government Furnished Equipment] are available'.[7]

A normal development programme *could* delay the aircraft beyond the point when they would be useful.

NAA was working on several options for the attack aircraft, not all of which made it onto the final product. The reference to cannon is distinct from the RAF's requirement for 20mm cannon as the main air-to-air armament, although NAA would have been working on the NA-91's cannon-equipped wing at about this time. Cannon was seen in this context as an air-ground weapon, and it appears a different configuration was considered. While the NA-91's cannon were to be buried in the wing, a mock-up was prepared for an underslung arrangement, which it is likely was developed for the 'attack' Mustang proposal. An NAA photograph dating from around this time shows a twin-underslung mounting for 20mm cannon with fairings over the breeches and exposed barrels (the photograph's ID number has the prefix '73', indicating that it shows an NA-73 model aircraft, pre-dating the allocation of a later model number to the 'official' attack Mustang programme). At around the same time, drawings (dated 3 May 1942) were prepared for a version of the NA-73 fitted with two 37mm cannon (37mm Automatic Gun, M4, the main weapon of the P-39, which, in that aircraft, fired through the propeller boss), one on each wing. This arrangement was in some respects similar to the RAF's installation of 40mm guns on

Hawker Hurricane Mk IId 'tankbusters', but buried almost entirely within the wing, necessitating only a bulge on the underside. This version was also fitted with dive brakes.[8]

Despite Materiel Division's reservations, it was felt that the NAA proposal was, according to General Hanley, Deputy Chief of Staff for the Air Force, the 'only possible source of additional interim planes in 1942'[9] in the light bomber category, and on 19 April, the Director of Military Requirements wrote to General Oliver Echols, Head of Materiel Division, with a formal requirement to procure 500 attack Mustangs, noting: '... It is desired that the P-51 airplane be converted to an interim dive bomber, without waiting for completion of the dive-bomber conversion project... those produced without dive brakes can be used as fighters, fighter-bombers, observation airplanes or in operational training units.'[10] In other words, the priority was to plan for production first, and finalise the details later.

The debate may have been the cause of some delay in the final contract for attack Mustangs, which was not signed until August; by this time, work had been ongoing on the variant for four months – NAA was investing a great deal of time and effort in this variant, and before it was clear that there would be an order. One can speculate that NAA had good grounds to hope for a British purchase in the event the US interest led nowhere, but in any event it represented a significant gamble on the company's part. It was an important one, though. Had the Mustang ceased production at this point, there was almost no chance it could be restarted.

The 500 machines were given serials 42-83663 to 42-84162, and the new sub-type was designated the A-36 by the Army and NA-97 by NAA. In service the first (and as it would turn out, only) model of the A-36 was termed the A-36A.[ii] Officially at least, the aircraft retained the name Mustang (see Chapter 10 for a description of the erroneous application of the name 'Apache' to the A-36).

---

ii At about the time that the A-35 and A-36 received their designations, it was decided to apply the 'A' suffix to the first service model rather than the second, and these two were amended accordingly. This promoted clarity, but since it was not retroactive, it has helped cause endless confusion in relation to the Mustang family, with NA-91 being 'P-51' but F-6A, and thus NA-99 being either P-51A or F-6B. (Fortunately, F-6C applied to both P-51B and C, the legacy of another short-term policy, which brought them back into alignment. RAF marks, of course, ran their own course and also contribute to the confusion).

Factory-fresh NAA Model NA-97, or A-36A in USAAF service, at the NAA factory at Inglewood. It has its dive brakes extended, demonstrating their form and arrangement. The first A-36A flight took place on 27 September 1942, with the first production aircraft – there were no prototypes.

Relatively minor modifications were made to the basic NA-73/NA-83 to produce the dive-bomber version. Some wing strengthening was incorporated, but there was much less difference from the basic NA-73 structure than was the case in the P-51/Mustang Mk IA wing, which needed large 'beams' to retain strength around the larger ammunition bays. The A-36A reverted to machine guns, but this time with four 0.50in Brownings in the wings, as well as two in the nose as in the Mustang Mk I. (This raises an intriguing question about tooling, and whether the production line switched back to Mustang Mk I tooling, with modifications, after the NA-91 run was complete, or whether parallel wing tooling was being developed for the A-36 during the NA-91's run.)

At the same time that fighters were looking for power at higher altitudes, a version of the Allison V-1710 optimised for low-altitude operations was developed specifically for the A-36, the -87 (F21R). This offered greater power, 1,325hp, for five minutes at maximum military power, between sea level and 3,200ft altitude.

The dive brakes closely followed the pattern of those developed for the Vengeance, with the co-operation of Northrop, which was building the

A-36A 42-83861, the 198th of 500 aircraft, in very close company with two of North American's other great product, the AT-6 'Texan' advanced trainer. With dive brakes stowed, the aircraft would be hard to distinguish from the NA-73/83 – the only visual clue apart from the serial is the bomb rack just visible below the wing.

dive-bombers not far away. (Indeed, Vance Breese, who undertook the first flights of the NA-73X, had also made the first flight of the Vengeance). The brakes took the form of folding, slatted panels on the upper and lower surface of each wing.

A Mustang Mk I, AM118, was fitted with the dive brakes and tested from May 1942, further indicating that NAA had been working on the idea without waiting for official approval. This could relate to the 'dive-bomber conversion project' mentioned above, or at least one stage thereof.

Bomb racks were fitted beneath each wing, enabling the A-36A to carry two bombs of up to 500lbs each, or 75-gallon (62.5-imperial gallon) drop tanks, or larger ferry tanks, which would extend the maximum straight-line range to an estimated 2,891 miles, (though it is unlikely that the large ferry tanks were ever used in service).

Though described as an interim machine, the A-36A promised to offer great accuracy, survivability and combat radius (particularly, as regards the latter, with its relatively high internal fuel tankage), and performance and combat utility far superior to the 'conventional' dive-bomber.

One A-36A, 42-83685, was allocated to the RAF for evaluation, where it received the serial EW998. It was tested from March 1943 but no British orders resulted and it was returned to the USAAF in July that year. It is seen here demonstrating dive-brake deployment and carriage of two 500lb bombs.

As for the Vengeance, at much the same time that the A-36 project was approved, Vultee proposed an 'A-31A', modified to address all the shortcomings that the AAF, and to a degree the British, had identified. According to the proposal, a prototype would be complete in July, and the old version would be superseded in October. The offer was accepted as the A-35, and further orders were placed with serials not far behind those of the A-36. While the Vengeance did see some operational use, it was not to be with the AAF (and the A-35 and its British equivalent the Vengeance Mk IV would only ever undertake second-line roles).

In the context of the Mustang's later brilliance as an escort fighter, the decision to order Mustangs as dive-bombers has, in hindsight, raised eyebrows. It has been suggested, both by later commentators and people who were present at the time, that the Army, deeply interested in the Mustang, placed the order to circumvent a lack of money in the fighter budget while exploiting the fact that there was cash left in the attack budget.[iii] As indicated earlier, more fighters were ordered at the same time as heavy bomber orders were being cut during 1942, but the priority was to concentrate on established types.[iv] At the time the Air Force favoured the P-39, P-40 and slightly later the P-47 as its main single-engined fighters.

It is apparent that following the US Army Air Corps purchase of A-36As, no further aircraft in the Pursuit category were ordered within the fiscal year of 1942. (Subsequently, the cancellation of orders in the 1942 financial year budget meant that some later fighter orders, including some Merlin-engined Mustangs, would be 'backfilled' and allocated blocks of '42' serials). However, it is equally clear from the ample available evidence that the AAF was serious

---

iii As an example, Peter C. Smith's notable book on the A-36A, *Straight Down!*, quotes NAA sources suggesting that, 'The defence budget for fiscal year 1942 had all been used up for purchase of aircraft in the "Pursuit" category. However, there was a loophole, soon exploited to the full by all concerned, for the "Attack" aircraft budget was still in surplus.' Smith quotes Stanley Worth, of the NAA design team, as saying: '"Dutch" Kindelberger... convinced "Hap" Arnold that the P-51A [sic]... with dive brakes, was just what the US needed. I don't believe that anyone really believed that dive brakes would work on a laminar flow wing. I know "Dutch" didn't!' The 'pursuit budget' theory is also mentioned in the 2012 MMP Books title *North American A-36A Apache*, and is very prevalent across internet sources.

iv For example, the Curtiss P-60 was cancelled in January 1942 in favour of more P-40s and P-47s.

about obtaining a dive-bomber variant of the Mustang to plug a gap in its attack inventory, with the possibility of major combined operations early the following year. Whether or not there was any formal bar to the ordering of Pursuit aircraft, aircraft for army support were an urgent new priority, especially with the delays and disappointments in the more traditional dive-bomber programmes. When viewed in context, the acquisition of the A-36A for the attack role makes perfect sense, and there is significant evidence to support it – while there is no contemporary documentary evidence to support the purchase of A-36As as a 'dodge' to acquire the Mustang as a fighter.

The value the AAF placed in the A-36A as an attack aircraft was borne out operationally. The A-36 was occasionally used in a fighter role, but the vast majority of its employment was exactly what it was procured for – as a fast, agile, army support aircraft capable of dive-bombing. Three Bombardment Groups were equipped with the type, two in the Mediterranean and one in the Far East (see Chapters 6–8). The only other operational use the type was put to was tactical reconnaissance.

There were numerous opportunities to substitute more conventional fighters for the A-36 – and these were not taken. The Director of Military Requirements had suggested in April (see above) that aircraft built without the dive brakes could have been used as fighters, but this was not taken up. Ultimately, it seemed there was little reason to add more fighter-variant Mustangs, while there were good reasons to develop the ground-attack version.

... and I'll Take the High Road

Hard on the heels of the US decision to order the A-36A, another very significant event took place. The commander of AFDU invited his friend, Ronald Harker, Rolls-Royce Hucknall's chief test pilot, to try out one of their (quite new) Mustangs. Harker was impressed with the aircraft's performance. Moreover, he had recent experience of the effect of the two-stage Merlin 61 on the Spitfire's performance and made an enthusiastic report to Rolls-Royce's management about the Mustang the next day (1 May 1942). Within two weeks, Rolls-Royce had made representations to the Air Ministry about the potential of a Merlin-powered Mustang.

Such developments would require some time though, and that month, the first of ACC's Mustang Mk Is were preparing to go into action.

Chapter 4

Preparing for Service

On 1 May 1942, the Mustang Mk I was officially released for service, and thereby became an operational type at last. There were in reality a number of caveats to this milestone. Oil cooling issues had not been fully resolved, and radiator baffles were being made available to prevent over-cooling that could take place in certain circumstances. The Mustang Mk I's armament was not fully satisfactory, as the starboard nose gun showed a tendency for stoppages due to a tight bend in the belt feed. In the condition in which the aircraft had been delivered, the wing 0.30in guns were liable to jump off the mountings and shoot through the wing skin. Specially manufactured stronger locking pins had to be fitted before the guns were considered safe to fire.[i] The exhausts initially fitted did not have the appropriate flame-damping qualities and replacements would not be available for some time.

Early that month, Lockheed indicated that 10–12 Mustangs would be fully modified to AC requirements by 10 May. The first, AG359, was to be a replacement for AG366 which had crashed at 26 Squadron on 1 May, and the rest were for 239 Squadron at Abbotsinch. The next ten after this were earmarked for 225 Squadron, which collected the Mustangs while at Abbotsinch and flew them down to Thruxton later that month.

---

i The installation of the wing guns was considered acceptable by both the AFDU and the A&AEE, though the latter experienced a number of stoppages, mainly due to faulty rounds. The former tested the guns under positive and negative G and suffered no stoppages. Although in later models, the canted guns with their solid feed channels were felt to be the root of too many jams. Not until the P-51D model was the installation of Browning machine guns in the wings changed significantly, with the guns mounted upright. New, flexible ammunition feeds enabled the guns to be fitted upright within the existing wing space, and requiring no changes to the wing surface.

The work-up period still had its dangers – at II (AC) Squadron, two Mustangs were seriously damaged and a pilot killed on 9 May when AG403, piloted by Pilot Officer Gosnell, struck Pilot Officer Willmett's AG488 while the former was taking off. Gosnell's Mustang climbed to 50ft before stalling and crashing inverted, and he later died of his injuries.

The first Mustang operation was flown by 26 Squadron – a reconnaissance on 10 May, with a 'rhubarb' flown on 14 May and another a week later. Much of the Mustang's operational ACC career would involve missions of this nature. Typically these included rhubarbs (offensive visual reconnaissance flights), 'rangers' (intrusion flights to divert air defences from other operations), and 'populars' (photographic reconnaissance missions). Other mission types would be added over time, and there was also plenty of flying on joint exercises with the Army.

With availability of a truly suitable aircraft at last, five new AC squadrons were formed on 15 June, in some cases spinning off from one of the existing squadrons. These were the reformed 63 Squadron (the number plate having previously been attached to a Fairey Battle squadron disbanded in April 1940), and the newly formed ACC units, 168, 169, 170

Mustang Mk I AM148 of 26 Squadron, the first front-line unit to receive the type. The usually matt-finish wings have been polished to maintain laminar flow.

A three-ship formation of Mustang Mk Is from 170 Squadron, demonstrating the short-lived chordwise yellow bands applied as identification markings.

and 171 Squadrons with new number plates. Not all received Mustangs immediately, but things were definitely looking up for ACC – it seemed Air Marshal Barratt's fears about re-equipment echoing the Tomahawk fiasco may have been unfounded. Squadrons were also expanded to the normal establishment of 18 aircraft during the summer months. (In fact, the limiting factor for new squadrons as of the beginning of August was the availability of maintenance personnel rather than aircraft.) Meanwhile 2 Group, Bomber Command, the other RAF force associated with AC, had begun to replace its Blenheims with the far more capable Mosquito (in its bomber variant) and its Bostons with North American's own Mitchells. (Less successfully, Lockheed Venturas were about to join the force as well.)

RCAF squadrons 400 and 414 also obtained their first Mustangs in June 1942, both 'jumping the queue' in receiving their aircraft as a matter of some urgency.[ii] Among the first pilots to get a taste of the new aircraft

---

ii This may well have been done with the forthcoming Operation *Rutter*, soon recast as *Jubilee*, in mind – see page 85.

was 414 Squadron's Pilot Officer Hollis Hills, an American who had volunteered for the RCAF. In the next few months, Hills' name would become part of the Mustang's history. The squadron's diary records that after his first experience of the aircraft, at Croydon on 5 June, Hills 'reported very favourably' on his new mount.

The following month, 309 'Ziema Czerwienska' Squadron became the first of several Polish units to operate the type, making the Mustang 'family' in the RAF rather a cosmopolitan one.

Modified Mustangs were now steadily arriving, though many still lacked seat armour. Attention turned to what could be done with the original unmodified aircraft, which were still held by seven squadrons. It had been suggested that these be disposed of to 41 OTU for use in training, but although AC Command had originally been amenable to the suggestion, it now resisted.[1] AC Command wanted the unmodified machines to be returned to the MAP for modification to the latest AC standard as a reserve against wastage (though ACC acknowledged that unmodified Mustangs were also potentially of use to help the new squadrons work up). However, on 12 July 1942, the Ministry pointed out ACC had earlier agreed to receive the unmodified machines on condition that once accepted, they could not be returned to the MAP for modification. The Ministry once again suggested passing the aircraft to the OTU.

AP170 of 309 Polish Squadron in April 1944, after the squadron had adopted 'WC' code letters. (via Wojtek Matusiak)

Group Captain Fitch replied that when the Mustang was first taken on, it was appropriate for unmodified aircraft to be used for training as a great deal of basic flying practice on the type was initially required. This was no longer the case, and the pressing need was for aircraft of the necessary standard for operational training.

This was no trivial matter. The expertise of the pilots carrying out AC missions was essential. Even after joining an AC unit, pilots would not conduct their first operation until they had completed several months of training specific to the entirety of the operations they would be involved in. This included blind flying practice, radio procedure and discipline, keeping fuel consumption low at high cruising speeds, and supervising the swinging of their aeroplane's compass. Every day pilots took part in range estimation and gunnery practice. Pairs of aircraft would go out over the sea and practise 'shadow shooting'. Formation flying was also practised incessantly so pilots could instinctively maintain station without having to concentrate excessively.

In July 1942, II (AC) Squadron staged a demonstration of their new Mustangs for the press at Sawbridgeworth. This, and the following sequence of photographs, is from that event.

AG623 'XV-W' carries out an extremely low 'beat-up' for the cameras.

AL995 'XV-S' undergoes a change of cameras while another aircraft flies overhead...

... and after having been put back together, runs up its engine. Note the white 'sighting mark' to help with photography on the trailing edge of the port flap.

It was therefore critical that Mustangs to full AC specification be available at both the OTU and the operational squadrons, so on 28 July, MAP agreed to accept all unmodified Mustang Mk Is back to 41 Group for conversion, on condition that they were returned in a serviceable condition.[iii]

While the training continued intensively, more operational sorties began to take place. A typical example was a free-ranging low-level 'rhubarb', carried out by three Mustangs from 26 Squadron on 14 July 1942. The pilots were Flight Lieutenant Dawson flying AG535, Flying Officer Giles flying AG462 and Pilot Officer Taylor flying AG415.

The three Mustangs were assigned the area around the Boulogne-Abbeville railway. They crossed the French coast at 11.27am and continued east until Rang-du-Fliers railway station was spotted, where wagons were lined up in sidings. The three pilots strafed the wagons but were unable to observe the results of their attack as there was a great deal of light flak from the station buildings. They continued at low level along the course of the railway until the next station, where more trucks were spotted along with an anti-aircraft gun on a flatbed car. The pilots concentrated their attack on the flak gun – Flight Lieutenant Dawson scored hits on shells stacked nearby for ready use, which exploded with a bright flash of yellow flame.

Nothing further was seen along the railway, but the pilots took note of 15 'invasion type barges' in a river estuary near Pointe du Hourdel. The flight turned north and strafed a water tower, before turning out to sea and returning near Le Touquet. A barge carrying out a landing exercise with around 40 soldiers on board was spotted and attacked in a dive from 400ft. While making this attack, Pilot Officer Taylor crashed or was shot down – the two other pilots did not clearly see what had happened, but Flying Officer Giles saw a cloud of sand bursting into the air near the barge, and Flt Lt Dawson saw scattered, burning wreckage while making a second pass. Dawson and Giles turned for home and returned to Gatwick at 12.21pm.

This mission illustrates how incredibly quickly things happened at high speed and low altitude. Besides the basic demands of this kind of flying, the

---

iii ACC squadrons failed to meet this condition, returning several aircraft with vital components removed, including one aircraft that had been stripped entirely of its armament.

pilots needed considerable skills and reflexes to identify targets and attack them when most of the time there was only an opportunity for a single pass. Safety was considered a high priority and both training and planning emphasised that no unnecessary risks were to be taken.

An area of training that was particularly important regarded emergency procedures. Forced landings in the event of an engine failure over land were practised. However, over water, ditching was discouraged as experience showed that 'if the Mustang must be ditched, it will go under like a shot'.[2] At 200mph, it was possible to gain 500ft by pulling straight up, just enough altitude to bail out. The procedure for an engine failing at 'zero feet' had to be practised intensively just to prove to pilots that it was possible to gain enough height to bail out, as long as they responded swiftly. Fast action was essential – in addition to pulling up as quickly as possible, the pilot had to find time to switch his IFF ('Identification Friend or Foe') to the emergency broadcast setting, jettison the hood and bail out. Pilots were also taught how to nurse a damaged engine long enough to get home.

The preparation was by no means over-cautious. Missions could be dangerous – two days after Pilot Officer Taylor was killed, a three-aircraft

Three Mustangs from 241 Squadron are welcomed back to their base at Bottisham, Cambridgeshire. This squadron operated Mustangs from April to October 1942.

popular took place with Flight Lieutenant Greville (a member of parliament in addition to his flying duties) and Pilot Officer McComas. Neither returned and no trace of them was found. The third member of the flight, Pilot Officer Watson, became separated from his compatriots in cloud shortly after the three had strafed soldiers on a beach near Hardelot. He headed for home, and reached Gatwick just after 3.00pm. Greville and McComas had simply disappeared.

Training itself was not risk-free – Pilot Officer G. D. P. Young, flying AG551, was killed during an air-firing exercise at Weston Zoyland on 30 May 1942. It would not be the last non-combat loss of a Mustang pilot. In August that year, Pilot Officer Kelly and Pilot Officer Manson of 26 Squadron were killed in a cross-country flying accident, probably as a result of a mid-air collision.

As the AC squadrons got closer to fully operational status with their new aircraft, the scope of training increased. No II (AC) Squadron at Sawbridgeworth was visited by Spitfires from North Weald to practise air-fighting tactics on 1 August 1942. Over the next two weeks, pilots took part in Artillery Reconnaissance ('Arty/R') exercises, mock low-level attacks on army and anti-aircraft units, formation flying and message dropping.

Competition was introduced in most elements of the training, with the most successful pilots rewarded with promotion to flight leader. Pilots were required to be thoroughly familiar with their own aircraft, make 'changes in their own aircraft for their personal comfort'[3] and attend to its performance. Each pilot was encouraged to keep his ground crew on their toes, including making sure the wings of the aircraft were 'polished and free from scratches'[4] and dents (the laminar-flow wings of the Mustang suffered particularly from any interruptions to the airflow). It was not just the machinery that pilots had to be familiar with; aircrews routinely formed pairs who tended to operate together as long-standing partnerships, planning and carrying out missions together. Generally, one would act as 'flight leader' and carry out the mission primary objective, while the other would act as 'weaver', keeping an eye out for enemy fighters and protecting the flight leader. Sometimes a pair would alternate the lead role during missions with several objectives or free-ranging rhubarbs.

The first operation with Mustangs for 414 Squadron was a patrol over the south coast on 30 June 1942, which proceeded uneventfully. In contrast to their AC duties, several Mustang squadrons were taken away from their usual AC duties and drafted in to the defence of south-coast towns against German 'tip and run' raiders. These operations consisted of aircraft crossing the English Channel at low level, carrying out a rapid attack and fleeing back to France before interception could take place. In the summer of 1942 there were not too many such raids, but later in the year, some Mustang squadrons found themselves doing little other than patrolling against the Luftwaffe.

For now though, the raison d'être of the AC squadrons was working with and on behalf of ground forces. Naturally therefore, a great deal of work was devoted to combined exercises. All of the Mustang squadrons took part in exercises of this type to develop tactics and hone the skills of both ground and air components. These ranged from small exercises lasting a few hours with Army brigades or Home Guard units, to large-scale rehearsals of major combined operations. An example of the latter was Operation *Dryshod*, which took place in August 1942. A number of Mustang squadrons took part, including 414 Squadron RCAF which had only received its Mustangs in the last two months. The reason for the relatively green squadron taking part in this exercise was soon to become apparent.

Mustangs from 414 Squadron flew to Abbotsinch on 1 August. No flying took place the following day, but the crews taking part were briefed on the nature of the operation – a full-scale practice invasion of France. It was to involve a mock 'English Channel' marked out on land, over which two infantry divisions and an armoured division, and all their equipment, would be theoretically transported. The operation commenced on 4 August, on which day 414 Squadron carried out 32 sorties of an hour's duration each. The following day, 31 sorties were flown and the day after that, 25 sorties.

The Mustangs' main task during *Dryshod* was tactical reconnaissance – happily, 414 Squadron 'did a fine job of obtaining information over strange country, and experienced little difficulty'. Nevertheless, it was apparent that all that training had to be put to some use – 'Pilots are becoming impatient to get into action,' the squadron's operations record book noted on 15 August. 'Practice flying is all right in its place, but our lads have been doing it for a year.'[5]

Operation *Jubilee*

The AC squadrons' pilots probably had little idea just how soon training would turn into reality and their recent experiences would be put to good use. Just three days after the squadron's diary had complained about a lack of real action, a number of pilots were briefed and sworn to secrecy about an operation that would be taking place from the following morning. Operation *Jubilee* was an audacious plan to seize and temporarily hold the port of Dieppe. It was not part of any invasion in itself, but would have considerable influence on later invasions.

For the operation, 35 Wing was formed for AC flying, and was made up of 26 and 239 Squadrons RAF and 400 and 414 Squadrons RCAF, all flying Mustang Is. The wing operated from Gatwick. For the two RCAF units, this would be the first time that Canadian AC squadrons had acted in their intended role, working with units of the Canadian Army in combined operations – the Canadian 2nd Division formed the main force. On the day of the assault, 414 Squadron pilots made 17 sorties to the Dieppe area, while 400 Squadron pilots flew 24 sorties, according to the squadrons' operations record books (ORBs).

Members of a Chinese military mission inspect a Mustang Mk I of 35 Wing, at RAF Odiham, 1942.

The Mustang squadrons were focused on deep, low-level tactical reconnaissance of road networks around and behind the objective. The Mustang pilots were charged with searching for any signs of enemy forces being moved in to repel the assault. The roads were largely clear, and the reconnaissance missions had little to report. They were far from uneventful, however.

The missions started early in the morning, at around 6.00am. Weather was good. Over the course of the morning, three of 400 Squadron's aircraft were holed by light flak. Equally, 414 Squadron's aircraft reported a lot of flak on most missions.

No. 26 Squadron flew 18 Tac/R sorties around Le Havre, Rouen, Abbeville and the mouth of the River Somme. Several ground targets were attacked – Pilot Officer Kelly, flying AG426, strafed two staff cars. The squadron had a bad day for losses though, with five pilots reported missing. A two-aircraft mission from 26 Squadron left Gatwick at 8.00am, and both were brought down over enemy territory. One of the pilots, New Zealander Flight Lieutenant Arnold George Christensen flying Mustang I AL977, was captured and later executed with 49 other members of the 'Great Escape' from Stalag Luft III.

German fighters were not slow to tackle the reconnaissance flights as they 'hedge hopped' across the French countryside. Flight Lieutenant Clarke's Mustang of 414 Squadron was hit in the radiator by a bullet from an Fw 190, and Clarke had to ditch in the sea. Clarke sustained a head injury and at the time remembered nothing of his incident (though later it seems the memories returned, and he spoke extensively with his son about the attack[6]). A destroyer brought him back to England. His weaver, Flying Officer Hills, had seen four Fw 190s shaping up to attack them as they approached the coast, but Clarke's radio was faulty and he did not receive the warning[7]. Hills was unable to prevent the first Fw 190 lining Clarke up and its first burst was enough to kill the Mustang's cooling system. However, when the second Fw 190 misjudged an attack on Hills and overtook the Mustang to Hills' left, Hills 'hit him hard' and 'knew that he was a goner'. The fight had taken place just above the rooftops of Dieppe, and the Fw 190 crashed within seconds.

Meanwhile, Pilot Officer Stover was bounced by another Fw 190 and forced to evade violently. Stover was manoeuvring so hard, and flying so low that he collided with a telegraph pole. It says much for the strength of the Mustang that he was able to evade the Fw 190 and fly back across the Channel, even with three feet torn from the starboard wing of his aircraft and part of the aileron missing. He crash landed successfully at Gatwick. Stover's partner on that mission, Flying Officer Horncastle, managed to get on the tail of the Fw 190, only to have all but one of his guns jam. He chased the Focke-Wulf, but was unable to do any damage with his one functioning gun. Almost comically, Horncastle was himself nearly brought down by a seagull as he pursued the Fw 190. The bird collided with his starboard wing leading edge when the Mustang was flying at high speed, and ripped a hole in the wing. Horncastle was able to return and make a normal landing, but was furious that he had missed his chance to make the squadron's – indeed, the Mustang's – first 'kill'. That honour instead fell to his squadron-mate, Hollis Hills, flying Mustang I AG470, with his Fw 190 now confirmed.

A photograph of a 613 Squadron Mustang from Twinwood Farm, Bedfordshire, taken with the reconnaissance camera of a second Mustang – hence the background being sharp and the aircraft out of focus – flown by Bill Hawkins. (Harrowbeer Local Interest Group)

As well as tactical reconnaissance, several missions were responsible for spotting for naval gunnery, including directing fire onto gun emplacements which were hitting the attacking forces. By lunchtime though, the Mustangs of 35 Wing had no more work to do. At 10.50am, a retreat had been called as all the forces landing were hard-pressed. The evacuation was complete by 2.00pm, but over 3,300 soldiers had been killed, wounded or captured. The Mustangs had flown around 70 sorties, with a total of ten aircraft lost.[iv] The operation had been a costly failure, but had at least indicated the extreme impracticality of attempting to seize an entire port intact ahead of an invasion.

The Last of the Allisons – P-51A/Mustang Mk II (NA-99)

Even as the Mustang was having its first taste of operations, the plan for the type's future was changing once again, which would lead to the end of the Allison Mustang line. However, a final development in the Allison Mustang would be produced even while its successor was planned.

As a result of Rolls-Royce's initiative in May, the British, and soon American, authorities were sold on the idea of a Mustang powered by the two-stage supercharged Rolls-Royce Merlin 61 (or the licence-built Packard equivalent) with its superlative high-altitude performance. Rolls-Royce Hucknall received AG518 for performance evaluation before the month was out, and soon received further Mustang Mk I airframes to use for the trial installation and development. By mid-June, US prototypes had been authorised and the implications for Packard's production plan were being studied.

Meanwhile, the continuing supply of US aircraft to Britain was interfering with the AAF's own needs for operational growth and replenishment, as well as training, including that for air-to-ground co-operation. The aircraft allocation discussion was accordingly once again opened in May between Portal, Arnold and Vice-Admiral John Towers, representing the US Navy (the subsequent plan being dubbed the 'ATP agreement' after the initials

---

iv The author's count of Mustang sorties during the Dieppe operation, 67, from the squadron ORBs does not fully tally with that of Richard Franks' *The Greatest Air Battle: Dieppe, 19th August 1942* – 73 sorties (Franks, Richard, *The Greatest Air Battle: Dieppe, 19th August 1942*, Grub Street, 2008).

of the men involved). The main focus was the remainder of 1942, but they also looked ahead into 1943.

The effect of these talks was to reduce the number of aircraft to be supplied to Britain under Lend-Lease, while protecting anticipated deliveries of light and dive-bombers, and to an extent of fighters.[8] In return, the US committed to send fully equipped squadrons to fight in the war against Germany, both from the UK and in the Mediterranean. The general principle was that of 'US crews in US aircraft', but Britain would still receive aircraft to support RAF squadrons already established on American types.

There was also some horse-trading. The agreement limited the supply of P-51s to Britain to 200 from June, which was itself only secured in exchange for 200 Spitfires to equip a second AAF Pursuit Group due to be based in Britain. This reflected the US Army's A-36A following the Mustang Mk IA (NA-91) on the production line, and meant that the RAF would receive only 93 of the 150 NA-91s, leaving the remaining 57 in the hands of the US.

Two of these aircraft were allocated to NAA to convert to prototypes of the Merlin version. In the long-term, production would rely on this project being successful. The ATP agreement indicated no Mustangs for Britain in the first quarter of 1943, but noted that this was 'subject to revision if additional production is created using Merlin 61 engines'.

By 25 June 1942, approval had been granted for Merlin Mustang production: 'The Joint Aircraft Committee in America had agreed that 1,200 Mustangs should be produced between January and October 1943,' stated the minutes of a July meeting in England. 'Mr [Charles Richard] Fairey had made a claim for 50% of the output as a condition of our releasing Packard Merlin engines... CRD said a Merlin 61 had been sent by air to the USA for trial installations.'[9]

The same meeting expressed doubt that Packard would be able to produce a Merlin with two-stage supercharger equivalent to the Merlin 61 in time for the projected beginning of production in January 1943. Furthermore, Kindelberger freely admitted that the timescale for the two-stage Merlin Mustang was ambitious, but nevertheless the future of the aircraft was clearly aligned with the Merlin.

In some respects, then, the P-51A can be regarded as a precursor of the Merlin Mustang. However, this is not the whole story, as several factors influenced the next step in the Mustang's development. There was a need to develop a fighter variant of the Mustang to American specifications, now the AAF was fully committed to the aircraft. This meant starting to prepare for the impending introduction of a Merlin-powered variant while continuing the improvement of the breed. An additional factor was the recognition of the Mustang as a potent ground-attack aircraft, but with less need for the A-36A's more specialist features, such as dive brakes.

The Army therefore found itself with an immediate windfall of a number of P-51s, and the anticipation of both the A-36A and a Merlin-engined fighter version to follow. In this environment, the AAF's Director of Air Defense authorised tactical trials of the P-51 (NA-91) on 13 July. The trials began on 7 August, and will be discussed below.[10]

'Dutch' Kindelberger wrote again to Materiel Division at Wright Field on 4 August 1942, in anticipation of being there in person on 9–10 August to discuss and, with luck, agree on a plan 'for the P-51 'A' development program'.[11]

Kindelberger indicated that an NAA representative had been contacted by General Arnold's office concerning the possibility of changing the order for A-36s 'to the P-51 type'. To do this and still be on track at the end of 1942, he suggested changing to an 'engine equivalent to the Allison F20R' and eliminating the nose guns, retaining the four wing-mounted .50s 'as specified for the P-51A airplane. Other desired changes could not be made and maintain production schedules.'

It is clear from the context that at this time, the 'P-51A' referred to in discussions did not mean specifically the exact model that later received that designation, but simply 'the next fighter version, following the P-51[no suffix]' whatever form it might take. The 'P-51A' at this stage might have had an Allison or a Rolls-Royce/Packard engine. And moreover, that Rolls-Royce might have been a single- or two-stage Merlin.

The real goal was the two-stage Merlin (Packard V-1650-3), but it was very unlikely that engines would be available to meet the airframe production plan, even if NAA had an airframe ready for it, which was not guaranteed either. Various solutions to the anticipated lack of engines were suggested, including shipping Mustang airframes to the UK to be fitted with Rolls-Royce built Merlin 61s.

Kindelberger's recommendation was to change to the Merlin 28 (the V-1650-1, with two-speed but single-stage supercharger, as used in the P-40F) as early as possible during the 1,200-aircraft order, noting that it appeared engines would be available then, and that the required new radiator would be the critical item. He suggested handling the further-developed Merlin 61 model separately, in light of the many factors affecting it.

The AAF elected to retain the A-36A as ordered, and the first flight took place on 27 September 1942, with Bob Chilton at the controls. There were no full prototypes as such, with the first production aircraft used for contractor's trials. The production P-51A that followed it was essentially the 'substitute' described in the letter, continuing with Allison power until the new Packard Merlin V-1650-3 was available. This aircraft was given the type number NA-99 by NAA.

The P-51A as it appeared used the Allison V-1710-81 (F20R), as per Kindelberger's initial suggestion, which had a war emergency power of 1,360hp. This was the improved version of the engine described in Kindelberger's February letter (see Chapter 3), which had been tried in the P-39J. It was now ready for service and was also used in the contemporary P-40M (and then N), while comparable 'E-series' Allison models went into the P-39M and subsequent variants.

The V-1710-81's critical altitude for military-rated power was 17,500ft, compared with 12,650ft for the Mustang Mk I's dash 39 (F3R) and 3,200ft for the A-36's dash 87 (F-21R), increasing the Mustang's performance markedly at medium altitudes.

The P-51A had moderate redesigns to its structure and aerodynamics, but retained the four wing-mounted 0.50in machine guns and the detachable bomb shackles of the A-36A. This broadened the role of the P-51A into fighter-bomber as well as pure fighter, though steep dive-bombing attacks could not be carried out as with the A-36A. Furthermore, combat drop tanks or ferry tanks could be fitted to increase range. (See Chapter 11 – Technical Description for more detailed information on the P-51A).

Thirty-five P-51A-10s were modified for photographic reconnaissance by the USAAF and were initially designated P-51-NA-11, but redesignated F-6B-1-NA when 'F' prefixes for photographic reconnaissance aircraft were standardised. These had similar modifications to the earlier P-51-based reconnaissance modification (aka P-51-2 or F-6A), with provision for two K-24 cameras, one in the rear fuselage for vertical photography and another behind the cockpit for oblique photography. Armament was retained.

Kindelberger's suggestion of a separate order for initial Merlin Mustang production was heeded, allowing it a special priority so there would be no barriers to progress. Once the programme was secure, the order for 1,200 Mustangs was adjusted, reducing the number of P-51As, with the rest to be built as Merlin-powered P-51Bs. The P-51A, and thus the Allison generation of Mustangs, accordingly went out of production in May 1943.

The resulting 310 NA-99s were built (beginning in February 1943) in three consecutive blocks, designated P-51A-1NA (43-6003 to 43-6102), P-51A-5NA (43-6103 to 43-6157), and P-51A-10NA (43-6158 to 43-6312). The pilots' notes refer to a P-51A-2, which had some of the features of -5 and -10 aircraft and would have been a field-upgraded -1. There is, however, no mention of a -2 in the USAAF's official designation list of 1944 so it is unclear if any aircraft were ever modified to that standard.

Fifty of these aircraft were issued to the RAF, as partial compensation for the USAAF's retention of 57 NA-91s by the AAF. In British service, the P-51A was designated Mustang Mk II, and it was used in the same tactical reconnaissance and light ground-attack role as the Mk I and Mk IA. The 35 F-6Bs were mostly issued to the 67th Tactical Reconnaissance Group in Northern Europe, becoming a rare example of Allison Mustangs used

FR901, one of the 50 P-51As passed to the RAF as the Mustang Mk II, testing long-range ferry tanks.

operationally by the AAF in that theatre, where Merlin-powered Mustangs were the norm. The majority of the remaining 225 P-51As were deployed to the China-Burma-India (CBI) theatre, while some remained in the US for training purposes.

Eglin Field Trials: P-51

The P-51 undertook trials into its tactical suitability at the Air Forces Proving Ground, Eglin Field, Florida between 7 August and 1 November 1942, as ordered on 13 July.[12] The three aircraft involved were 41-37323, 41-37324, and 41-37325 – the fourth through sixth machines from the production run of 150 cannon-armed P-51/Mustang IA fighters.

The purpose behind the Eglin trials is not entirely clear, although by the time they took place, the future of the Mustang clearly lay with the Merlin-engined variants. It is possible, therefore, that the tactical trials were conducted to determine how the forthcoming Merlin-powered fighters could be employed, as much as the existing Allison-powered aircraft.

Heavily retouched NAA factory photograph of a P-51 over the Californian coast in 1942. Note the thickening of the carburettor scoop where the air filter is fitted.

It is also not clear if the Army had a role in mind for some or all of the P-51s it now 'owned'. Late the following month a report was compiled on a prototype set of modifications, equipping the P-51 with cameras for army support operations.[13] This suggests that the Army was at least considering a similar tactical reconnaissance role to the British.

By the time of the North Africa campaign, '... air force leaders already believed [that] observation or reconnaissance aircraft had to be ranked with the fastest fighter types available to the enemy... Brig. Gen. Paul L. Williams, commanding the XII Air Support Command, recommended the use of P-51s, modified for photography, normally flying their missions in pairs...

'Maj. Gen. George E. Stratemeyer, visiting North Africa as Arnold's representative, thought that the equipment of tactical reconnaissance squadrons "should consist of our best and fastest type fighter aircraft." He thought that the P-51 would be "ideal" for the purpose.'[14]

The trial report concluded that the P-51 was 'the best low altitude American fighter aircraft yet developed'. The report went on to say that 'pilots become completely at home in this aircraft immediately after the first take-off due to the remarkable sensitivity of control, simplicity of cockpit, and excellent flying characteristics'. It was also noted that the P-51 was faster than all standard US fighters up to 15,000ft, with the exception of the P-47C-1.

The report was in many respects glowing, but the P-51 was felt to be not without shortcomings, some of them serious. The rate of roll was considered 'not as rapid as is desired for combat operations,' and the view over the nose was deemed 'not sufficient to allow full deflection shooting in a turn'.

The report also made a number of recommendations for areas that could be improved. These included reducing the power loading of the aircraft, in particular, by reducing excess weight in the structure and increasing engine power. Eglin Field also recommended replacing the four 20mm Hispano cannon with four 0.50in machine guns, as the cannon were considered to be 'functionally unsatisfactory'. (Indeed, the gun armament of the A-36A/NA-97, as the next production variant after the NA-91, consisted of 0.50in guns rather than cannon, despite 20mm guns being considered. The wing gun arrangement for the A-36A was subsequently adopted virtually unchanged on the P-51A and B/C, somewhat to the disappointment of the British).

P-51 s/n 41-37324, one of three aircraft to take part in tactical suitability trials at Eglin Field in late 1942.

Significantly, in view of the contemporary plans for a Merlin 61-powered Mustang, the Eglin Field report called for 'an engine which will permit satisfactory tactical combat maneuvering between twenty-five-thousand (25,000) and thirty-thousand (30,000) feet'. The report went on: 'The absolute ceiling of the subject aircraft at the date of this report was found to be approximately thirty-one-thousand (31,000) feet. It is believed that the fighting ceiling of this aircraft is twenty-thousand (20,000) feet as the engine loses power very rapidly above eighteen-thousand (18,000) feet. This limited ceiling is the most serious handicap to this aircraft, and every effort should be made to increase the power and critical altitude of the engine.'

The US report, like the British reports, was effusive in its praise for the P-51's handling qualities and ease of flying. The American pilots reported that 'a pilot flying this plane for the first time feels immediately at home when this ship leaves the ground, and he has a feeling that he has flown this ship for a large number of hours'.

British and American trials did not agree in all matters. British trials at the AFDU and A&AEE were very concerned about the rearward view with armour fitted, while the Eglin Field tests considered this 'somewhat restricted but not dangerously so'. On the other hand, one British testing establishment had remarked on the forward view as good, due to the Mustang's narrow nose when compared with other single-engined fighters.[v] Eglin Field did not concur, requiring that 'every effort must be made to increase the angle of view over the nose'.

Finally, Eglin Field disagreed with the British test centres over the P-51's climbing ability. The British establishments were unimpressed with the rate of climb with Mustangs fitted with the V-1710-F3R, while Eglin Field considered that the P-51 had the 'ability to climb well at a high indicated speed'.

Of course, time had passed between the early British tests and the US tests at Eglin, and the latter had a somewhat different purpose. While the British establishments were focusing on fitting the Mustang Mk I for service, by the time the Eglin tests took place it was known that the next major production version would be powered by high-altitude rated Merlin engines. This could well have put a significantly different cast on the testing at Eglin Field.

The US test centre was able to compare the P-51 in mock combat against a number of American types, and a captured Mitsubishi A6M 'Zero'. The Mustang was found to be superior in speed to the 'Zero', P-39D and experimental XP-47F (a P-47 with laminar-flow wings) at all altitudes,[vi] and the P-47B and P-38F up to 15,000ft. Its acceleration in dives and maximum permissible speed was greater than all types it was measured against, and it was similar in turning characteristics to the P-39 and P-40F. Tactically, the P-51 had a significant advantage in that its speed at low altitudes enabled it to break away from combat and re-engage at will.

---

v   In fairness, the view over the nose was later criticised in British circles, but when considering its tactical reconnaissance role rather than in the air-to-air fighter role.

vi Although the XP-47F's wing was designed according to 'laminar flow' principles, the surface as manufactured was insufficiently free of distortion to reap the full benefit of the low-drag potential. The XP-47F may have been intended in part as a testbed for the proposed XP-69.

Eglin Field Trials: A-36A

Three of the first A-36As were made available to the AAF Proving Ground at Eglin Field between November 1942 and April 1943, arriving just as the trials on the P-51 were being completed.

As with much of the testing of Mustang variants previously, the Proving Ground test pilots had many positive conclusions about the A-36A. In the AAF Proving Ground Command report, it was remarked that the A-36A was 'very pleasant to fly, being extremely stable on each axis' and that it was both 'an excellent minimum altitude bombing and attack aircraft' and 'an excellent fighter'.[15]

However, the testing centre felt that the aircraft was 'an inferior dive bomber' due to what the Proving Ground Command perceived as excessive speed in the dive, even with the dive brakes extended. Furthermore, test pilot Herman Watters was killed in December when A-36A 42-83666, the third production machine, suffered structural failure during a test at Eglin.[vii]

Even before this tragedy, the testing centre had recommended that the dive brakes be deleted, and that bombing attacks not be made at more than 70° dive angle. The Army had clearly wanted the dive brakes to be fitted to the aircraft, yet when it started to reach squadrons, there appeared to be a concerted effort to ensure they were not used. The war diary of the 86th Fighter-Bomber Group noted in November 1942:

'A-36 Aircraft began to arrive. One of the first orders out by [sic] the 23rd Provisional Training Wing prohibited aerobatic missions and forbit [sic] use of dive flaps and dive in excess of 30°. This order was strictly enforced throughout the entire training period.'

It has often been reported that A-36As had their dive brakes wired permanently shut. This was not the case – in fact, the dive brakes could

---

vii Whether this represented a vindication of Materiel Command's reservations about ordering the aircraft without a development programme is unclear. The A-36A did go on to have a relatively high accident rate for stateside aircraft, at 274 accidents per 100,000 flying hours. This compares with rates of 245 for the P-39 and 188 for the P-40 and does not seem especially high given that the A-36 was a dive-bomber and therefore potentially more liable to accidents than fighters. (The figure for all other P-51 models is 105 accidents per 100,000 hours). Accident figures for other army dive-bombers are, sadly, not available. Squadrons operating the A-36 on the front line do not appear to have been concerned by excessive losses to accidents, though later on, some pilots declined to use the dive brakes (see Chapter 6).

not have been physically fixed in the closed position, because this would have impeded access to the ammunition trays. It has also been postulated that a procedure of opening the dive brakes before entering the dive was introduced to minimise loads on the wings. The Northwest African Air Forces (NAAF) tactical bulletin No. 23[16] indicated that dive brakes should be 'opened immediately before the roll-over' but did not state whether this was for safety or tactical reasons. Captain John Harsh of the 526th Fighter-Bomber Squadron recommended that entering the dive 'is best accomplished by turning the ship onto its back and pulling the nose through the target, which requires the use of dive brakes to kill the accelerated speed and allow time for complete sighting'.

'Low Attack' – the British Flirtation with Close-Support Mustangs

A debate was taking place within the RAF in the second half of 1942 as to the best aircraft for close support of Army forces. The failure of the 'bomber-reconnaissance' type for ACC (see Chapter 2) had left a void in this respect. In Britain as in the US, the fighter-bomber type was now seen as the answer. While the 'Hurribomber' had proved its worth, a successor with better performance was needed.

In July, Fighter Command's 11 Group Headquarters held a conference on 'Requirements of Fighter aircraft in the event of invasion of Continent', anticipated for the following spring.[17] The Mustang and Typhoon were proposed for close support, and the former had much to recommend it in that role as well as fighter reconnaissance, though the availability of the Typhoon in large numbers spoke in favour of the Hawker aircraft. Nevertheless, the Mustang Mk I's superlative low-level performance (and lack of high-altitude performance) had marked it out for further development in air-to-ground combat, in the UK as in the US. (At the same time, the Westland Whirlwind was being modified to carry stores, but this could only provide two additional squadrons of fighter-bombers.)

An engine of the type selected for the A-36A, the F21R, was trialled in Britain on Mustang I AP222 at the A&AEE between 25 October 1942 and 7 February 1943. During tests on climb and level speed performance, it was found that the maximum speed at 1,000ft was increased from 360mph to 377mph with the F21R engine, and this speed could now be attained from sea level up to 4,000ft. However, the revised engine reduced the ultimate top speed from 394mph to 377mph, and lengthened the time to climb to 20,000ft by three minutes. The service ceiling was also reduced from 30,000ft to 25,000ft. Interestingly, for comparative purposes, the engine was converted back to equivalent F3R status by changing the supercharger gear ratio, neatly demonstrating the modular nature of the V-1710 engine.

The F21R engine was tested at full throttle at all heights, involving a measure of 'overboost' beyond normal limitations. Further tests were being carried out with a modified induction manifold intended to increase boost, but during these tests the engine failed.

It is unclear what the exact purpose of these tests was, but a 'data card' dated July 1943 indicates that at one point, it was anticipated that the RAF's Mustang Mk Is be fitted with the F21R engine, although this was superseded by another card with the same date reverting to the F3R.[18] Indeed, during the Mustang Mk I's service the RAF had established that it was possible to increase its performance at lower altitudes with the existing engines through judicious use of overboost. This was achieved by removing the automatic boost control, and could apparently be done without harming the engine's excellent reliability. Below around 11,000ft, using full throttle without boost control raised the power to as much as 1,440hp,[19] and improved the top speed considerably. At 4,000ft, this rose to around 382mph from around 367mph.[20] (Given that the October 1942–February 1943 tests with a F21R engine had been conducted with the boost control removed, it is possible that this contributed to the realisation that the boost control could be deleted on service aircraft.) There was a certain irony to this, as the Air Ministry had decided that boost controls were necessary after Mustang deliveries began, and ordered that they be retrospectively fitted to 465 aircraft.[21]

The aircraft's proven low-level prowess meant that, in late 1942, the Mustang was also mooted, along with the Typhoon (which also had good low-level and poor high-level performance), as a possible Hurricane replacement in the 'tank busting' and ground-attack role. As part of this exploration, NA-83 AM130/G (the 'G' indicating that the aircraft was to be kept under permanent guard) was modified to accept rocket projectiles and tested at the A&AEE in December 1942.

AM130/G (the 'G' indicating that the aircraft was to be kept under guard) during rocket-projectile trials in December 1942, demonstrating the bulky nature of the first layout.

AG357 in flight in 1943, testing the second incarnation of the rocket projectile installation.

The rocket installation included a heavy blast plate and drag-inducing mountings, and reduced the top speed to a pedestrian 291mph. Performance could not be expected to improve dramatically even after the rockets had been fired due to the clumsy mountings, and indeed with no rockets but the rest of the equipment still fitted, AM130/G was only capable of 302mph. Perhaps surprisingly in view of this, handling was little affected.

The rocket installation was clearly unsuitable in that form, and a modified set-up was fitted to NA-73 AG357. The blast plates were deleted and the rockets rails were attached to faired pylons. This worked slightly better, increasing speed around 10mph in each condition.

In a further development along these lines, AM106/G was fitted with a special 'low attack wing' and was tested in this form from 4 May 1943. The 'low attack' wing was conceptually similar to the 'universal' wing used on the Hurricane Mk IV. Essentially, the wings had been redesigned to accept two 40mm Vickers 'S' anti-tank guns, two 500lb bombs, two long-range fuel tanks, or two Mk III (smoke-laying) containers, while retaining two 0.30in guns for sighting (as well as the two 0.50s in the nose – though at some point AM106/G had its nose guns removed and the apertures blanked off).

With 'S' guns fitted, AM106/G's maximum speed was reduced to 304mph at 2,000ft and 341mph at 10,000ft – though it is worth noting

AG357 in July 1943, testing a revised arrangement of rocket projectiles with blast plate deleted.

AM 106/G during trials of the 'low attack' wing in May 1943, here fitted with the 40mm Vickers 'S' anti-tank gun.

that this was nearly 60mph faster than the Hurricane IID. Its range was reduced by around 40 miles but was still over 900 miles. Handling characteristics with 500lb bombs or smoke containers was similar to a standard Mustang, and entirely satisfactory. The take-off run and climb away were longer than standard, but well within acceptable limits. One problem discovered with faster aircraft such as the Mustang or Typhoon was that with the slow rate of fire of the large guns there simply wasn't time to get off enough shots in one firing pass.[viii] This made rockets a better option, as while they were less accurate than the S-gun, up to eight could be fired in one pass.

One A-36A, 42-83685, was evaluated in Britain from March 1943, where it was known as the 'Mustang Mk I (Dive Bomber)' and given the serial EW998. It was returned to the USAAF in July 1943, and crashed on 24 July 1944. No orders for A-36As were forthcoming from the RAF, though a number were lent to 1437 Flight, which used them in the reconnaissance role in the Mediterranean theatre (see Chapter 6).

---

viii The recoil of the S-gun tended to impart a nose-down trim which had to be corrected before the next salvo was fired, so the gun could not in practice maintain its theoretical rate-of-fire.

Ultimately, none of the ground-attack modifications fed through to service RAF Mustangs, and the Typhoon eventually became the main ground-attack type. Later versions of the RAF Mustang would, however, acquire the bomb racks developed for US variants, as fighters in general adopted a broader, multi-role philosophy, and some Mustang IIIs (Merlin-powered P-51B/C) did serve briefly with the 2nd Tactical Air Force as fighter-bombers before being called back to Air Defence of Great Britain (ADGB) to help intercept V-1s.

Eglin Field Trials: P-51A

Tactical trials on the P-51A followed on the heels of the A-36A trials. A report from 8 June 1943 by the USAAF School of Applied Tactics, Orlando, Florida highlighted the improvements in performance that had been realised with this latest version. The maximum level speed was 410mph at 18,000ft, 30–40mph faster than the Mustang Mk I's best speed, and at 3,000ft greater altitude, indicating that the aircraft was now a true medium-altitude fighter. Bomb racks led to a reduction from the 'clean' P-51A's top speed of 15mph – impressively, though, still faster than the Mustang Mk I. In addition, the rate of climb was also better than that of the Mustang Mk I.

The P-51A was similar to previous models in its fine handling and its ability for new pilots to quickly master it. It was found to be easy to fly in formation although the canopy frames obscured vision in some positions. A 'clear vision' panel had been introduced to the port side panel of the windscreen, which could ensure the pilot could still see should snow, sleet or rain obscure the canopy. The panel was located in an area of negative pressure, which meant that it could be opened without the elements entering the cockpit. (Ironically in view of its name, the edges of the panel partially obscured the view forward, and it was deleted on the P-51B.)

The School of Applied Tactics noted that the P-51A was good for escort duties, with its large fuel supply and excellent fighting qualities. This was significant given the contemporary concerns around the need for effective long-range bomber escort.

The report was not completely without negatives – heat in the cockpit at lower altitudes was still a problem, and the seat was found to be uncomfortable for long flights.

The P-51A's combat range (the range for a typical mission, rather than total range) was an impressive 420 miles. This included 210 miles or 45 minutes at maximum cruise, 15 minutes at emergency maximum power at the target area, and 210 miles or 60 minutes at minimum cruise, with a reserve of around 20 gallons (16.7 imperial gallons) at the end of the sortie.

The School of Applied Tactics compared a P-51A with a Lockheed P-38G, Bell P-39N and Q, Curtiss P-40M and Republic P-47C – significantly, the P-40 and P-39s in the trial used virtually identical models of V-1710 to the P-51A. According to the school, below 22,000ft the P-51A was 'considered to have the best all-round fighting qualities of any present American fighter. Its main advantages are its fair rate of climb, quick acceleration, very high level speed and exceptionally high dive speed.'

The report continued: 'In comparative combat trials with the P-47C at heights from 10,000–15,000 ft, the P-51 was found to have a smaller turning circle without manoeuvre flaps, and with manoeuvre flaps a very much smaller turning circle. At all speeds the P-51A has a slower rate of roll than the P-47C. At the above mentioned altitudes the P-51A has no difficulty in outfighting the P-47C under any conditions. Both these aircraft have high diving speeds and fast acceleration in the initial stages of diving, but the P-51A handles better and is faster in a prolonged dive.'

The P-51A was practical in other respects. Maintenance was comparatively straightforward as the main components were easily accessible. It was found to be quite possible for a crew of nine men to service a P-51A completely with fuel, oil, oxygen, and ammunition and conduct a radio check in 15 minutes. However, as the P-51A had 'laminar flow' wings it was pointed out that the surface had to be kept 'scrupulously clean', and dents or dirt would impair performance considerably.[22]

Chapter 5

Army Co-operation Command Rides On

Following the excitement of Operation *Jubilee*, the Mustang squadrons settled back into their routine of training and operational flying. The Luftwaffe, however, had begun a series of low-level pinprick raids on the south coast of England with Ju 88 bombers and Fw 190 fighter-bombers, and the raids were succeeding in diverting resources away from attacks on the enemy.

The RAF had to pull a number of fighter squadrons away from their normal duties to counter the increasing activity. The Mustang's excellent loiter time made it well suited to these missions, especially as they were generally carried out at low level where the Mustang Mk I performed best. Frustratingly, towards the end of 1942 and into 1943, the Mustang units were increasingly pulled away from the specialist role they were beginning to perform so admirably. From October 1942, several of the squadrons became devoted almost entirely to patrolling for raiders.

In the vast majority of cases, these patrols passed without contact or incident, but occasionally, aircraft were encountered. On 28 October, 414 Squadron's Hills and Champlin chased two Messerschmitt Bf 109Fs across the Channel to Cherbourg. Hills, the first Mustang pilot to shoot down another aircraft, was unable to add to his tally on this occasion.

The fighter patrols continued throughout November, hampered by bad weather. Luftwaffe attacks on Channel convoys also increased, adding to the burdens of the Mustang squadrons. On a few occasions, Mustangs were vectored onto radar plots, and very occasionally made contact, but success was elusive, and the efforts were not without cost. On 3 November, 414 Squadron lost a veteran pilot in unfortunate circumstances – Flying Officer Horncastle was killed in AG654 when the Mustang's engine failed on take-off.

There were some positive results from the interception patrols – on 4 September, Flying Officers North-Lewis and Cooper of 26 Squadron had been lucky enough to catch the Ju 88 they had been vectored onto, and dived after it as it 'wave-hopped' back across the Channel. North-Lewis closed to 250 yards and subjected the Junkers to a three-second burst. Fragments started to fall off the starboard engine, followed by a stream of white smoke and four or five balls of white flame. Cooper lined the Ju 88 up and fired two short bursts. The Junkers was only 30ft above the waves at this point, and vanished into the haze hanging over the sea's surface.

The following year, on 23 May, 414 Squadron's Squadron Leader Godfrey and Pilot Officer Potts were directed to intercept 17 Fw 190s bombing Bournemouth. The Mustangs sighted and chased the *Jabos* across the Channel, and were gaining slowly but had to withdraw when the French coast came in sight.

These actions were relative rarities though. The raids had begun to tail off in the early months of 1943 and by the summer, most squadrons were able to resume regular offensive operations once more. The flavour of missions carried out varied between Mustang squadrons. While all took part in a mix of rangers, rhubarbs and populars, the frequency of each varied, with the occasional special task.

'Populars' – Photo Recon Missions

Populars were essentially photo-recon missions with specific targets, usually requested by the Army. They could be offensive or not, depending on the importance of the target and the urgency of the information required. Planning was essential, but as AC squadrons, a fast response could be crucial. An experienced unit with the right facilities available could plan and launch a mission within an hour and a half of receiving the request, and the resulting photographs could be processed and assessed rapidly, for example by the Army Air Photographic Interpretation Service (APIS).[1]

According to Roy Nesbit: 'In 1942, an Army Photographic Interpretation section had been formed at the Central Interpretation Unit (CIU), with the task of examining all photographs taken of areas within 30 miles of the European coastline from Den Helder in Holland to the Spanish frontier'.[2]

While some squadrons had been assigned to coastal defence, II (AC) Squadron RAF spent much of the same period photographing the Dutch coast for 34 (Photographic Reconnaissance) Wing, with instructions not to take any offensive action unless attacked.

Initially the AC Mustang Mk I carried a single, oblique camera, which was later complemented with a vertical camera. These were automatic in operation (thanks to an electric motor) and photography was initiated by the pilot. The aim was to take a series of photographs at fixed intervals, while flying a fixed course to ensure good overlap between images. Images were often taken of the coastal areas, ensuring an up-to-date understanding of defences. While the lead Mustang took photographs, the weaver would remain half a mile offshore.

It was not as straightforward as it might sound to carry out a photo-recon mission at low level. A pilot could do everything by the book, and still end up with photographs taken too low, with insufficient overlap, not covering the target properly, or simply too blurred. Any such failure meant that someone would have to go out again and repeat the task. Often, by the time a photographic run was well under way, nearby flak batteries had 'woken up', and the pilot was faced with braving an intense barrage while flying straight and level, or attempting to evade at the risk of ruining the photographs.

The constraints of coastal photo-recon missions were often difficult to adhere to – Squadron Leader A. E. Houseman and Flight Lieutenant G. Kenning were unable to photograph the approaches to Domburg and its radar station from 1,000ft due to low cloud on 14 November, so had to take the images at 350ft. The resulting photographs were sharp, with good overlap, but were of little use to 34 Wing as a result of the lower altitude.

Poor conditions spoilt several sorties, and Pilot Officer Cunningham was lost during one such mission. The weather between the Hook of Holland and Westkapelle was too poor for really good photography – there was no interception, and Cunningham simply disappeared on the flight back across the North Sea. The flight leader, Flight Lieutenant Hall, saw him following on leaving the Dutch coast, but five minutes later Cunningham was nowhere to be seen. Sergeant Smith was lost in similar circumstances on 29 December 1942. It was likely he was shot down, as flight leader Flying Officer Davies found bullet holes in the starboard wing of his Mustang, AM113, on returning to North Weald – having had no idea he had been fired upon. Agonisingly, although Davies returned with photographs, they were not sufficiently detailed.

Other sorties had better success, but the chances of the photographs being sufficiently good were against the Mustang pilots, especially in the winter months. Visual reconnaissance, which could still be backed up by oblique photos, comprised the majority of Mustang sorties.

Rangers and Rhubarbs

It was not just the Mustang Mk I's range and speed that suited it to tactical reconnaissance – its armament, although lighter than the latest RAF aircraft, was highly effective against most ground targets. ACC's Mustang squadrons increasingly utilised this feature as 1942 progressed, and they engaged more often in directly offensive action. Eventually, their operations developed into a dedicated campaign against enemy communications – road, rail and river transport networks – across the German-held territories of Northern Europe. The increasingly common ranger and rhubarb missions used the aircraft's hitting power to the full. Rangers were intended to keep defences such as fighters occupied or diverted from intercepting other operations, while rhubarbs were aimed at destroying targets of opportunity such as communications and infrastructure, as well as carrying out a visual reconnaissance of the areas flown.

And ACC missions were beginning to range further than ever. On 21 October 1942, four Mustang Mk Is of 268 Squadron led by Wing Commander A. F. Anderson penetrated into Germany during a reconnaissance of a variety of targets including the Dortmund–Ems Canal. This was the first time in the war that a single-engined fighter based in the UK had crossed the German border.

In a typical raid, a flight of Mustangs could be away from their base for three hours and 40 minutes, fly up to 90 miles into Germany and among them destroy or damage several locomotives, goods barges and other vehicles such as staff cars and motor launches. One mission over France and Germany involving just two Mustangs caused the damage or destruction of five locomotives, the same number of goods barges, and a motor launch.

An example of a successful rhubarb was that carried out by Hills and Champlin of 414 Squadron on 13 October 1942. The two, who had become a veteran pairing during their time at the squadron, spotted a long train made up of 20 cars, 20 tanker wagons and a large locomotive near Étretat.

A low-level, close-in attack was made and the pilots saw an explosion in the train's cab, after which the train stopped, wreathed in steam. They went on to Bolbec and strafed gas containers before re-crossing the Channel. No flak or enemy fighters were encountered for the whole mission, emphasising the value of maintaining surprise.

On 9 November, after a spell where the squadron mainly took part in fighter patrols (see above), both men were withdrawn from the RCAF and transferred to the US Navy. Hills became an instructor, thanks to his valuable combat experience, and later joined VF-32 flying Grumman F6F Hellcats, shooting down four Mitsubishi A6M 'Zeroes'.

On 26 November 1942, Flying Officer Bethell scored 268 Squadron's first and second air-to-air victories on the same day, by shooting down a Messerschmitt Bf 109 and shortly afterwards a Junkers Ju 52 transport, which crashed in flames. Much later, during a ranger in the Paris area in August 1943, Flight Lieutenant Stover of 414 Squadron bounced a Junkers Ju 88 that was flying over Moiselles aerodrome, shot it down, and attempted to attack a second Junkers. This attack failed when his guns jammed. The Mustang pilots were under instruction to avoid air combat, but this was not always possible and though rare, some air-to-air victories were occasionally scored to add to the tally started during Operation *Jubilee*.

Trains were increasingly a favourite target of the Mustang squadrons. It was estimated that, given the availability of materials and repair facilities, a locomotive with its boiler holed by 0.50in bullets would be out of service for four to six weeks. The boiler was frequently seen to explode, and sometimes escaping steam blew the fire out of the furnace and into the cab, killing or injuring the crew. According to Allied intelligence at this time, it was becoming increasingly difficult for the Germans to find experienced train crews that were prepared to continue working in areas within range of Allied aircraft.

Pilots were warned not to attack locomotives near stations or other locations where flak defences might be concentrated, although it appeared that this was not always possible. Attacks on trains were safer for the Mustangs and more likely to result in success out in the country where railway lines were largely single track. This meant that a damaged train would hold up other traffic, maximising the disruption caused. If the train exploded, it could also damage the track, necessitating more repairs before the line could be reopened.

Furthermore if trains were mobile, it meant that they had steam up. This meant that more damage was likely to be done if the boiler was perforated, and it was a good way for the pilots to tell instantly if they had damaged the train severely.

On 27 November 1942, 26 Squadron put on three rhubarbs – one of three aircraft, one of two and a rare lone intruder mission. The first two targeted marshalling yards[i] in northern France, while the individual mission tackled the railway in the vicinity of Montivilliers. The three-ship attacked three trains, one of which was seen to issue a large amount of steam and another of which blew up. The two-Mustang mission attacked four trains and in two cases saw a large column of steam coming from the boiler. The single-ship also strafed an individual train and saw the steam issuing from the punctured boiler.

The following May – the same month that the 17 Fw 190s were chased back to France – Flying Officers Hutchinson and Mossing of 414 Squadron ranged over to Brittany where they attacked and damaged five locomotives, though Mossing damaged his wing by colliding with a tree. The pilots were becoming skilled at managing their fuel by this stage, and after two and three-quarter hours in the air, both Mustangs still had 30–35 gallons (imperial) left in the tanks.

On 9 November 1943, Flying Officer Dunkerley of II (AC) Squadron and Wing Commander Anderson (who had been CO of 268 Squadron) crossed the French coast near Cabourg and Dives and flew parallel with the railway to Mézidon, where they spotted three locomotives and around 20 wagons. The trains were strafed, with hits to locomotives and wagons observed, despite much light and medium flak, and the two Mustangs went on to look for more targets. However, Dunkerley's aircraft was hit by flak as the Mustangs flew over a village, and crashed in flames. Anderson's aircraft was hit in the leading edge of one wing, causing the ammunition

---

i This would appear to go against the injunction not to attack trains in stations, but marshalling yards were likely to be more open and flak defences easier to spot – in any event, on this raid on the marshalling yards, little flak was experienced. It would appear from the next example that guidance on safety was sometimes disregarded if there was felt to be sufficient tactical advantage in doing so.

to explode. The aircraft remained airborne, however, and remarkably Anderson continued to look for targets. Contrary to the usual emphasis on safety and not taking unnecessary risks, Anderson strafed a railway signal box between Mézidon and Cabourg, and on re-crossing the coast, attacked a flak tower on the beach.[ii]

Planning for Success

The 'daylight intrusion' missions can sound haphazard, as though the aircraft were simply casting around for targets. This was far from the case. Extreme care and effort went into planning and managing the operations. Fortunately, the strategy and tactics of ACC Mustang squadrons in this period were recorded by a USAAF officer, Colonel Clare W. Bunch, Colonel, AC, Operational Engineering, NAAF, who wrote a detailed report to inform the NAAF, interviewing Wing Commander Peter Dudgeon, who had commanded 268 Squadron. The following section draws significantly from this report in the context of ACC's activities during the period before the command was disbanded.[3]

The overall aim was the destruction of designated targets with the minimum of casualties. Routes were meticulously designed with the aircraft's movements carefully indicated. The aircraft followed a preset zigzag course designed to bring them parallel to their targets, such as canals and railways. Defensive tactics involved sending a sufficient number of aircraft into a target area to overwhelm defences and reporting systems. This caused confusion through the multiplicity of plots – it was usually impossible to dispatch interception for all reports in an area, and by the time intercepting fighters had reached a plot, the Mustangs would be long gone.

It was imperative that the Mustangs followed their flight plan assiduously, as the rendezvous with the other squadron aircraft after recrossing the enemy coast depended on it. This was the time when interception by enemy aircraft was most likely, and the maximum protection offered by numbers

---

ii One of the advantages of the Mustang Mk I's armament was that the pilot could select the option of wing or nose guns only, as well as the full armament. It is not recorded in the mission report, but Anderson may well have been able to continue the mission after his wing ammunition detonated by selecting the nose guns only, it being likely that the wing guns would no longer have been useable.

was important. Indeed, the only Mustang to have been lost to Luftwaffe fighters before ACC was supplanted by the 2nd Tactical Air Force, was shot down on the return journey over the sea. The recrossing was generally again made at maximum speed, while weaving. Speed was not sufficient protection from ground fire, and 'jinking' was the best way of surviving the concentration of light flak at the coast. Maximum cruising speed was maintained until the Mustangs had put 40 miles between themselves and the enemy coast. It was recommended to use cloud cover if available.

In fact, cloud cover was an essential part of these missions, and if there was insufficient cloud, missions could be called off. Full cloud at 500ft was considered ideal conditions. This required considerable skill and concentration on the part of the pilots. The risks involved were later tragically demonstrated when three pilots of II (AC) Squadron were killed during the flight to Thruxton for an exercise on 25 May 1943. A formation of ten aircraft flew into a wall of sea fog at Kimmeridge, St Alban's Head, and the formation leader ordered the Mustangs to climb. Unfortunately, Flying Officers Hirst, Miller and McLeod failed to clear a hillside and crashed.

The most usual formation for AC Mustang missions was made up of pairs in line-abreast, though four line-abreast and two or even three flights of four-abreast were tried. The formation flew to a given point off the enemy coast at which point it broke into smaller groups which made their way independently to their assigned area for attack. Crossings of the coast were made as near to simultaneous as possible. The point of landfall was so important that if it was missed, pilots were ordered to return immediately as it would throw off the entire flight plan. Landfalls were chosen meticulously in areas known to have less flak coverage.

If radio silence was broken for any reason on the outward journey, this would also result in the mission being called off immediately due to the element of surprise being lost. This was relaxed somewhat when over enemy soil as complete concealment was not possible once over occupied territory.

The flight to around 40 miles off the enemy coast was typically made at 200mph and a height of 25–50ft. The Mustangs then increased their speed to 250–275mph (maximum cruise) and remained at that speed at all times over enemy territory. In fact crossing the enemy coast was recommended to be made at a shallow dive to increase speed, and pilots were encouraged to direct bursts of gunfire at any gun emplacements that were on their path. The aircraft would then return to tree-top height, taking advantage of whatever natural cover was available.

The attacking pair generally alternated roles, with one aircraft making the attack while the other provided cover, constantly scanning the skies for enemy aircraft to avoid the possibility of a surprise interception. Attacks were always from one side of the railway or canal to the other, never along its length. Surprise was key to these attacks, to the extent that pilots were ordered never to repeat an attack even if the first pass had not been successful.

At 270mph and 'zero altitude', the search area was relatively limited and targets appeared quickly. The pilots needed experience and constant alertness to pick out a target in time to make an attack – inexperienced pilots were required not to exceed 250mph until they had picked up this important skill. Over time the pilots developed tricks to make their difficult job a touch easier. It was found that lowering the flaps 5° had little effect on speed, but made the aircraft fly a little nose-down, which made it easier to see over the cowling.

The pre-planned zigzag course was made up of legs of around six minutes, which was the minimum time required for a report of the Mustangs' presence to be reported and interception launched. This meant that any interception was always around six minutes out of date in its information, and the Mustangs would be miles away when the intercepting fighters made their rendezvous.

Success was significant – in 18 months of operations, Dudgeon reported to Colonel Bunch that 268 Squadron claimed as destroyed or severely damaged, 200 locomotives, over 200 barges and a number of aircraft on the ground.

The successes were not achieved without risk, even with the emphasis on safety – 268 Squadron alone lost eight aircraft up to the end of May 1943 one of which was shot down by fighters, five shot down by flak and two which disappeared without the reason for their loss being known. No AC Mustang was intercepted over enemy territory during this period, despite raids being carried out over Holland, occupied France, Belgium and Germany (though one aircraft was shot down over the English Channel). The most distant raid involved a flight of over 1,000 miles.

In addition to the physical damage to enemy resources, a vast amount of information and photographic data was brought back – indeed, this remained the chief purpose of the operations. Partly because of the need to return with information or photographs, the pilots were required not to be reckless – and there were enough dangers in the missions even when carried out with caution.

Mustangs Over the Sea

There was considerable variation in the nature of missions flown by the Mustang squadrons in 1942 and 1943. Despite ostensibly being an AC force, the Mustang squadrons spent a surprising amount of time on maritime operations.

In late 1942 and early 1943, Coastal Command aircraft had been attacked over the Bay of Biscay by Arado Ar 196 floatplanes while on air-sea rescue (ASR) patrols. The floatplanes tended to alight on the sea, acting as a decoy to await patrolling Whitleys and Sunderlands, which they would then attack with their heavy armament of 20mm cannon. To combat this, a detachment of 400 Squadron RCAF moved to Trebalzue in Cornwall in January 1943 to provide an escort. The presence of 400 Squadron's Mustangs may have helped spur a decision to withdraw the Ar 196s after a short period.

In March 1943, II (AC) Squadron began a period largely devoted to 'Lagoon' missions. These were reconnaissance missions specifically to spot enemy shipping, so that attacks could be directed. Typically the patrol area was from the Hook of Holland to the island of Texel, and although photographs were taken, any sightings were radioed immediately to RAF Duxford. Sightings included a convoy of five merchant ships, each flying a barrage balloon, heading Westwards from Katwijk on 29 March, a fleet of seven fishing boats off The Hague on 9 April, and two destroyers off the Hook and ten flat barges off Westhooft on 11 April.

The squadrons engaged in these missions often did not get to hear what had happened as a result of their actions, but pilots from 414 Squadron had a stroke of luck on 27 April. The unit's ORB for 1943 reports that 'Wing Commander Davenport, Officer Commanding 16 Squadron, [another AC Mustang unit] landed here with gen on some shipping he and three of his pilots had seen whilst doing a popular in vicinity of St Malo. Shipping

Mk I AG589 in which, during a shipping patrol, Flying Officer Ferris of 400 Squadron RCAF was shot down by an RNZAF Typhoon over the English Channel. Here, the aircraft wears the original factory-applied camouflage, with the fuselage roundel in the original position and no squadron markings.

was reported to Controller M. W., and strike was laid on. By 1800 hours, a 2,000 tonner, two trawlers and a converted yacht had been sunk. A good show which gives an indication of the support we can expect when one of our shipping recces <u>does</u> see something.'

The Mustangs did not just gather intelligence for attacks on shipping, sometimes they took part. In April 1943, Westland Whirlwind 'Whirlibombers' were accompanied on anti-shipping sweeps by 414 Squadron's Mustangs. Later, Beaufighters and Mosquitoes were escorted on 'Instep' shipping strikes by the Canadian squadron, which detached aircraft from Portreath to Predannack for that purpose.

The 'Insteps' could be dangerous. On 6 June 1943, Flying Officer Doherty was shot down by a Fw 190. On 17 June 1943, Pilot Officer Vaupel, flying AP206, was shot down in error by a Spitfire of 42 Squadron, the day after Pilot Officer Potts had disappeared from a four-ship escort formation. Morale was taking a hit at 414 Squadron – it probably came as some relief when rhubarbs started up again later that month.

In addition to offensive operations, a number of air-sea rescue patrols were carried out by Mustang units, assisting the standing ASR services. As with the interceptor patrols, the amount of territory to cover and the limited number of aircraft meant that sightings were rare. When contact was made, however, the Mustang pilots often demonstrated great courage and calmness.

One pilot of 400 Squadron was so dedicated to ASR operations during January 1943 that he remained orbiting over ditched aircrews for three and a half hours. A daylight bombing operation had suffered badly at the hands of German fighters, leading to four or five Lockheed Venturas ditching, possibly along with some of their Spitfire escort according to the squadron's ORB. Flight Lieutenant Knight stayed with the dinghies as long as he possibly could, hours after the remainder of his flight had turned back to refuel. Knight was unwilling to stop orbiting as, although rescue was in progress, when light began to fail there was still one man in the water. He only turned back when barely enough fuel remained to get him back to Middle Wallop. He was then fired on by coastal defences, preventing him from crossing the English coast. He was told to climb above the cloud and bail out over Southampton, but elected to try and save his Mustang. He was talked back to Middle Wallop and carried out a wireless-controlled descent through the cloud, landing safely as the last of the light departed.[iii]

On 29 May 1943 Flying Officers Blakeney and Flight Lieutenant Amos spotted an upturned dinghy in the Channel with ten men clinging to it, possibly the crew of a ditched US bomber. The pair orbited the dinghy until the men were rescued by an ASR launch (a Supermarine Walrus amphibian had reached the scene earlier but been unable to land).

On 7 June 1943, 414 Squadron's Commanding Officer arranged a visit for off-duty pilots to visit an ASR launch station near their base of Portreath. The visit was good for building the squadron's faith in the RAF rescue services and no doubt boosted a sense of mutual understanding. The pilots were treated to a trip around Mounts Bay in one of the RAF launches.

---

iii Unfortunately, 400 Squadron's ORB does not record if Flight Lieutenant Knight received any commendation for this feat, or indeed what the fate of the man in the water was who Knight risked his own safety for.

A most uncommon type of mission was undertaken by II (AC) Squadron on 2, 3 and 4 July 1943, referred to in the squadron's ORB as 'Distill' operations. Two formations of four Mustangs and one of eight aircraft were required to patrol over the North Sea for Junkers Ju 52 minesweeper aircraft that had been reported in the area. The Ju 52 minesweepers, nicknamed 'Mausi' by the Allies, carried a large electrically charged degaussing ring, which caused magnetically triggered mines to detonate.

No sighting of the Mausi took place during any of the three missions, but on the third, two convoys were spotted and the Mustangs, present in some strength for once, did not miss their chance to attack. Flight Lieutenant Hall and Flying Officer McPherson strafed the first convoy's escort vessel, seeing the after end blow up. A straggling vessel was also attacked, with hits scored around the waterline and superstructure.

Equipment and Organisation

Once the gates were thrown open in June 1942 with the formation of new squadrons and the general availability of fully equipped Mustang Mk Is, relatively little further change took place during ACC's ranging missions over occupied Europe.

In support of Operation *Torch* in November, 225 and 241 Squadrons, now with Hurricanes, moved to North Africa,[iv] as did ACC's two 'bomber reconnaissance' squadrons (Nos. 13 and 614), still on Blenheims since the planned dive-bombers (see Chapter 3) never arrived. (The dive-bombers were still nominally represented as late as the spring 1943 plans for the invasion target-force, but apparently with little conviction.)

A few additional squadrons received Mustangs as new equipment after this period – 168 Squadron, which had been formed from a flight of 268 Squadron in June, received Mustangs in November after having worked up on Tomahawks. A newly formed 430 Squadron joined the other two Canadian ACC squadrons on 1 January 1943 – its Mustangs had been handed over the previous day by the short-lived 171 Squadron, which had

---

iv This did not represent the end of 225 Squadron's association with the Mustang – see Chapter 6.

received the aircraft only two to three months previously.[v] Meanwhile, 231 Squadron remained in Northern Ireland on Tomahawks until March–April 1943.

A most significant change in organisation was to take place, however. As Chief of Air Staff Portal explained to the Chiefs of Staff Committee in April 1943:

> With the formation of Headquarters, Expeditionary Air Force, and the adoption of the Composite Group organisation, the task of Army Co-operation Command will have been completed and its existence will be terminated.
>
> Army Co-operation Command was established in December 1940 to organise, experiment and train in all forms of land/air co-operation. The Command has done most valuable work during its existence and thanks very largely to its efforts and to the lessons learned in the fighting in North Africa,[vi] British technique in the combination of land and air operations has been transformed and extended to embrace a much wider range of action than hitherto. Furthermore, in the European theatre we are now passing from the phase of development to the phase of action, and our organisation must be adapted accordingly.
>
> It is of the highest importance that the store of knowledge and experience which has been built up in Army Co-operation Command over the past 2 1/2 years shall not be lost. Full use will therefore be made of the present staff of Army Co-operation Command in building up the new organisation within and under Fighter Command HQ. The existing training formations of Army Co-operation Command will be retained whilst the training of fighter pilots generally and of light bomber crews will be extended to embody the latest lessons of combined Army/Air operations.[4]

---

v   The decision to disband 171 Squadron and pass its Mustangs to the new 430 Squadron was in order to have another Canadian squadron in the army support role.

vi The Allied Air Support Command, later Northwest African Tactical Air Force, was formed following discussions on structuring the Allied air forces at the Casablanca Conference in January 1943, working alongside a bomber force and a coastal air force. This was retrospectively considered the First Tactical Air Force (although, confusingly, a later organisation based in France was given that name).

All AC squadrons were incorporated into the new organisation, along with fighters (primarily fighter-bombers) and the tactical bombers of 2 Group to form a complete unit dedicated to integrating with army operations. It was designated the Second Tactical Air Force, usually abbreviated to 2 TAF. (The term 'Tactical Air Force' was adopted because 'Expeditionary' was considered to point too much to its purpose.) Perhaps surprisingly, Air Marshal Sir John d'Albiac, leading 2 Group since the previous December, was put in command, while Air Marshal Barratt became the head of Technical Training Command.

In the Mustang Mk I, ACC had received and honed an aircraft that did everything they needed it to with aplomb and which could be relied on totally. The tough airframe could survive flak and fighter attacks, and even collisions with the scenery. The straightforward Allison engine was a mechanic's dream and could take a great deal of punishment without letting go.

The previously mentioned USAAF officer, Colonel Clare W. Bunch,[vii] reporting on RAF AC operations just after the command had been superseded, remarked: 'According to them, the Allison is averaging 1,500 hours between bearing failures as compared to 500 or 600 hours for the Merlin. The Allison, they have found, will drag them home even with the bearings ruined.'[5] He went on, 'The record of the Mustang I is excellent. The pilots all like to fly it and its success has been due to its simplicity, reliability and the fact that it is faster than any contemporary aircraft at low and medium altitudes.' Bunch described the Allison Mustang as 'excellently fitted for long-range, low altitude daylight intrusion'.

The Mustang units were formed into reconnaissance wings, 35 Wing in 11 Group then 84 Group, and 39 Wing (RCAF) in 83 Group. The fighter-reconnaissance squadrons, and indeed, the 2 TAF leadership, were clear that the Allison-powered Mustang was the most suitable aircraft for this function.

In addition, 16 Squadron and some of the old 34 Wing staff transferred to the new 34 (Photographic Reconnaissance) Wing along with 140 Squadron – 16 Squadron was earmarked to convert to high-flying PR Spitfires, but initially kept its Mustangs. While waiting for a change

---

vii   Bunch was the Colonel, AC, Operational Engineering, Northwest African Air Forces.

of equipment, 16 Squadron conducted useful low-level reconnaissance and ASR work, and also continued 'train busting'. In the latter part of August 1943, two pilots on one rhubarb attacked 12 trains.[6]

As 2 TAF came into being, the cannon-armed Mk IA was released to squadrons. These had been accepted at North American from July to September 1942, and arrived in Britain between November 1942 and January 1943. Three squadrons – 268, 168, and 170 – exchanged their Mustang Mk Is for IAs in the three months from June 1943. In November, 63 Squadron also received Mustang Mk IA aircraft and II (AC) Squadron replaced its Mk Is with the Mk IA in February 1944. (Nevertheless, the lack of new Allison Mustangs was beginning to tell and a few squadrons started giving them up at this time – though 309 Polish Squadron, for example, would return to the type later on.)

It had become an accepted principle that fighter-reconnaissance squadrons should be equipped with the fastest single-seater aircraft at heights up to 5,000ft, with a range of 600 miles when operating at or below 5,000ft. The 2 TAF command felt that the equipment of fighter-reconnaissance squadrons with Mustang Mk I and Mk IAs prior to the invasion of France was evidence that this principle had been fully

A Mustang Mk IA, destined for the RAF, prior to delivery.

A Mustang Mk I in RAF service. These aircraft were retained as a reserve for the existing ACC fighter reconnaissance force and did not equip front-line squadrons until June 1943. (Doug Gordon)

understood, not least because the high diving speed and stability of the Mustang made it ideal for low-level oblique photography.[7]

The 2 TAF was a formidable weapon which would prove a great success, but this should not detract from any recognition of ACC. During the previous two years, Barratt and his organisation cajoled and coaxed the RAF and Air Ministry into forming and equipping a highly specialised AC air arm. The AC Mustang squadrons had proven the wisdom of this approach and carved out an important role for themselves. They were an elite force, skilled and practised at intricate roles that nobody else could perform. The dark days of 1940 and 1941, with morale at rock bottom and training virtually at a standstill, had been well and truly consigned to the past. In addition, as Portal suggested, ACC had made more of a contribution to the general practice of air support for ground forces than might appear on the surface. Much is rightly made of the development of air-ground co-operation in North Africa, for example, ahead of the D-Day operations, but the contribution of the UK-based squadrons to this discipline should not be overlooked.

Chapter 6

North Africa and the Mediterranean

The Mustang was well established in British service over Northern Europe in late 1942, when the so-called second front was opened by Britain and the US.

Despite all the planning for an invasion of North-West Europe in late 1942 or early 1943, the British had effectively vetoed this idea by the end of July 1942.[i] The scheme that took its place was a revision of Operation *Gymnast*, one of a series of plans formulated in January of that year. It is not exactly clear why *Roundup*, the previously preferred 1943 invasion of France, fell out of favour. However, the change meant that the A-36As ordered by the AAF with operations such as *Roundup* in mind would not go into action in support of an invasion force crossing the English Channel.

From 8 November 1942, Operation *Torch* landed 735,000 troops in Tunisia, Algeria and Morocco in an attempt to gain control of French North Africa, and, with the British 8th Army, form a 'hammer and anvil' to crush the German forces in North Africa.

No Mustang squadrons went into action when the landings themselves took place, but a number of US Army units were working up to operational status on P-51s (F-6As) and A-36As, and would soon begin to deploy to North Africa. Other units would be equipped with Mustangs in theatre.

One RAF squadron, No. 225, which had operated Mustangs under ACC, transferred to North Africa among the first wave of units arriving in the aftermath of the invasion, reaching Algiers on 13 November, five days after

---

i The chief British objections, according to the official US Army Air Force History (Craven and Cate, 1955) were 'a shortage of landing craft, and the time factor', added to the fact that in 1942, US forces would not be in a position to carry their share of the load.

the landings began. However, the squadron had given up its Mustangs before leaving England and converted to Spitfire Mk VCs. This squadron would soon, however, operate Mustangs again.

The first units to receive Mustangs in North Africa were the two US Army tactical reconnaissance squadrons under the 68th Reconnaissance Group. The 154th Observation Squadron and the 111th Observation Squadron (later redesignated 'Reconnaissance Squadron (Fighter)', then 'Tactical Reconnaissance Squadrons'[ii]) went ashore the day after the invasion, but did not receive any Mustangs until the following year.

The two US Army Observation Squadrons were initially equipped with Douglas A-20 twin-engined tactical bombers, but subsequently adopted single-seat fighter aircraft in the form of the Bell P-39. Later, the US Army's first Mustangs to enter active service arrived. These were the cannon-armed P-51s originally intended for the RAF but retained for US service. In the reconnaissance role they were fitted with a K-24 camera in the rear fuselage and another behind the pilot's head.

In March 1943, the 111th and 154th Observation Squadrons received their first Mustangs. The two squadrons were still adjusting to flying fighter-reconnaissance aircraft, which were a different kettle of fish from the twin-engined adapted bombers they were used to. The 154th obtained its first six P-51s towards the end of the month, but on 3 April, one of the Mustangs spun in and, according to the squadron history, 'really smashed up all over the field'. Lieutenant Howard Kenner was killed.[1]

On 7 April the 111th took its single-seaters (P-51s and P-39s) to Guercif, French Morocco for practice gunnery and further training.[2] Only two days later, the first US Army Mustang combat operation took place – Lieutenant Alfred C. Schwab Jr, flying 41-37328, successfully photographed Kairouan airfield and returned safely.

Tactical reconnaissance missions steadily increased on the new aircraft. The squadron retained six Mustangs, although by the end of May this comprised five P-51s and one A-36A. The US Army only had a maximum of 55 P-51s converted to reconnaissance specification, so the

---

ii Although the decision to rename all observation groups and squadrons as reconnaissance units was taken on 2 April 1943, the 111th and 154th do not appear to have switched to the new title until at least May or even June. The change to 'Tactical Reconnaissance' was made in November 1943.

P-51 s/n 41-37320 was adapted for photographic reconnaissance by the Photographic Laboratory, Experimental Engineering Section, at Wright Field, Dayton, Ohio in August 1942. (Dana Bell)

The camera installations on the prototype photo-recon Mustang – the top picture showing the oblique camera mounted aft of the cockpit and the lower image showing the vertical camera in the lower fuselage. (Dana Bell)

newly arrived A-36A may have been the only available replacement for the P-51 destroyed in early April.[iii]

The squadron was in the thick of the action with its P-39s during the Tunisian campaign, providing a constant stream of aerial photography to General Patton's HQ, and also staging attacks on Axis ground troops and vehicles.

One preoccupation of Allied commanders during the North African campaign was to restrict shipping between Italy and Axis-held islands, and the remaining Axis-held North African ports of Bizerte and Tunis. This enabled the continued supply of forces fighting in North Africa and represented a potential escape route to withdraw troops and equipment if North Africa fell. Reconnaissance showed that shipping leaving Palermo during the night would arrive in Bizerte and Tunis in the morning, before they could be intercepted by anti-shipping aircraft.

The Allies' reconnaissance aircraft early in the campaign, such as the Marauders of 14 Squadron, often found themselves driven away by enemy fighters before they could locate and report shipping movements. Therefore the NAAF command suggested issuing some P-51s to 14 Squadron for shipping reconnaissance. It was felt that these aircraft could speed in below the fighter umbrella, locate any shipping and return to Bône in time for a strike to be launched. One American and six British pilots trained during April and May. Axis forces in North Africa surrendered before the Mustang flight could become operational, though the squadron continued to establish the flight for possible use in the future.

The RAF's 225 Squadron returned to Mustang operations during the spring of 1943. Initially this unit mainly undertook shipping reconnaissance, but also took part in numerous tactical reconnaissance sorties as requested by the Army. The squadron's Spitfires were not suitable for some of the missions the squadron was increasingly called upon to perform, so four P-51s were borrowed from the US Army.

On 4 May, the 1st Army requested photographs covering a large area of Tunisia on the 9 Corps front to help locate minefields and hostile artillery.

---

iii Supply of Allison-engined Mustangs was never ample, and by this time A-36A production had already begun to swing over to P-51As at the Inglewood plant. The vast majority of P-51As were allocated to the China–Burma–India theatre, and so no more new Allison Mustangs would be available to the Mediterranean theatre.

'Broad brush' photographic reconnaissance of this type was not the sort of task that 225 Squadron, as a tactical reconnaissance unit, had been brought into theatre to deal with. Nevertheless, the unit obligingly set up a 'shuttle service' of pairs of aircraft, each leaving when the last had returned to cover this area.

Four pairs of Mustangs and one pair of Spitfires successfully photographed the area around Massicault, Tebourba and Saint-Cyprien. The information they brought back was invaluable, revealing as it did the presence and location of 140 enemy guns. This was the area in which the final phase of the battle for Tunis was fought, so the photographs were crucial to Allied progress.

The squadron was able to respond to demands from the four Army corps in theatre (two British, one American and one Free French) extremely quickly. It found, in contrast to European operations, that Tac/R operations were best carried out at 4,000–7,000ft as this was out of the range of light flak, while maps were often found to be unreliable, making targets hard to find at low level. The 225 Squadron Mustangs were fitted only with vertical cameras, as the Army had found that vertical photographs were much more useful than oblique images. To add to 225's success in Tac/R sorties, Flying Officer Rumbold, flying Mustang 41-37361, claimed an Fw 190 damaged during an encounter with enemy fighters on 5 May during a shipping reconnaissance.

The squadron experienced its most intensive period of work between 18 April and 12 May 1943 but continued to operate some Mustangs until July (the last two, 41-37424 and 41-37366, were transferred to the 111th Tactical Reconnaissance Squadron on 29 July).

After the Allied victory in North Africa following the Axis surrender on 11 May, attention turned to Europe and the islands of the Mediterranean. These comprised small islands, which had to be overcome so as not to leave a threat to the Allied invasion forces' flanks, and Sicily, the next major target.

On 24 May, the US 111th Squadron moved eastward to Nouvion, Algeria where the personnel learned that they were now to operate independently from the 68th Group. During the squadron's 26 days at the airfield, groundcrews completely serviced over 50 P-39s and P-51s in anticipation of forthcoming operations.[3] It was probably when the 111th moved to

Nouvion that it took over some P-51s that had been operated for a short time by the 154th Reconnaissance Squadron, which was converting to the Lockheed P-38.[iv]

On 29 May, 14 Squadron's Mustang flight finally became operational, and marked its first sortie with the destruction of a Junkers Ju 52 transport off the Sardinian coast. The unit was finding it difficult to keep more than two or three of its Mustangs serviceable at a time, as it lacked enough maintenance staff to manage both the Marauders and the additional single-seaters. Spares also created difficulties, with tailwheels being particularly problematic. (This was not unique to 14 Squadron – US P-51 and A-36A operators were known to fit tailwheels from captured or crashed Fw 190s to their Mustangs due to trouble with the factory-supplied units, which were frequently defective and in short supply.)

The original purpose of 14 Squadron's Mustang flight had passed, but it was quickly found that Axis shipping moving along the eastern coast of Sardinia was well protected by fighters operating in Italy and Sicily. The modified tactical bombers used by the RAF and US Army for much of their tactical reconnaissance could not survive in this environment, so the Mustangs were the ideal solution.

With its Mustangs, 14 Squadron could safely cover the north Sicilian coast and Sardinia, and report shipping movements to the Northwest African Strategic Air Forces in time for strikes to be dispatched. The Strategic Air Forces even put strike forces on standby waiting for the reconnaissance flights to return, to ensure they could find and destroy the reported convoys before they attained the safety of Palermo or Cagliari.

This became even more important with the impending invasion of Italian islands. Palermo was the only port the Axis could use to reinforce Sicily if the forthcoming invasion went to plan, so it was imperative to interdict shipping using that route. The Mustangs lasted until June, when they were probably turned over to USAAF tactical reconnaissance units.

The British experience had shown the value of the Allison-powered Mustang variants. In May 1943, Colonel Bunch of the NAAF interviewed Wing Commander Peter Dudgeon (recent commander of 268 Squadron and now on the staff of ACC, while it was in the process

---

iv In its reconnaissance version, which would later be designated F-5.

of becoming 2 TAF). Bunch produced a report indicating the strengths and tactical use of the Mustang as it could be applied to the North African and Mediterranean theatre.

Tellingly, the Colonel focused on the advantages of the Allison-engined Mustangs over those powered by the Merlin, which were already beginning to come off the production line at that time. He explained:

> In view of the British experience, it is felt that we have a plane excellently fitted for long-range, low altitude daylight intrusion and for a medium altitude escort fighter to accompany our medium bombers. Actual combat has proved that the aircraft can run away from anything the Germans have.
>
> It is suggested that the Allison-engined P-51A may lend itself better to a combination of low-altitude fighter-intruder and a medium bombardment escorter than will the Merlin powered P-51B due to the inherent difficulty of operating the Merlin engine at the low RPMs necessary for a low fuel consumption.
>
> In view of the British operation and the fact that we have an approved war emergency rating on the 1710-39 engine of 56, it is suggested that immediate steps be taken to remove the automatic boost controls from our P-51 airplanes in this theatre and that instrument dials be marked with the proper limits...
>
> The British... have had exceptionally good service out of these engines and due to its smoothness at low RPMs, they are able to operate it so as to obtain a remarkably low fuel consumption giving them an operational range greater than any single engine fighter they possess (the fact that the Merlin engine will not run below 1600 [rpm] prevents them from obtaining an equivalent low fuel consumption and therefore limits its usefulness for similar operations). [4]

Pantelleria and Invasion of Sicily

The US Army's 111th Squadron barely had time to get used to the unusually good facilities at Nouvion before they moved again, to Korba on Cap Bon. During the period leading up to the Allied invasion of Sicily the 111th took part in dawn-to-dusk tactical reconnaissance operations. Just before the invasion was due to commence, the squadron's personnel were briefed on the operations, and the fact that if successful the squadron would soon be moving to a forward base in Sicily. Few had any regrets at the thought of leaving North Africa.

The Allison V-1710 (vee-layout, 1,170cu in capacity) 'F' series, with spur reduction gear seen to the right. This engine was the one intended for the Mustang from the start and offered a step up in power, compactness and – crucially – reliability over the earlier 'C' model. (Mike Gleichman)

The fourth RAF Mustang Mk I, AG348, in factory fresh condition, demonstrating features of very early NA-73s such as the short carburettor intake scoop atop the nose and fairings for the nose guns. This aircraft was one of four delivered to the USSR for evaluation, despite the desperate need for Mustangs to equip RAF ACC. Contrary to many claims, AG348 did not become the first of two XP-51s.

After its testing by the USAAC, XP-51 41-039 went to the NACA at Langley, Virginia, in December 1941 for aerodynamic testing. It is seen here at Langley in November 1943, having gained a coat of Olive Drab paint, with (L–R) NACA test pilots John P. 'Jack' Reeder, Herbert H. 'Bob' Hoover, Mel Gough, and Willie Gray.

A well-known but undeniably attractive photograph of the first NA-83 model Mustang Mk I on a test flight before its delivery to the RAF. When being flown in the US, despite the RAF camouflage and serial being worn, British national markings were temporarily covered with USAAC markings. (US Library of Congress)

A 'mixed bag' of P-51s for the USAAF and Mustang Mk IAs for the RAF having their final preparations before delivery. The aircraft were painted in the open. Ironically, the beautifully DuPont-finished RAF aircraft would be stripped and repainted as soon as they arrived in the UK, as the Dark Earth/Dark Green/Sky camouflage had been superseded. (US Library of Congress)

Another well-known, beautiful image. This time a P-51 flying over the Californian hills near NAA's factory. This is one of the 57 aircraft retained by the USAAF on the entry of the US to the Second World War, rather than transferred to the RAF as had originally been planned under Lend-Lease. The serial has been obscured with temporary distemper but is visible as 41-37416, the 96th of 148 NA-91s. (US Library of Congress)

The dive brakes of the A-36A (shown here on the Comanche Fighters' aircraft, 42-83731) – the upper brake extended in the first photograph, and stowed in the second. (Jim Buckel)

The neat bomb rack installation introduced on the A-36A, which enabled it to carry a pair of bombs of up to 500lb. (Jim Buckel)

Two superb air-to-air photographs of the Comanche Fighters A-36A – the first image showing the dive brakes deployed, the second showing them stowed. (Doug Fisher)

A beautiful Charles E. Brown air-to-air photograph of AG633 'XV-E' of II (AC) Squadron.

Factory photographs of the third production P-51A, 43-6005, just after completion.

The camera installation on the prototype photo-recon Mustang showing the oblique camera mounted aft of the cockpit. (Dana Bell)

A-36 aircrew in training pose in front of an A-36A in summer 1943 – red-outlined national markings were in place from June to August.

Captain Paul Striegel of the 525th Squadron, 86th FBG, just returned to his squadron after bailing out during the invasion of Sicily. He won the DFC for his exploits during the next month but was killed in September during the invasion of Italy.

Corporals Leland Guise and Ed Masingale feed a belt of 0.50in ammunition into the ammo tanks of an A-36A in North Africa, July 1943.

A long line of 1st Air Commando P-51As in 1944, many with nose art, including 'June Bride' and 'Late Date Dollie'.

First Air Commando P-51A 'Euna', showing the five-stripe identification markings unique to that unit.

Planes of Fame's beautiful P-51A wearing the markings of the 1st Air Commando's 'Mrs Virginia' in company with the same operator's P-40N wearing Flying Tigers colours, in a scene that could be from 1944. (Doug Fisher)

Mustangs of 400 Squadron RCAF at their Dunsfold base in late 1943 and early 1944 – rearming, maintenance and loading/unloading the vertical camera.

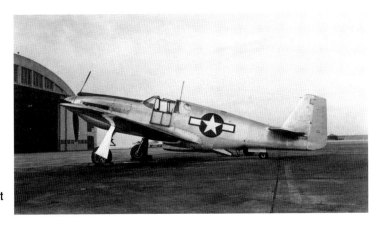

The US Navy acquired this P-51, 41-37426, for evaluation, issuing it with BuNo 57987.

Comanche Fighters
A-36A 42-83731
during its visit to
Duxford in 2002.
(Adrian Balch)

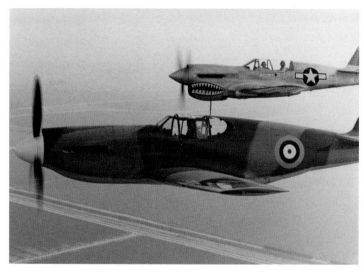

The Planes of Fame
P-51A 43-6251, in
its long-term colour
scheme representing
an early RAF Mustang
Mk I.

43-6251, in its current
colours from 2010 as
'Mrs Virginia' of the
1st Air Commando,
Burma. (Doug Fisher)

P-51A 43-6274 at the Yanks Air Museum, Chino, in the colours of AX-H, an F-6B of the 67th TRG in England in 1944, complete with a K-24 camera. (Jim Buckel)

P-51A 43-6006, 'Polar Bear', taking off in 2006 – the deeper P-51D radiator scoop is apparent from this angle. (Jim Buckel)

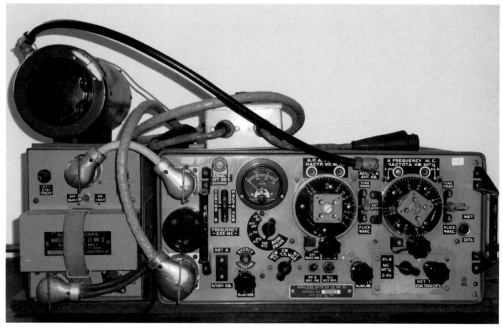

Wireless Sets 19 Mk II for communicating with army units, as carried by RAF AC Mustangs.
(Richard Howes, Pye Telecommunications Historic Collection)

Cockpit of the P-51 modified for photo-recon (later termed F-6A). The box next to the instrument
panel marked by pen is the camera switch box, and the device on the right sidewall indicated
by pen is the rear camera control. (Dana Bell)

The cockpit of the Comanche Fighters A-36A 42-83731, representative of most Allison Mustangs. (Jim Buckel)

The nose 0.50in guns of A-36A 42-83731 – note the left gun further forward. This installation was the same on the Mustang Mk I. (Jim Buckel)

The A-36A's dive brakes, upper and lower. (Jim Buckel)

The Allison V-1710-81 engine of P-51A 43-6251 – note the free space underneath that had been occupied by the nose guns and ammunition boxes in earlier variants. (Doug Fisher)

A 'stateside' A-36A, 42-83678, in a revetment for testing and aligning guns. The markings on the nose are the 'buzz number', individual aircraft letter, squadron number and field letter, common to stateside aircraft.

Just before operations for the invasion of Sicily, and the related attacks on the island of Pantelleria, 70 miles to the southwest of Sicily itself, the A-36A dive-bomber Mustang joined the fray. The 27th Fighter-Bomber Group (16th, 17th and 91st Fighter-Bomber Squadrons, in August redesignated the 522nd, 523rd and 524th) and 86th Fighter-Bomber Group (525th, 526th and 527th Fighter-Bomber Squadrons) had arrived in North Africa in May 1943, having worked up from November the previous year.[v]

The 525th Squadron's war diary recorded the powerful weapon these squadrons and their aircraft would become: 'after flying a succession of

---

v The names of these groups changed on several occasions, from Bombardment Group (Light), to Bombardment Group (Dive) to Fighter-Bomber Group, and those of the squadrons from Bombardment Squadron to Fighter-Bomber Squadron. The names Fighter-Bomber Group and Fighter-Bomber Squadron are used here for simplicity and as the most appropriate description of the activities of the units in the Sicilian and Italian campaigns.

planes which included A-20s, A-31s and A-24s, they received their new A-36s… Axis rail and motor columns would soon discover what a deadly team the plane and the pilots would make.'[5]

It was during this phase, as the invasion of Sicily was beginning, that the A-36A gained its unofficial name of 'Invader', which became extremely prevalent for a period. Lieutenant Walsh of the 527th suggested the name, which was immediately adopted by the 86th Fighter-Bomber Group (FBG). Although unofficial, the name gained wide acceptance and appeared in publications as diverse as a USAAF aircraft recognition guide and UK Cabinet Office reports on the progress of the war. The media took up the name with some enthusiasm, as did manufacturers of components used on the aircraft who repeated the name in advertisements. This no doubt caused some consternation to the US Army's senior commanders, who had resisted giving the A-36A a separate name (and in any case, the name Invader had been allocated to the Douglas A-26). The Associated Press quoted Walsh (of Felt, Idaho) indicating his inspiration for the name, stating 'when the invasion comes we all expect these ships to be right in there from the start.'[vi]

Later the group's bar invented a cocktail named after the Invader, which was composed of gin, cherry brandy and grapefruit juice and according to the war diary was 'very potent'.

The first sortie of the campaign, and indeed the war, by an A-36A squadron was carried out on 6 June, when aircraft of the 27th Bomb Group carried out a reconnaissance over Pantelleria. The tiny island had become the focus of considerable Allied attention for several reasons – the island's airfield could have been used to help evacuate troops from North Africa to bolster forces elsewhere and its radar stations and airfield could present a significant threat to the invasion of Sicily. It was also of interest as an experiment in heavy bombing as a prelude to seaborne invasion.

---

vi The decision taken by the author to refer to the aircraft in the Mediterranean theatre typically as 'Invaders' (with inverted commas) reflects the very common usage of the term at the time, appearing as it does almost constantly through some units' war diaries. This is in no way intended to suggest that the term was official – much as the use of 'Camel' to refer to the Sopwith F.1 was widespread but frowned upon in official circles, for example.

A soldier poses with a new-looking A-36A in 1942 or early 1943, probably in the US, while an Interstate L-6 Cadet trainer/liaison aircraft taxies past.

The day after the reconnaissance sweep, the 27th carried out the first of many dive-bombing missions over the island. The majority of these were focused on gun emplacements, of which Pantelleria had many and which constituted a significant threat to invading ground and sea forces. On 11 June, the island fell when the garrison surrendered, its position hopeless.[vii]

After a number of A-36A missions had been conducted, the NAAF drew up a tactical note outlining the best known use of the aircraft.[6] This document noted that, 'the P-51 was designed fundamentally as a low-altitude fighter,' but that with the addition of bomb racks and dive brakes, 'it became an excellent fighter-bomber, capable of delivering its bomb load with extreme accuracy'. The units in action so far had adopted fighter formations of 12 aircraft in line-abreast, with a distance of 50 yards between each aircraft. The report noted that the excellent range and accuracy of the A-36A meant it could be used against strategic pin-point targets, and its high speed meant that calls for close army support could be responded to more quickly.

The tactical note set out the best attack methods then known, remarking that the accuracy of the bombing varied with the steepness of the dive. The flight leader would signal the rest of the aircraft to open their dive brakes, which they would do immediately before rolling over into the dive. Each pilot would sight individually onto the target, but trying to keep as small a gap as possible to the aircraft in front.

For heavily defended targets, the dive would begin at 10,000ft, recovering at 4,000–5,000ft, and for more lightly defended targets, the dive would begin at 6,000–8,000ft with recovery 'on the deck'. The latter, naturally, was more accurate but more dangerous.

On 3 July 1943, the 86th joined the campaign when two of its pilots took part in a mission by the 27th to dive bomb a panzer division in the South-West of Sicily. Lt Robert Kirsch of the 527th Fighter-Bomber Squadron (FBS) and Lt Gilliland of 526th FBS accompanied the 27th FBG to help

---

vii The surrender of the garrison following air attack solely, with no ground invasion, represented a brief 'victory' for supporters of strategic bombing who had continually downplayed the need for close support aircraft such as the A-36A – ironic considering the large-scale invasions to come, in which ground attack aircraft were to prove so pivotal.

A trio of A-36As flies over the Californian landscape, in training for operations in Europe or the Far East.

gain experience for the 86th FBG before they themselves went into action as a group shortly afterwards.

Flying personnel from all the squadrons converged on Korba on 6 July and immediately began flying combat operations. The 527th conducted an armed reconnaissance over Licata, while the 525th's first mission of the campaign was a 12-ship rhubarb aimed at disrupting the roads and railways around Sciacca.

Over the next few days, all of the A-36A Squadrons went into action. Axis forces on Sicily were hit hard – missions included strafing and bombing the railway station, warehouses and factories at Mazala; bombing and strafing military tents and a fuel dump at Agrigento; and bombing railway yards at Canicattì. German fighters attempted to oppose the attacks; Captain Stell of the 526th was attacked by three enemy aircraft who set upon his A-36A after he had been wounded in the leg by flak. Captain Reginald Winters, the squadron's CO, came to Stell's rescue and drove off the fighters.

A-36A 'A-V' of the 225th Squadron, 27th FBG in markings applied upon arrival in North Africa.

A 'radiophoto' transmitted to American media by the US Signal Corps of A-36As taking off from their North African base to attack targets in Sicily in July 1943.

A more unconventional defence was experienced by the 527th as their formation of 12 A-36As approached the coast at wave-top height. 'Flak guns lobbed shells over sea, trying to get hits with water spouts and ricochets on our deck-flying machines,' recorded the squadron's war diary.

1437 Strategic Reconnaissance Flight

In addition to 14 and 225 Squadrons, one more RAF reconnaissance unit operated in the Mediterranean theatre with borrowed USAAF Mustangs. This was 1437 Strategic Reconnaissance Flight which had operated Martin Baltimores from Sorman in Tunisia.[viii] By June 1943 the Baltimores were felt to be unsuitable for the work in hand, being too slow and lightly defended to avoid or fight off enemy fighters in the thick of the invasion zone.

Much as with the American reconnaissance groups in theatre, the RAF considered that fast, single-seat aircraft would be more effective than modified medium bombers.[ix] Therefore 1437 Flight was re-equipped with borrowed USAAF A-36As. Although the A-36A was designed as a dive-bomber, it was just as capable of carrying out armed reconnaissance as the RAF Mustang I or the American P-51.

Between 4 and 9 July, six A-36As loaned from USAAF 12th Air Force arrived at Sorman. RAF national markings and code letters were painted onto aircraft but the US Army Olive Drab colours appear to have been retained, as were US serial numbers, at least at first. The aircraft obtained were 42-83829, which was coded 'E', 42-83898 'B', 42-83906 'D', 42-84018 'C', 42-84019 'A' and 42-84117 'F'. Later, RAF serials were applied to the aircraft that remained, and these included HK946, HK947, HK955 and HK956. The nose guns were removed and cameras fitted in the rear fuselage. Unlike some US Army units, the RAF was happy to call the A-36A 'Mustang'.

The Allies' push through Sicily, following the invasion on 10 July 1943, required as much information about enemy defences as possible, and perhaps as a result only a short time was spent working up on the new aircraft. Despite being hampered by lack of spares and the small number of airframes, the flight was ready far more quickly than 14 Squadron had managed with its own Mustang flight. A mere three days after the last aircraft arrived, the flight was ready to start operations.

---

viii For more details on 1437 Flight's period of operations with A-36A aircraft, see Chapter 5 'Nought Feet' of Peter C. Smith's history of the A-36 (*Straight Down!*, pp. 98–115). This chapter draws heavily from 1437 Flight's ORB, AIR 29/869 at the National Archives, Kew.

ix This was of course a lesson that had been learned some years previously in North West Europe, though converted twin-engined bombers had remained competitive in the Mediterranean for longer.

Despite being a strategic reconnaissance unit by background, 1437 adopted tactical reconnaissance methods similar to those developed by ACC in England, with two-ship formations made up of a flight leader and weaver. The aircraft were also armed, and able to make their scouting missions offensive in nature if suitable targets presented themselves.

On 11 July, five of the six aircraft of 1437 Flight flew to Luqa, Malta. The next day, low-level photo reconnaissance missions over Sicily commenced, providing information for the Army. The first mission flown was a reconnaissance along the coast to Catania, followed the next day by an assessment of enemy road movements between Palermo and Enna.

The 'Invaders' of Sicily

The invasion of Sicily began on 10 July, and the A-36As flew several armed reconnaissance and dive-bombing missions to the island. Lieutenant Kirsch of the 527th lost control of his aircraft and crashed it into another on take-off, killing two enlisted men of the 310th Bomb Squadron. Lieutenant Kirsch was lucky to get out of his own aircraft before the two 500lb bombs exploded. He described the incident to the *Buffalo Evening News*: 'My left landing-gear crumpled as I was going down the runway and I veered off into the parking area at about 90 miles an hour. I hit the plane dead centre and they both caught fire immediately. I managed to get out and start running and got about 50 feet when the first bomb went off. It knocked me on my face, and like a darn fool, I got up and started running again.'

There was more bad news to come for the group that day – the 526th Squadron CO Captain Winters was killed in action. Captain Glenn Stell took over.

Over the succeeding days, the A-36As would find themselves fully occupied. Their work involved shooting up convoys of motor transports and railway traffic and bombing enemy positions in the front line identified by the Army. At this stage, the A-36A was very much a 'battlefield' aircraft and would continue to be so for some time – later on in the Italian campaign, the use of fighter-bombers would change to attacking targets further behind enemy lines, but for the time being the Invaders were in the thick of the fighting around the front line.

On 14 July, the 111th Squadron's 'air echelon' travelled to Gela, Sicily in Douglas C-47s with the unit's P-51 and P-39 aircraft acting as escort.

A-36A 'El Matador' in Sicily in 1943, the aircraft of Flight Officer R. Bryant (right) with crew chief, Sergeant Dan Perry. (US Air Force Museum)

The advance parties of the A-36A squadrons also arrived and began to set up the airfield to receive the main groups and aircraft. Any relief from moving out of the unpleasant conditions of North Africa was short-lived – the airfield was bombed on the first night and most of the station's personnel spent the night hunched in a drainage ditch.

The following day, the 111th surveyed the results of the previous night's raid. Several of their aircraft had been damaged, some irreparably, by shrapnel, and many unexploded bombs littered the field. Gingerly, the squadron's groundcrews started the process of inspecting and patching up the aircraft. The airfield was too vulnerable, so a satellite field was quickly created some five miles away, known as Gela West. The new airfield had been a cotton field, and according to some of the men newly stationed there, the dispersal area still was. The area was in use even before all the mines had been cleared, and the field was close enough to the front line that artillery could be heard quite clearly.

That day members of the 525th Squadron bivouacked in an olive grove outside Comiso airfield. The Allies had apparently achieved the element of surprise in the attack (no doubt helped by Operation *Mincemeat*, where a corpse purporting to be that of a British officer was planted near the Spanish coast with papers suggesting that Greece was the target for Operation *Husky*). The airfield showed every sign of having been deserted in a hurry. There were many German and Italian aircraft, some of them serviceable, parked around the field and abandoned meals were evident on plates in the mess. Two Junkers Ju 87s even tried to land, apparently unaware that the airfield was in enemy hands. The other part of the squadron was at Gela, and the two halves did not join up for several days.

A few days later, the A-36A squadrons of the 27th FBG joined those of the 86th on Sicily itself. The fight they joined was degenerating into a slog after rapid initial gains – German forces had created a line of defences from the coast to the foot of Mount Etna, rendering the few roads that existed impassable to the Allies. The A-36As were used to bomb and strafe these defences directly and they also took on the role of escort fighters for medium bombers attacking targets on the island.[x]

The 525th's war diary outlined the squadron's work during this stage of the campaign: 'While based on Gela Airfield, Sicily, the squadron came into its own, doing wonderful work in support of the 7th Army's drive through Sicily. Flying from daylight to dusk they molested enemy convoys, gun positions, troop concentrations, strongpoints and road bridges.'[7]

The association with Allison Mustangs and 'train busting', along with attacks on other communications, continued. Lieutenant Fernandez of the 525th had a lucky escape on 19 July 1943 when a train he was strafing blew up, damaging his A-36A. He was able to coax his aircraft out to sea where he bailed out, and was picked up by a rescue launch.

The remainder of the Sicilian campaign consisted of strenuous activity in close support of II Army Corps, working with the first division. This included specific targets and free-ranging missions seeking targets of opportunity. Roads to the north of Nicosia were patrolled, and the Invaders

---

x The use of the 'attack' A-36A as an escort fighter is interesting, as it demonstrates a significant degree of flexibility in the use of aircraft from a command point of view. The suitability of the A-36A as an escort fighter was identified in the Northwest African Air Forces' tactical note on the use of the aircraft, but the switching of roles as necessary indicates the local Air Force commanders were not thinking rigidly – though one explanation could simply be a shortage of 'conventional' fighters, especially those with the range to escort bombers over long distance.

A staged photo-op for the 86th FBG in Sicily, with mechanics servicing and rearming the A-36A 'Vulture II'.

bombed a motor transport convoy and later an enemy strongpoint south-east of Petralia. Later, landing barges were strafed, followed by bombing and strafing enemy ships and seaplanes in Milazzo harbour.

Several dive-bombing missions in squadron strength were made to Messina harbour, which was heavily defended by flak. Hits were claimed on a cruiser and two destroyers and Lieutenant Sittler was awarded a Distinguished Flying Cross (DFC).

Reconnaissance from Forward Bases

After the first few missions had been flown from Malta, 1437 Flight moved back to Sorman for a spell. During this phase, missions generally involved ascertaining enemy movement on Sicily's northern and eastern coast roads and associated inland roads, but it was quickly established that the 240-mile round trip wasted too much flying time and put too much strain on the pilots. On 18 July 1943, therefore, the flight began to move groundcrew and equipment to Luqa in order to operate from the island as a forward base, although Sorman remained the unit's official home.

On the same day, and the next, reconnaissance over the north-east of Sicily was carried out. Little build-up of enemy forces was seen at this stage. By 20 July, the forward base was fully established at Luqa. The flight began looking at roads north of Etna, but still no large-scale movement of forces was seen.

By 24 July, the flight was generally staging two recces a day from Luqa. The A-36As would typically strafe any motor transports or troop concentrations they located, again mirroring the offensive reconnaissance methods used in Northern Europe.

However, increasing amounts of flak were experienced as enemy forces were pushed back, organising their considerable strength in anti-aircraft guns to cover the planned withdrawal. Missions consequently became increasingly dangerous for 1437 Flight. It was not uncommon for the pilots to experience intense flak for the whole time they were over enemy-held territory. On occasion the A-36A pilots returned the favour by strafing anti-aircraft positions.

By the end of July, reconnaissance missions typically covered communications routes between Messina and Milazzo, and south of Messina. Late in the month, the Flight suffered a blow to its operations when it lost a pilot, and two aircraft were put out of action. The ever-dangerous flak was the cause, as Flight Sergeant Stanley and Flying Officer Jones were both hit as they began a photographic reconnaissance run near Messina. Stanley's aircraft caught fire over the target. Jones's A-36A was severely damaged and limped to a forward landing ground. It was assessed as having 'Category II' damage, meaning it would need considerable work to repair and would be out of action for some time. Jones, fortunately, was uninjured but Stanley failed to return and was posted missing. It later transpired that Stanley had survived and been taken prisoner.

The decision was taken to move the flight to Francesco on Sicily itself, which helped bring the unit nearer to its operational area, but the situation with aircraft was serious. The unit had never had an overabundance of airframes, but with the loss of two of the original six, and a further two undergoing engine changes, only a pair of A-36As was now available.

Missions now turned to Italy itself as well, and began to cover the southern extremities of the peninsula and the east coast. These established that the eastern coast of southern Italy was not heavily defended and not used extensively for transporting troops and equipment. There was less flak than there had been on Sicily, but enemy fighters were now more of a threat and several attempts to intercept the A-36As were made without success. On 1 August, a reconnaissance of the coast from Marina di Monasterace discovered little road transport, but did see a lot of railway rolling stock. Flying Officer Griffiths and Warrant Officer Leggo strafed rail cars in a siding and attacked two locomotives, one of which was seen to explode.

The valuable reconnaissance work continued despite the paucity of aircraft, but the flight's difficulties were bound to increase. Flight Lieutenant McLaren's A-36A, originally 'F' 42-84117 was hit by flak during a mission over the north of Sicily and although McLaren succeeded in bringing the aircraft back as far as a temporary airstrip at Lentini, it was another case of serious damage and the A-36A would not be fit for operations for a very long time. To make matters worse, McLaren was injured in the forced landing and would not be flying again soon.

The flight was now down to half its original complement of Mustangs although there were plenty of pilots, even after McLaren's injuries. The availability of spares was becoming a problem as well, and the chances of any more A-36As being made available was slight – the USAAF needed all it could get, and the type was out of production. In the middle of August, two Spitfire Vbs were assigned to the flight to supplement the A-36As. However, these were used only for training and practice (and later dropping messages to troops), as the Spitfires were considered to be inferior to the Mustangs and not suitable for the challenging operations the unit was required to perform.

Striking at Communication Routes

Fighting to wrest control of the roads continued. On 28 July, A-36As from the 27th FBG attacked heavy traffic on the Troina-Randazzo road, and dive-bombed bridges and roads north and west of Cesarò. The road from Troina to Randazzo was one of the two key routes to Messina assigned to the American Army forces on Sicily, so clearing it for an assault on the 'Etna Line' was important. The 27th FBG's fighter-bombers also struck an airfield at Falcone and buildings near Randazzo that day.

During August 1943, offensive missions carried out by the USAAF's FBGs mainly consisted of attacking enemy communications and transport to hamper their defence of the 'Etna Line', as well as supporting the Army directly. The A-36A squadrons found that their accurate dive-bombing with 500lb bombs could create effective road blocks, denying certain routes to enemy supplies and reinforcements. Attacks on railways were made, focusing on dive-bombing bridges and marshalling yards and strafing trains. Maritime transport was also a common target, with shipping and harbour facilities dive-bombed and strafed by the fighter-bombers. During August, pilots of the 527th Squadron Lieutenants Westfall and Stone were credited with sinking a 50,000-ton transport ship at Bagnara, south-west Italy. Two direct hits and a near miss were observed at the stern of the former liner. Pilots overflying the quay the next day reported the ship had sunk, though there was later some doubt raised as to whether the ship had been as large as supposed.

The A-36A squadrons were proving themselves to be a potent force, but things did not always go according to plan. On 4 August 1943, a mission to bomb the German stronghold at Troina led to the bombing of Regalbuto by mistake. Captain Striegel of the 525th realised the mistake on entering his dive but was unable to prevent the rest of his flight from bombing the town, where there were a large number of Allied troops, not to mention civilians. Fortunately, the 527th bombed the correct target, for which Captain John Harsh was recommended for the DFC. The squadron's bombing was accurate and powerful. The squadron was later told that their bombing had directly helped US forces occupy Troina, an incredibly 'tough nut', which was defended by the 15th Panzer Grenadier Division and elements of the Italian Aosta Division.

Once Troina had been captured, the next focus was Randazzo, which became known as 'flak alley' for obvious reasons. Second Lieutenant Lyle Hood of the 527th FBS experienced this to his discomfort, reporting:

We were returning towards friendly territory when all at once we were in the midst of a terrific flak barrage. It came so thick and fast that we were very much surprised. Immediately, we began evasive action but couldn't get completely away from it. One burst came extremely close to my plane while I was in a steep turn. Three pieces of flak hit my plane. One hit in the canopy and one in each wing. The concussion from the burst felt as though I had been hit on top of the head with something heavy. The shattered glass and a piece of metal hit the right side of my head, and a piece of glass hit my right wrist. Both wounds bled for a while but before reaching our base they had stopped bleeding.[8]

The 86th and 27th FBGs conducted a variety of missions as August progressed in support of the advancing Army as it moved on the crucial, strategic port of Messina, without which no assault on Italy would be possible. The port, surrounding area and associated facilities were pounded mercilessly, with the dive-bomber squadrons hitting associated targets several times a day. In addition, the 86th hit bridges, gun emplacements, troop concentrations and road traffic with their accurate and devastating mix of dive-bombing and strafing. The 27th FBG even began to focus on the next step in the war – the invasion of mainland Europe. The group's A-36As, supplemented by Curtiss P-40s, began to strafe and bomb shipping, barges and small vessels in the narrow strait between Sicily and the toe of the Italian boot and some targets on Italy itself, among the very first of the campaign. Belatedly, the Allies realised the extent to which Axis forces were evacuating troops and equipment to face the Allied armies again on the mainland, and the interdiction of shipping and boats in the Straits of Messina hoped to hamper this activity.

On 17 August 1943, Messina fell, effectively ending the campaign. Until the end, USAAF 'Invader' missions included reconnaissance, bombing railway yards, bombing supply dumps and attacking landing barges. During this phase of the war, the 86th Bomb Group alone had flown 2,375 combat sorties during five weeks of combat. The A-36As had bombed with decisive results at Troina, Randazzo, Milazzo, Cesarò and Messina and also attacked the enemy's withdrawal along the southern Italian coast.

Interestingly, despite the success of the A-36 as a 'pure' dive-bomber, there were moves by some senior pilots to limit their use. On 4 August 1943, Lieutenant Dorris of the 526th told the squadron's assistant operations officer that he did not intend his flight to use the dive brakes. This evidently went against previous practice to the extent that the squadron considered that this might even be in contravention of orders from the group's CO, Colonel Paul. Further investigation brought to light that there were no orders insisting on use of the air brakes, but it is revealing that some senior officers thought there were.

The Toe of Italy

For 1437 Flight, reconnaissance missions over north-east Sicily continued right up to the final withdrawal of the last Axis forces from the island. From 16 August 1943, the flight began a series of missions to reconnoitre the inland roads around the mountainous regions in the toe of Italy. Unfortunately, the Axis forces had been able to transport a significant proportion of the flak batteries that had made life so difficult over Sicily, across the strait and re-established them on the mainland.

On 17 August, Flying Officer Griffith and Flying Officer Gilliland were scanning the mountain roads in the southern tip of Italy when they stumbled across a valley where a number of tanks and armoured vehicles were concealed. This was a valuable find, but well-protected, and Griffith's aircraft was seriously hit by light flak before Gilliland put the guns out of action by shooting them up. Griffith ditched his aircraft in the sea and was picked up by a Walrus flying boat. He returned to the unit unharmed, but one more A-36A had been lost.

By this time, the flight was mostly operating with two aircraft. Efforts were made to recover A-36A 'C' which had suffered a forced landing at Pachino in July 1943. The aircraft had been patched up enough to get it to Francesco, but further work would be needed to get the machine to a maintenance unit in North Africa.

With the flight's available aircraft, reconnaissance was carried out as comprehensively as it could manage. The pilots were able to establish that much of the winding, mountainous road network was unsuitable for heavy road traffic. Thirty reconnaissance sorties were carried out during the month, good for a unit with only two serviceable aircraft. Message drops were also made to British troops, in a further parallel with the AC Mustang units located in Britain at that time.

Chapter 7

The 'Underbelly of the Axis'

For the units operating Mustang variants in the Mediterranean, the action continued without respite. As soon as Sicily was secured, the full force of the Allied assault was turned toward the 'underbelly of the Axis', as Churchill referred to Italy.

The A-36A squadrons now began 'staging' to Sicilian airfields nearer the action. On 22 August, A-36As of the 86th FBG escorted a formation of B-26s from Termini Imerise on Sicily to Salerno and back – aircraft from the 27th were also intended to provide an escort for the rear formation of B-26s but failed to make contact.

When the bombers started their bomb-run, the force was attacked by a dozen enemy fighters, identified as Messerschmitt Bf 109s and Macchi C.202s. Captain Striegel and Major Tarrant of the 525th turned toward the enemy formation and soon each were tenaciously pursuing a fighter. Striegel chased a C.202 for some miles, scoring numerous hits at close range, although only two of his guns would fire. Striegel broke off the combat at the Italian coast, and the Macchi was last seen issuing smoke and losing height. Tarrant, meanwhile, latched onto a Bf 109 which broke and fled after Tarrant had fired a few bursts.

Lieutenant Lynam, of the 527th, had allowed his A-36A to lag slightly, and was set upon by a Messerschmitt Bf 109. Two of his squadron mates, Lieutenant Yetter and Lieutenant Dungan, immediately turned into the attack, and Yetter scored some hits on the Bf 109. The enemy fighter dived away, smoking. Captain Gilliland, Lieutenant Fager and Lieutenant Wright of the 526th scored three confirmed victories and two probables among them, marking their squadron's first air-combat victories. No B-26s from the forward formation, which the 86th was escorting, were lost.

A-36A 'Ole Eagle Eye' of the 27th FBG in Italy during winter 1943–44.

Two days later, Captain Striegel added ship-busting to his air-to-air victory. The war diary of the 525th records that:

> On a mission to bomb railroad yards at Sapri, Italy, Capt. Striegel performed a feat worthy of the DFC. When approaching the target, he observed a naval vessel, either a cruiser or destroyer, in a cove South of Sapri. Realising its value as a target, and yet not wishing to divert the whole formation from the assigned target, he led the flight into the dive, but saved his bombs, and coming off the target, he proceeded to the vessel and bombed it and strafed it at low level, scoring direct hits on the stern, setting it on fire and causing it to sink. Lt. Griswold, his wingman, also strafed the vessel.

On 26 and 27 August 1943, the two groups operating A-36As moved to Barcellona, near Milazzo. This enabled them to cover the invasion areas and provide direct support for amphibious landings. The versatility of the 'Invader' was such that the two groups were able to provide their own escorts without requiring fighters from other groups to cover them.

Usually, one squadron would be assigned as the escort and provide top cover, while the other two would bomb and strafe.

On 3 September, British forces were due to land at Calabria, and six days later the main invasion at Salerno would begin. The A-36As were charged with helping to maintain constant air cover over the landing beaches. However, just before the first landings, the 525th lost their courageous and effective CO, Captain Striegel. During the dive-bombing of a target at Lamezia, Striegel's A-36A was apparently hit by flak. The aircraft was seen to explode in the dive in a 'huge red ball of fire'. Major Gunnison took over Striegel's role.

As the 8th Army was landing, with little opposition, at Calabria, the 527th undertook a 12-ship sweep over the roads of southern Italy. The squadron bombed rail yards at Bagnara, Calabria and caused a large explosion in what was believed to be an oil dump. Further attacks were made on barges and shipping near the invasion area.

After the landings at Calabria, but before the main invasion could begin, the Italian government surrendered, this being announced on 8 September. It would now be a German force of occupation that the Allies would primarily be opposed by.

On 9 September, the main invasion at Salerno began, and A-36As contributed to blanket air cover for the American forces that were then landing. Each squadron was assigned an area to patrol, and even given the shorter distance from Barcellona, auxiliary fuel tanks were needed to provide the required endurance. The A-36As covered the beaches until 7.00pm, which the 527th diary records as 'gruelling, tiresome work'.

The 527th Squadron had begun to style themselves 'Captain Harsh's Flying Circus', in honour of their CO. The 'circus' was pleased to break up the beachhead cover by flying an armed reconnaissance on 11 September. South of Gioia de Colle, the squadron spotted a row of bombed-up Junkers Ju 88s about to take off, no doubt heading for the invasion beaches. The A-36As dived in strafing and bombing, and destroyed at least ten of the Ju 88s as well as a building on the airfield. Later on, it was back to patrolling the beaches.

Two days later, A-36As of the 27th were providing close air support to troops on the beachhead when they fell victim to the standing patrol, in another of the not-uncommon friendly-fire incidents that marred the

Mediterranean campaigns. That day, the group had moved to Capaccio, near Salerno itself. A fighter-controller informed a flight of Lockheed P-38 Lightnings that some unidentified aircraft, possibly 'bandits', were present over the beach at low altitude. The Lightnings dived from their combat air patrol altitude of around 11,000ft to the co-ordinates they had been given, where it was now claimed the 'bandits' were Messerschmitt Bf 109s attacking American troops.

The Lightnings spotted the unidentified aircraft at around 3,000ft and went into the attack. Just as the Lightnings opened fire, the flight leader, Captain Smith, realised that the 'Messerschmitts' were actually American aircraft. He called the P-38s to break off, but one Mustang had already been hit. One of the aircraft burst into flames causing the pilot to bail out, although he reached the beach safely and was picked up by US troops. Aircraft recognition remained a perennial problem in the theatre, and this was neither the first nor the last time that Mustang variants would be mistaken for Messerschmitt Bf 109s.

By September 1943, the RAF's 1437 Flight could only carry out the most important reconnaissance missions due to the lack of spares for its overworked aircraft. Having moved forward again to Milazzo, from where sorties over Italy could more easily be staged, missions commenced on 13 September.

The first mission involved two A-36As, scouting road networks between Taranto and Policastro for the British Army. A large troop encampment was discovered near Lagonegro, including significant numbers of tanks and motor transports. After strafing the camp, flak became intense and the two Mustangs headed for home. However, Squadron Leader Welshman's A-36A took a hit to the engine. The A-36A's engine got Welshman back to Milazzo East, once more proving the ability of the V-1710 to take damage and continue to function, finally dying only when the aircraft was lining up to land. Fortunately, the squadron leader was able to land safely. Again though, the flight had lost another aircraft to a lengthy period of repairs.

This incident left the flight with only one serviceable aircraft, and only three in total. Thereafter, 1437 Flight was unable to carry out further operations and, despite dogged attempts to secure more aircraft or spares for the unserviceable Mustangs, the unit was ultimately disbanded on 13 October.

An A-36A of 1437 Strategic Reconnaissance Flight, in company with RAAF Kittyhawks, in Italy, 1943. It was one of a handful borrowed by the RAF from the USAAF.

From the fourth day after the landings (D+4), the A-36A squadrons and the remaining Mustang reconnaissance unit, the 111th, began to operate from Sele airfield near Salerno. Enemy forces were still very close by so there were risks involved in transferring to the airfield and operating from it. Axis forces regularly shelled the invasion beaches and the airfield was in range. To add insult to injury, the area was thick with mosquitoes and other insects. As with the move to Sicily, the A-36As helped escort transport aircraft moving personnel and equipment, as well as taking part in numerous bombing and strafing missions.

The 86th FBG flew its first combat missions from Italian soil on 15 September 1943, operating from a forward base at Sele, although the aircraft flew back to Barcellona after the day's operations were complete.

On 16 September, Lieutenant John Gee led a flight of the 527th A-36As which bombed an airfield south of Rome. Gee later reported the sortie to the *Hamilton Press*, indicating that the flight had spotted 'that some 20 to 25 Messerschmitts had just landed and hadn't had time to disperse. They were in two groups. We buzzed down on them and three of our ships scored direct hits on one group and there was a very near miss on the other group. All you could see was parts and dust from the first group. We circled around and could see that the first group was completely wiped out.' It was estimated that around 14 aircraft had been destroyed or damaged.

In spite of the successes, losses were heavy during the first fighting on Italian soil. On 18 September, the 525th lost two of its best pilots, Lieutenant Strainis and Lieutenant Fouts – Fouts failed to return after a strafing mission near Colliano, while Strainis was seen to bail out but his parachute did not open. The 526th lost three pilots in two days to the heavy flak north of Salerno.

Despite the losses, the A-36As were making their presence felt. On 20 September, German troops and vehicles were seen massing for a counter-attack, but before they could strike, aircraft of the 526th set upon them, bombing and then strafing. The Army later confirmed that the attack had been a complete success and had broken up the counter-attack. As late as the 22nd though, Axis forces were dangerously close to the beachhead – that day it took aircraft of the 527th some time to land as a bombardment of the beaches was taking place and attempting to put down nearby would have been too risky.

That day the 525th was lucky not to lose a second squadron commander in a matter of weeks. Major Gunnison was forced to bail out over the sea after his aircraft sustained damage caused by the explosion of an ammunition dump the squadron was bombing. Fortunately, he was picked up by a fishing boat and returned to the squadron the following day.

The 111th was also doing sterling work in direct support of the hard-pressed armies on the ground. The reconnaissance Mustangs spent this period directing naval artillery fire onto targets requested by the 5th Army, showing the benefits of tight co-operation between air, sea and ground forces.

By the end of September, rain had set in, and so little flying could be achieved that moving the A-36A units based at Sele to an all-weather base was considered. Many new pilots began to arrive and some of the more experienced men began to be rotated out. Missions continued to focus on hampering enemy communications, including bombing roads and strafing military road traffic. The Invaders also bombed areas of towns where the enemy was believed to be concentrated, and bridges. Sometimes several missions were required to do sufficient damage to bridges, which could be difficult to hit squarely from the air. The

P-51 of the 111th TRS 'Snoopers' in Italy, 1943. (Grahm Nordlund)

527th obtained a small Dachshund cross as a mascot, and named him 'Rhubarb' as he consistently operated at minimum altitude.

On 12 October 1943, the 525th Squadron and 86th Group HQ moved to Serretelle base, near Battipaglia, while the 527th and 526th moved to Pomigliano airport near Naples along with the 111th Tactical Reconnaissance Squadron (TRS) and their reconnaissance P-51s and A-36As. This enabled the units to carry on flying missions when more temporary fields were rendered inoperable. The runway at Pomigliano had been deliberately damaged by the retreating Germans, however, so the units based there enjoyed a week's stand-down while it was repaired. The tough fighting on the ground meant that the front line moved little, and the squadrons were to remain at their new bases for some time. After several short spells at various airfields where conditions were poor and facilities limited, the relatively long stay at the well-equipped Pomigliano and Serretelle at least allowed the crews to experience something of a home-from-home.

The usual variety of missions continued, including bombing of rail yards, bridges and vehicles. On 17 October, the 527th destroyed two bridges in one day, while the following day Lieutenant Forst of the 526th shot down two Fw 190s while the rest of the squadron strafed an airfield, destroying many more aircraft on the ground.

One of the most dramatic incidents of the campaign thus far took place on 25 October 1943. A-36As of the 527th attacked a railway station that was storing so much in the way of ammunition that the resulting explosion reached thousands of feet into the air.

Lieutenant Colonel Yancey Tarrant described the mission:

The four of us went in on the deck, as was customary, and flew over water until time to turn inland and begin looking along the road nets[i] in that territory… We then saw an enemy troop train which apparently had about a thousand soldiers on it. From my position in the flight it was impossible for me to get my guns on the cars, so I pulled to one side in order to give the leader of the second element a better shot without having to worry about hitting either me, or my wingman with his bullets.

Both he and his wingman raked the train and covered at least three quarters of its length. Just ahead was another small station into which I fired about three hundred rounds with no apparent damage except what could normally be expected. At this point, the leader of the second element had dropped behind and I again moved over to give him a shot at the station ahead. This is normal procedure as it not only gives all members of the flight a shot at some of the targets, it spreads the expenditure of the ammunition in such a manner that all the ships have some left in their guns in case they are jumped by enemy fighters. I watched him turn onto the target and saw his tracers going in and around the box cars. As I turned my head to look to the front for another target there was a terrific explosion. The first sensation I had was that the whole side of the airplane was gone, and that something had hit me quite a blow on the side of the head and face. After being stunned momentarily, I came to enough to realise that the sliding panel of the canopy was in my lap, and that the left side of the ship was still apparently intact. I looked back just in time, at about five hundred feet, to see a ship come out of the explosion, roll over on its back, and head straight down. Its guns appeared still to be firing.

… The target must have been quite a large ammunition dump. The blast and concussion were not comparable to anything I have ever seen before, and the smoke and flame went up to at least three thousand feet. My own

---

i   Presumably 'road networks'.

ship was at an altitude of approximately two hundred feet, and at least three hundred yards to the right [sic] of the station. The impact was so powerful that it practically caved in the right side of the airplane. The wingtip was creased and dented, although nothing struck it. The removable panels to the cowling were caved in and the stramer[ii] to which they are attached was bent... Along the aft section of the fuselage the skin was pushed in, and most of the bulkheads had been bent... The vertical stabiliser had been strained, and the rudder moved about an inch and a half to one side. The horizontal stabiliser and elevators had been sprung out of trim. In spite of this damage, all the controls were only slightly sluggish and stiff in their reaction. Upon reaching the airfield, a normal landing was made without any difficulty.

Towards the end of October 1943, the main road south of Mignano and across the river at Roccamonfina became the focus for a concerted effort on behalf of the Army. The bridges were successfully destroyed, leading to German troops being trapped in a triangular pocket. The interception of desperate communications from the commander of the trapped Germans allowed American troops to spot the opportunity and close the trap – the following day one regiment captured more German troops than the total number captured in the entire preceding three weeks. Army HQ passed on to the FBGs that, 'General [Mark] Clark knew of the splendid work being done by the Invader planes, [and] was extremely pleased by the bombing results obtained'. By this time, some of the A-36A pilots had well over 100 combat missions under their belt.

On 11 November 1943, the 27th dive-bombed Civitavecchia, a stronghold of Axis army forces, and bridges at Pontecorvo. Frustratingly, the bombs were extremely hard to place on the target due to high winds and it took repeated attempts from several squadrons to finally destroy them. At least one aircraft was lost due to small-arms fire – Lieutenant Price had to bail out near Isola del Liri during a rhubarb mission, and his A-36A, 42-84124, crashed into the side of a mountain. The 27th returned to the docks at Civitavecchia repeatedly over the next few days and weeks – soon the crews knew the target so well they barely required any briefing.

---

ii Sic – stringer

Unusually, a fighter-bomber attack was made on Pomigliano on 12 November – a flight of Fw 190s swept over the field just after breakfast, dropping fragmentation bombs. Fortunately no one was hurt but one of the 111th's P-51s was damaged along with a P-38.

The Invader continued to make a name for itself. On 21 November 1943, Blue Network Radio's George Hicks made a broadcast devoted to the work of the aircraft in Italy: 'When you're at the front with the 5th Army, crouching behind a hill, one of the great pleasures of the war is to see American fighter-bombers come in to dive behind the hill beyond where the German artillery is stationed,' he said, adding that the A-36A 'is credited with saving the Sele River front at Salerno by its pin-point dive-bombing of troops, gun positions and truck lines. The pilots... say dive-bombing is safer once you learn the skill, because you are a harder target to hit. And it's more accurate.'

The strategy of the aerial war the A-36As were fighting was evolving. In November 1943, the pilots were told that they would be concentrating more on supporting ground forces. Air Vice Marshal Arthur Coningham told the 86th and 27th that they had 'proved the efficiency of fighter-bomber units and have become one of our most lethal weapons... Most of your work hereafter will be Army support. We have always believed it is better to hit the enemy in the kidneys than in the front where he is expecting it. From the Italians we have learned that the Number One German fear is being strafed by Allied aircraft. Your work of the future will be largely in supplying the demand of this priority.'

In confirmation of this doctrine, following an attack on Atina on 30 December 1943, it was confirmed that a command post of the German 44th Division was completely knocked out. The Army sent a message to the A-36A squadron responsible expressing its gratitude and praise. Some missions began to be carried out further behind enemy lines, such as a rhubarb to the Rome area and an attack on gun emplacements near Lake Maggiore flown by the 27th on 2 December. However, despite Coningham's preference for a shift to interdiction, the focus of many A-36A missions would remain closer to the front for the time being.

A major reason for this was the desperate tussle over Cassino, which was about to be fought. The town, and hill overlooking it, were central to a defensive cordon, the 'Winter Line', that German forces had constructed across the country. From 9 December 1943, the A-36A groups began bombing bridges in the vicinity of the town, although the first major battle there would not take place until 24 January.

As Christmas approached, Humphrey Bogart and his wife visited the forces fighting in Italy and provided an unusual gift for the 525th to deliver to the opposing forces. This was a signed 100 lire note, pasted to a 500lb bomb that was dropped during a mission on Christmas day.

Anzio and the Winter Line

As the new year began, the offensive on the Winter Line ramped up. During January, the CO of the 86th FBG, Lieutenant Colonel Harold Kofahl flew five missions, three on the same day when the group was called upon to exert extra effort. It was unusual for the group CO to fly combat missions, and this indicated the pressure that the A-36A groups were under.

Most missions conducted during this period were dive-bombing sorties. On 2 January 1944, the 525th bombed gun emplacements on Mount Chiaia, silencing the artillery. Four days later, the 526th struck at dug-in German positions at Monte Trocchio and Aquino, to which the Army responded: 'Army delighted – enemy casualties [in] two days 150'. On 9 January, German counter-attacks on the slopes of Monte Cedro forced Allied troops back, and pin-point strikes were requested on gun positions and troops. The 527th attacked the gathering threat, and the bombs disrupted the counter-attack. Once again, the A-36A pilots received the congratulations and thanks of their colleagues on the ground.

Towards the end of January, the 27th FBG joined the 111th TRS and units of the 86th FBG at Pomigliano. The group was now increasingly using P-40s to supplement its A-36As, as the NAA dive-bombers were in short supply. Production had moved on to the P-51A (equipped with bomb racks but not dive brakes) even while the A-36 units were arriving in North Africa, and there would be no more fighter-type aircraft capable of true dive-bombing to follow the A-36A.

Another offensive began at Anzio at the end of January, and again, the skills of the 111th TRS in naval gunnery spotting were in demand. The landings at Anzio were intended to outflank the entrenched German forces, but instead the Allies found themselves encircled and facing another tough fight to link the two fronts. The reconnaissance pilots were called upon to direct the fire of warships lying off the coast onto the Axis lines, as a withering hail of gunfire was constantly poured onto the Allied army units stuck on the beachhead. This struggle went on until May when the Allies finally broke out.

Among the reconnaissance Mustang pilots taking part in this significant battle was First Lieutenant Maurice Nordlund. On 14 February, Nordlund was airborne above the beachhead, adjusting naval artillery fire on enemy positions. During the mission he encountered severe flak, which caused considerable damage to his aircraft. Despite this, Nordlund was able to carry on with his gunnery spotting to relay precise information to the ships laying down the bombardment. His information led to several German artillery positions being completely destroyed, and Nordlund was awarded the Air Medal. The sortie was a testament both to Nordlund's bravery and the strength of the F-6A, which on this mission, as on so many other occasions, was able to bring its pilot home even when damaged.

While several of the A-36A units were devoted to the attacks on the Winter Line, some joined the fighting over the Anzio–Nettuno front. The 525th was assigned the role of covering lines of communication to and from the forces surrounding the beachhead.

The weather was so poor at this time as to severely hamper operations. Even when the Mustangs and 'Invaders' could get off the ground there was no guarantee that they would have the weather to do the job when they got to the target area. At the end of January 1944, armourers from the 86th FBG suggested painting mission markings on bombs as well as aircraft, as some 500 pounders had been over enemy territory up to five times!

A new method of locating targets and quickly attacking them was also pioneered between the 86th FBG and the 111th TRS at this time. Two Mustangs of the 111th would fly ahead of a group of A-36As as they scouted the road networks around Cassino. The reconnaissance aircraft would probe for possible targets, check that they weren't 'flak traps', and direct the A-36As' bombing and strafing. This was first tried on 27 January, and the 527th reported a 'pretty good bag' of motor transports.

As February progressed, the A-36As' tactics developed. The methods resembled more and more closely the model pioneered by the RAF's Mustang Mk Is. Large formations were replaced by two-ship rhubarb

First Lieutenant Maurice Nordlund of the 111th TRS 'Snoopers' with his P-51 in Italy, 1943. Nordlund was awarded the DFC and Air Medal for reconnaissances carried out under challenging circumstances. (Grahm Nordlund)

sorties, which enabled more ground to be covered, and was a more effective way of hampering enemy road and rail transport.

By this time, the shortage of A-36As was acute. The 525th was told that it would have to give up its Invaders for Curtiss P-40s, and its existing aircraft would be shared out among the 526th and 527th FBSs and the 111th TRS. It appeared that the squadron commanders had drawn lots for which of them would give up their coveted Invaders, and the 525th lost. Later in the month the 27th FBG handed over its remaining A-36As to the 526th and 527th as well. Its squadrons converted to the P-40, though before long the Republic P-47 became the fighter-bomber of choice in the theatre.

On 9 February 1944, the 526th bombed the monastery at Monte Cassino, 'the target being covered in fanlike pattern of bombs… causing great loss to the enemy in personnel and equipment'.[1] In fact, it was unclear whether or not German forces were actually using the monastery at this point (although Allied commanders were increasingly confident that they were) and the 500lb bombs carried by the A-36As cannot have caused much damage to the 10ft-thick masonry itself. It would take a concerted attack by heavy bombers a week later to destroy the monastery completely. Nevertheless, the battle for Cassino was now well and truly under way with the A-36As in its midst.

The precision bombing that the A-36A was capable of was used to considerable effect on 13 February, when aircraft of the 526th dive-bombed factory buildings in Carocetta, which had been acting as a German Army HQ. British Army units were close by the factory, which meant all bombs had to be placed very near the target. There were 11 direct hits scored on three buildings, and one of the squadron's pilots declared it the 'best bombing we ever did'.

In March 1944 the battle for Cassino continued to rage, and the remaining A-36A squadrons were in the thick of the action. Their activities were not all concerned with hitting the enemy though. During the month, the first of many supply drops was made to friendly troops, using para-bundles and containers adapted from A-36 combat tanks to deliver food and medical supplies. According to a memo setting out the lessons of the Cassino assault, 're-supply of ground units with A-36 aircraft using either para-bundles or belly tanks proved to be practicable'. It was important for the target to be clearly marked, and for pilots to be well briefed with accurate photographs of the area of the drop, but the effectiveness of aerial resupply using an aircraft capable of pin-point delivery was well proved.

USAAF groundcrews load A-36 combat tanks with food and other supplies to drop to isolated 5th Army units fighting on the slopes of Monte Maggiore, and an A-36 dropping one of the canisters in December 1943.

More conventional missions included bombing marshalling yards used to route supplies to the enemy, dug-in enemy positions at Cassino itself, and nearby railway bridges.

On 18 March more food and other supplies were dropped to Indian and New Zealand troops cut off on the slopes of Monte Cassino. Twenty packs were dropped directly on the troops' location, though four 'hung up' and had to be brought back. However, the main interest that day was caused by the eruption of Vesuvius, which dominated the skyline around Naples. That day First Lieutenant Nordlund of the 111th earned a DFC to add to his Air Medal, after conducting a photographic reconnaissance over Atina. Once again, Nordlund's aircraft was battered by flak on the approach, and once again he pressed on with his mission, securing photographs of enemy positions that proved highly useful in planning operations.

The DFC was proving to be a great motivation to fighter-bomber pilots. The day after Nordlund's medal-winning mission, General Saville presented around 40 medals to members of the 86th FBG, including a DFC to Lieutenant Colonel Cassidy. Cassidy's award had a distinctly positive effect on morale – one of the new pilots was heard to say, 'Boy, what do I have to do to get one of *them*?'

During April 1944, A-36A missions consisted chiefly of cutting railways north of Rome – the 86th FBG conducted over 1,000 sorties in this month, all but one of which were dive and glide bombing attacks on rail communications (the exception was a strafing attack on Canino landing ground). One example was a mission flown in extremely bad weather to bomb a railway at Attigliano. Despite the conditions, this was a success with many rail wagons destroyed along with a station, the tracks were cut in numerous places and a group of large buildings at the mouth of the Tiber were destroyed into the bargain.

That month a detachment of 18 men and four aircraft of the 111th TRS moved to the Nettuno airfield at the Anzio beachhead, specifically in support of that front. The Mustangs provided reconnaissance and artillery support under difficult conditions, with the airfield frequently subjected to bombing raids and artillery bombardment.

After months at Pomigliano, the remaining A-36A squadrons moved to Marcianise, which was barely 30 miles from the front line. The reason for the move was that P-47s could not operate from temporary runways with a full bomb load, so the A-36As had to make way.

During May 1944, the 86th FBG continued to attack rail communications, but the focus shifted towards road transport as well. During the month, the group created 49 road blocks, destroyed 224 motor transports and 18 railway wagons (along with a further 55 damaged). The A-36As also bombed strategic towns and conducted close-support missions, including nine bombing and two low-level strafing.

On the night of 11 May, a large-scale offensive aimed at finally dislodging Axis forces from Cassino was launched. The artillery bombardment could be heard from Marcianise. The 527th conducted a bombing raid on a German Army brigade HQ near Piglio in an attempt to disrupt the Axis forces' response to the major assault, and the 'Invaders' scored several direct hits on the buildings in question. This was the first anniversary of the 86th FBG's landing in North Africa – it was hard to believe that only a year had passed since the group had arrived in theatre, so much had happened in the meantime.

The fighting in the new offensive was eventful for everyone. On 15 May, Lieutenant Dean Gilmore of the 111th and his weaver were flying above the battle providing artillery co-operation support. Gilmore's adjustment to the fire enabled Allied guns to silence two 88mm-gun batteries, one heavy gun battery and a dual-purpose gun position. However, while Gilmore was adjusting fire on a fifth target, 12 Messerschmitt Bf 109s attacked the pair. Gilmore damaged one Bf 109 before he and his wingman were able to withdraw.

By the 17 May, the Allies had finally prevailed over Cassino, and the remaining German forces there had withdrawn. The focus of missions immediately changed back to hampering enemy transport, as Allied forces pushed towards Rome. On 24 May, the 86th FBG destroyed 134 motor trucks and damaged 74 more. In fact one armed reconnaissance by the 526th destroyed 30 trucks and tanks, after which the flight ran out of ammunition. Undaunted, the flight leader called in a group of P-40s to continue the attack and led them into the dive himself.

The following day produced similarly spectacular results for the 86th FBG, with its A-36As and P-40s destroying 216 motor transports and damaging a further 253. That morning, the Anzio beachhead finally linked up with the main Allied forces. After the front had been bogged down for so long, the bomb line was moving almost hourly, and the A-36As made the most of it, routing German road convoys as forces retreated to the next defensive line. In fact, from April to June 1944, approximately one third of the vehicles destroyed by all units of the 12th Tactical Air Command were claimed by members of the 86th Group during the drive from Cassino.

Rome and the End

The victory at Cassino and the rapid push north meant that the A-36A and F-6A squadrons were back to the 'base-hopping' that had characterised the early part of the campaign. The 111th TRS moved to Ponte Galera,[iii] close to Rome, then Follonica before moving briefly to Corsica and then on to Northern Europe. The 86th FBG moved to Ciampino near Rome, before decamping to Orbetello.

June continued as May had ended, with rapid movement of the front line as the Axis forces broke. On 5 June 1944, Rome was taken. Lieutenant General Mark Clark, the Officer Commanding the US 5th Army, wrote to the 12th Air Force: 'I wish to convey to you the 5th Army's appreciation and admiration of the magnificent air support which we have received throughout the offensive operations which have resulted in the capture of Rome and the destruction of so much of the enemy's forces and material.'

However, the dwindling supply of A-36As meant that the Invaders would not accompany the 86th FBG on the push towards France. On 23 June, the group received its first P-47. The 526th undertook its last mission on the type that had served them so well on 7 July. This was a textbook example of the A-36A's precision capabilities – the squadron dive-bombed a moving train, scoring six direct hits. As a coup de grâce, the Invaders strafed another troop train and shot down a Bf 109 as it lined up to land. Briefly, the squadron passed its A-36As to the 525th, which itself flew what was probably the last A-36A mission in Europe on 15 July. An eight-ship formation bombed railways with results not observed. One last motor truck was destroyed by strafing on the way home.

---

iii The squadron diary spells this as 'Ponte Galera' and suggests it was to the north-west of Rome, though it is probable that the squadron's new home was actually Ponte Galeria, to the city's south-west.

Personnel of the 34th Air Depot Group in Pisa, Italy, 1943. Units like this were responsible for maintaining and issuing aircraft to squadrons.

The pilots were overwhelmingly disappointed to lose their A-36As and almost as disappointed that they were replaced with P-47s. The 526th's diary recorded that 'today was a mournful day for everyone. We transferred our A-36 airplanes to the 525th Squadron. These aircraft have been a source of pride for the squadron for more than a year and there is much doubt on the part of the pilots as to whether any other airplane can do this type of work as well as the A-36'. The pilots devoted much energy to creating derogatory nicknames for the P-47, which included 'Republic's Repulsive Fat Boy', 'Old Overbolt' and 'Flying Milk Bottle'.

Chapter 8

China-Burma-India

The third major theatre of operations where Allison-powered Mustangs operated was the so-called China-Burma-India (CBI) theatre.[i] In this theatre, Mustangs would act as fighter-bombers, perform pin-point close support for ground forces and, for the first time, also carry out genuine long-range bomber escort.

The US had interests in China before the war, but after the opening of hostilities in the Pacific, it became crucial to US plans. It was regarded as a potential base (via India and Burma) for attacking Japan, or for forces crossing the Pacific or from Australia. Furthermore, Chinese resistance to Japanese domination tied up forces that could otherwise be arrayed against the US in the Pacific, and supporting China therefore aligned with American war aims.

India, on the other hand, was critical to the British. It stood as a bulwark against a Japanese link-up with German forces in Persia and was a vital source of industrial resources and manpower for the Allied war effort.

Burma, as a 'wedge' between India and China, therefore found itself vital to US, British and Japanese interests. The Burma Road, running the length of the country north–south was, until 1942, the chief overland means of the Allies providing materiel to China. Moreover, Burma itself was of huge value to Japanese expansion, mainly through its production of rice, which was needed in vast quantities to feed the Imperial Army.

The defence of Burma, however, had partly suffered from British policy in the late 1930s, which ranked defence of the Empire third behind defence of the United Kingdom and preserving trade routes to Britain.[1] The British government felt that if the homeland could be preserved, occupied areas of the Empire could potentially be retaken when the threat to the homeland

---

i In fact, CBI was not a single theatre in the true sense of the word – for example, Allied forces in the region did not have a single command structure.

had been neutralised. Britain also overestimated the strength of countries adjacent to Burma – Singapore, Indochina and Thailand – which would in theory have made any seaborne or overland invasion unlikely. Finally, the British overestimated Japan's reliance on formal communication routes – railways, roads and rivers – which could be easily defended. The country's mountainous, jungle terrain was felt to be all but impassable, especially in the monsoon season, which generally lasted from May to October. The British felt that if they were able to delay an invasion force until the monsoon set in, it would give time to bolster defences.

As it turned out, Japanese forces were able to move directly through the jungle and circumvent Allied defences with relative ease. In the spring of 1942, the Japanese invaded, pushing the Allies (mainly British, Burmese and American-led Chinese) out of all but a few outposts in the far north of the country.

The Allies responded by reinforcing India's air defences, while the US began to build upon its existing air power in the theatre, based around the American Volunteer Group (AVG), which had been employed in protecting the Burma Road. The 10th Air Force was initially to be composed of a heavy bombardment group (the 7th), a medium bombardment group (the 341st) and two fighter groups (the 51st and the 23rd, the former AVG), which were mainly equipped with P-40s. By the end of 1942, the 10th had 184 fighters in theatre, but of these, around 20 were worn out, obsolete P-40B models, and four were Republic P-43 Lancers, used only for reconnaissance.[2] Moreover, the 10th Air Force was imbalanced, being split into two 'task forces', one based in India and the other in China, with more fighters based in China and relatively few – two squadrons only – in India.

A second US Air Force in theatre, the 14th, was activated in March 1943 under Chennault's command, to be based around the elements of the 10th based in China (including the 23rd Fighter Group).[ii] There were now dedicated air forces in both China and India, and work to supplement forces in the latter would lead to a group operating Mustang variants – the 311th – being earmarked for the theatre. The choice of fighter-bombers for CBI was a natural one, with close support of ground forces being particularly relevant in jungle warfare. During the retreat north in

---

ii On paper, the units of the 10th were not transferred to the 14th until April.

Typical terrain in Burma, demonstrating the need for supply drops from the air.

March 1942, Hurricane fighters from 17 Squadron RAF had proved their worth in support of the Army, while three squadrons of dedicated fighter-bomber Hurricanes had been allotted to the first Allied offensive in the Arakan region of western Burma in early 1943. This potentially contributed to the later shape of air forces in CBI relying heavily on fighter-bombers.

A P-51A undergoing maintenance at the airfield in Kurmitola, established to support the front-line airfields in Assam and Burma. In this theatre, P-51As were increasingly used as long-range bomber escorts.

In May 1943, a new command structure was implemented, which contributed to a more cohesive Allied strategy. Previously, command had been divided between forces in India, under British command, and those in China, under American command. The introduction of South East Asia Command (SEAC) under Admiral Lord Louis Mountbatten promised to end the previously piecemeal approach. (In reality the complex US–Chinese command structures meant that Stillwell generally continued to report directly to the US Joint Chiefs of Staff.)

Preparations for Counter-attack

With Burma overrun, the Allies took to supplying China via the so-called 'Hump' route, by air over the Himalayas, and this lifeline needed to be defended against Japanese aircraft operating from Burma. Construction of a new route, the Ledo Road, from Assam to Kunming in China, began, and this also had to be defended against air and ground attack. America was committed to supporting China militarily, and at this stage in the war, air power was the only means at the Allies' disposal to provide direct assistance, while the geography of the region made even this immensely challenging. Meanwhile, some Allied commanders, notably Stilwell, harboured hopes of retaking Burma and using it as a springboard into China.

Others started to develop the methods needed to achieve this. Colonel Orde Wingate, a British artillery officer, had studied Japanese tactics and proposed a technique of hit-and-run warfare to take the fighting to the occupying forces in Burma. He created long-range penetration groups (LRPGs) which would hit the enemy far behind the lines and disappear before they could be intercepted. Wingate's soldiers were popularly known as the 'Chindits', a term based on the name of the Chinthé, a mythological beast which was half lion and half griffin. 'This lion-griffin beast was portrayed as a statue which guarded Burmese pagodas, and symbolised to General Wingate the unique cooperation required between ground and air forces. This name was given to Wingate's 77th Indian Brigade in 1943.'[3]

During the first Chindit mission, Operation *Longcloth*, which ran from February to June 1943, it became clear that the LRPGs could do a great deal to damage the Japanese occupation force. However, only by dedicated air supply and support could the LRPG concept succeed. The LRPGs had to move fast through difficult terrain, which meant that instead of artillery and tanks they would need the support of bomber or ground-attack aircraft. Wingate, swiftly promoted to General, requested the necessary air resources in the summer of 1943 – bombers for air support, Douglas Dakota transports for resupply and light aircraft to evacuate casualties.

The subsequent negotiations would eventually lead to an exclusively American air force providing support to an exclusively British and Commonwealth ground force. It did not start out this way. Initially, the RAF indicated that it could provide the bombers for military air support of the forces on the ground.[iii] However, the British air forces were already overstretched and the CBI theatre was a relatively low priority, so the transport and light aircraft could not be spared. Winston Churchill, at

---

iii British bombers in theatre did not have radios that could communicate with Wingate's forces, and doubts began to grow that the RAF had the ability or the will to provide the necessary close support. According to Van Wagner (p. 53), Cochran requested 12 B-25H bombers be added to the Air Commando's complement instead, and this was approved on 21 January 1944.

the 'Quadrant' conference, therefore discussed Wingate's request with President Roosevelt, who approached General 'Hap' Arnold to discuss the necessary resources for Wingate. Quadrant also saw the decision to form a US LRPG.[iv]

Arnold saw in this model of warfare a further opportunity to set the theatre alight. Instead of the relatively modest forces requested, Arnold allocated a more ambitious army support unit including fighters, fighter-bombers and gliders as well as the aircraft previously mentioned. The force that began as 'Project 9' would be an experiment in close co-operation between a fast-moving ground force and a flexible, responsive air support operation. The reasons for Arnold's sudden, wholehearted support for this relatively new style of air warfare are unclear, but in the UK the final touches were being applied to the new Second Tactical Air Force, which Arnold would have been party to, and this may have provided some influence to his thinking.

Arnold appointed Colonel Philip Cochran and Lieutenant Colonel John Alison to form the air component, giving the two imaginative and aggressive officers carte blanche to build up the force in the best possible way. Cochran evidently impressed Arnold on their first meeting. He later wrote: 'In my office Cochran still wore his Natal leather boots with the trouser tops stuffed in. In North Africa he had originally headed a unit of replacement pilots, but before anyone was aware of it he had them up at the front fighting as a unit. Later he commanded a squadron of fighter pilots who were frequently so far ahead of our other forces that it was humorously remarked that they were fighting a war of their own.'[4]

Alison, on the other hand, according to Arnold: 'Had been an outstanding fighter pilot with the 14th Air Force in China and had also fought the enemy from England, Russia and the Middle East. He was short, slender, and self-possessed. He knew his business.' With these experiences in mind, the two men built what was to be known as the

---

iv The 5307th Composite Group (provisional), established in September 1943, was to have been a US LRP Group under Wingate's command. However, Stillwell reacted against the only US ground force in the region being under British control. Although 'Merrill's Marauders' as the group became known trained with Wingate in December 1943, it was separated from the Chindit force before its next operation.

The offensively spirited Colonel Philip Cochran, veteran of North Africa and the driving force behind the 1st Air Commando, with his P-51A.

1st Air Commando Group,[v] under the nominal command of the 10th Air Force, but in fact with almost total autonomy. Arnold claimed he explained the mission and sent them off with the words: 'To hell with the paper work, go out and fight.'[5]

The first aircraft allocated to the small fighter-bomber force within the 'Air Commando' were 30 P-51A Mustangs. (The Mustangs were actually the third choice after P-38s or P-47s[6] – this meant, however, that the already well-established use of the Mustang in support of ground forces would continue.) The 1st Air Commando would spend the following months training intensively and taking part in joint exercises to prepare themselves for their unorthodox mission. On 1 October, the fighter force moved to Seymour Johnson Field in North Carolina. The unit's personnel would begin to arrive in India just after Christmas 1943.

The 311th Fighter-Bomber Group Arrives

Meanwhile, the more conventional air forces in India under the 10th Air Force were being laboriously built up, following the splitting of its assets between India and China. September 1943 saw the arrival of the 311th Fighter-Bomber Group, under Colonel Harry R. Melton Jr, equipped with A-36As, and soon P-51As as well. The aircraft were initially based at Assam in India. The arrival of the 311th was indicative of a general strengthening of fighter-bomber resources in CBI, which included another group of P-40s (the 80th Fighter Group, with P-40Ns) to which was added a squadron of Lockheed P-38s, the 459th.

The 528th and 529th Squadrons of the 311th Group received A-36As, and the 530th was equipped with P-51As. The deliveries of new aircraft were not free from complications. The A-36As appear to have arrived in good condition, apart from some damage being caused to their tailwheels as they were being lightered ashore.[7] The P-51As, however, suffered badly from the journey and consequently may have taken longer to prepare for operations. The P-51As had been transported to Karachi on the decks of aircraft carriers, but two shipments of the aircraft were found to be

---

v   The force was originally known as Project 9, then Project CA 281, 5318th Provisional Unit (Air) and 1st Air Commando Force before finally settling on 1st Air Commando Group (Van Wagner, R.D., *1st Air Commando Group: Any Time, Any Place, Any Where*, Military History Series 86-1, USAF Air Command and Staff College, 1986).

in 'non-operational condition because of saltwater corrosion and storm damage,'[8] and needed to be overhauled. Furthermore, one of the squadrons was temporarily disbanded in order to transfer its maintenance personnel to the 459th, allocated to the theatre to provide long-range escort with P-38s. The Allies had hitherto managed not to surrender air superiority over Burma, so escort fighters were not as high a priority as they might have been.

Nevertheless, the arrival of the Mustangs, with other more modern types, represented a significant boost to the strength of the 10th Air Force. According to the AAF history:

> Thus the fighter strength of the Tenth Air Force was greatly increased in the space of a few weeks. The number of squadrons jumped from two to seven, and instead of having old-model P-40s for every conceivable kind of mission, P-40Ns, P-51As, A-36s,[vi] and P-38s were available, and all had superior altitudes. For the first time there could be a division of labor among the fighters in the Tenth. Versatility of the fighter force promised to make it more effective in countering enemy moves in Burma. P-38s of the 459th in the south soon gave bombers their first long-range fighter escort, while in Assam the P-40s took over patrol duties, interpolating an occasional bombing and strafing mission. P-51As and A-36s engaged largely in air support to ground forces moving down from Ledo in advance of the road-builders, but they frequently flew reconnaissance and patrol missions.[9]

Meanwhile, the RAF was building up its strength with Hurricane fighters and fighter-bombers, which had arrived in large numbers during 1942 and 1943 (followed by other types, which, incidentally, included Vultee Vengeance dive-bombers).

Action was not to be long in coming. The Japanese had employed the period of limited operations of the monsoon season to repair damaged airfields and build new ones. When the rainy season ended, therefore, Allied escort and offensive missions were strongly opposed. The first mission to be carried out by the 311th was a dive-bombing and strafing

---

vi The A-36 did not, of course, have a superior altitude to the P-40 though they were the exception in this respect among the 10th Air Force's new types.

mission in the Sumprabum region. It was something of a baptism of fire, despite an increase in fighter cover. According to Weaver and Bowen: 'American fighter patrols were increased from four to eight planes but with little effect. On 16 October, three A-36s of the 311th failed to return from a mission over Sumprabum.'[10]

Despite this unfortunate start, the 311th had begun a spell of frequent attack missions in support of ground forces. Targets were generally identified by intelligence tracking Japanese movements and aerial reconnaissance.

Mustangs of the 14th Air Force into Action

In November, the 23rd Fighter Group (FG) of the 14th Air Force in China also gained some Mustangs, in time to take part in some ambitious raids on Formosa. The P-51As, 16 in total described by Weaver and Bowen[11] as 'old and worn',[vii] were allocated to the 76th Fighter Squadron based at Suichuan.

The 14th Air Force had five main aims:

- To destroy Japanese aircraft.
- To destroy Japanese military and naval establishments in China and encourage Chinese resistance.
- To disrupt Japanese shipping in the interior and off the coasts of China.
- To cause serious damage to Japanese establishments and concentrations in Indochina, Formosa, Thailand, Burma, and North China.
- To break the morale of the Japanese Air Force while destroying a considerable percentage of Japanese aircraft production.[12]

It was therefore little related to the activities of the 10th Air Force in India and Burma, though dependent upon it for sustenance. On 23 November 1943, the first operational P-51A mission took place when seven aircraft of the 23rd FG took part in a raid on Yoyang railroad yards and warehouses. Two days later, they participated in an attack on Shinchiku airfield.

---

vii It seems unlikely that these aircraft were in fact old or heavily used given that no P-51As had yet been in service, and indeed, they should have been new aircraft. It is possible, however, that those aircraft received by the 23rd FG were among those that suffered from atmospheric and weather damage in transit to theatre and therefore seemed decrepit.

Colonel Clinton D. Vincent had planned a low-level strike on the airfield, a bomber base on Formosa, for some time, but conditions had prevented the raid from going ahead until this point. Eight of the 23rd FG's P-51As were detailed (with eight P-38s) to provide close escort to 14 B-25s, sticking to the bombers until they had made their attack and then strafing the airfield themselves. (It seems that once again, only seven of the P-51As actually took part in the mission, one having to abort.)

The raiding force was attacked by fighters identified as Nakajima Ki-43 'Oscars' and Kawasaki Ki-45 'Nicks' – one Ki-45 was shot down and another probably shot down, while two Ki-43s were probably shot down, for the loss of two Mustangs and another two damaged. The raid caused damage to hangars, barracks and other buildings, and dispersal areas on the airfield.

The 23rd FG's P-51As attacked Kowloon shipyards on 1 December 1943, then seven of the fighters, along with some P-40s, escorted B-24s to attack White Cloud airfield on 23 December during which 11 Japanese fighters were claimed.

Five days later, a force from the 14th Air Force, including four P-51As, attacked shipping on the Yangtze at Chiuchow. A cargo ship was claimed sunk with a further two damaged, and an armed launch was set on fire.

Further organisational changes took place at this time. In November 1943, Air Command South-East Asia was formed to control all Allied air forces in the theatre. The new arrangement was under the overall charge of Air Chief Marshal Sir Richard Peirse. The following month, part of the 10th Air Force was integrated with the RAF's Third Tactical Air Force, which existed to provide air support to the 14th Army.

Long-range Escort

Meanwhile, the 10th Air Force sought to protect the 'Hump' air supply route, and hamper Japanese forces in Burma by attacking military installations, supply routes, and lines of communication. This was essential both for softening up Burma for a future invasion, and to prevent further Japanese advances into India.

For the Mustangs, hampering the Japanese advance meant both attacking targets directly and escorting bombers. The 311th FBG demonstrated the P-51A's prowess as a medium-altitude escort fighter with the first of the type's long-range bomber escort missions to Rangoon (Yangon). Maintaining attacks on the city was essential to the Allied strategy of rendering it useless as a port and centre of storage and distribution of supplies to the interior. Until late 1943, all bombardment missions were flown without escort due to the lack of fighters with suitable range and performance.[13] The increase in Japanese fighter strength had, however, rendered this approach untenable and the Mustangs, with their long-range and air-to-air capabilities, were sorely needed.

It appears that at first the P-51As sent to CBI were regarded purely as fighter-bombers in the same vein as the A-36, and little or no thought was given to using them as escort fighters. Initially, only the 459th Squadron with its Lockheed P-38s was earmarked for escort duties. According to Weaver and Bowen,[14] however, in late November, 'at the last minute' a decision was made to move the 530th from Assam to Bengal to join the Lightnings of the 459th.[viii]

The P-51A would become increasingly closely associated with attacks on Rangoon over the coming months. On 25 November, B-24s of the 308th Bombardment Group attacked the city, supported by Mustangs from the 530th fitted with drop tanks to enable them to make the 900-mile round trip. On the same day, B-25s of the 409th Squadron attacked the airfield at Mingaladon, again with support from the 530th's P-51As. The Mustangs claimed one enemy fighter destroyed and four probably destroyed. Two P-51As were shot down and two others damaged, but most importantly, the B-25s were able to bomb the airfield successfully and none were damaged by attacking fighters.

Two days later, NAA B-25 Mitchell bombers were escorted on a raid to Insein by 10th Air Force Mustangs, along with Consolidated B-24s and Lockheed P-38s. This attack met stiff resistance from Japanese Army fighters, and six fighters (including two Mustangs) and three heavy bombers were shot down (none of the B-25s were lost), while the fighter escort claimed 13 enemy fighters destroyed.

One of the Mustangs that had been shot down, however, was that of Colonel Melton, CO of the 311th Group. According to Weaver and Bowen,

---

viii The 459th had earlier received some personnel from the 311th after one of the group's squadrons was disbanded.

Melton 'was seen to bail out and land in territory where natives were generally friendly'. In fact, Melton became a prisoner of war and later died when the ship transporting him to Japan was sunk.

On 1 December, the Mustangs of the 530th were once again earmarked to escort B-25s, this time for a raid on Myitnge bridge. By now, the squadron had only 10 P-51As available, and even these were delayed from taking off by fog, which prevented them from making contact with the bombers before they reached the target. The B-25s sustained heavy losses due to massed fighter attacks, and the P-51As only arrived as the bombers were returning, still under pressure from Japanese interceptors. The Mustangs engaged, losing one of their own number.

Mercifully, the final raid on Rangoon, on 4 December, met with no opposition so further losses were avoided. During the raids between 27 November and 4 December, eight Mustangs had been lost and more were damaged.

A number of lessons were learned from these raids. For example, it was found that if fighters transited to the bomber base the night before an escort mission, it would avoid difficulties such as those experienced on 1 December where the fighters failed to link up with the bombers. Co-operation with P-38s was also developed, wherein the Lightnings provided high-altitude 'umbrella' cover, while the Mustangs stuck closer to the bombers.[15] Resistance to the daylight raids had been intense and losses had been relatively heavy – on 28 November alone six B-24s were lost and the same number seriously damaged – while the RAF's concurrent night raids with Vickers Wellingtons suffered much lighter losses (three Wellingtons lost from 66 sorties). After the series of raids on Rangoon, the US heavy bomber force switched to night raids on Bangkok. As the Mustangs of the 311th were not needed for escort duties for the time being, they reverted to more of a fighter-bomber role. Throughout December 1943, the 311th undertook numerous attacks on shipping and port facilities in Burma and occupied China alongside other fighter-bombers and tactical bombers.

As 1944 began, aircraft of the 311th FBG struck repeatedly at targets in Burma. On New Year's Day 1944, 11 A-36As and 15 P-51As bombed and strafed the airfield at Myitkyina and the following day scored several hits on Loilaw bridge and the approaches to it. The day after that, the Mustangs hit warehouses and an ammunition/fuel dump at Sahmaw airfield.

In the next few days the A-36As and P-51As carried out ground-support missions at Sumprabum and Taihpa Ga and hit army bivouac areas and supply dumps at Kamaing. There were more attacks directly against Japanese troop concentrations and encampments over this period as the Japanese launched a new offensive in Burma. An encampment estimated to contain around 5,000 soldiers and large quantities of supplies was bombed and strafed on 11 January 1944, causing a great deal of damage. Similar missions in and around Lalawng Ga, Shaduzup, Ngamaw Ga and Sawnghka saw the 10th AF harrying Japanese troops on the ground.

The Mustangs in theatre continued to act as fighter-bombers and escort for tactical bombers throughout January and February 1944. In northern Burma on 20 January, more than 40 A-36As and P-51As of the 10th AF bombed and strafed storage dumps along the railway in the Mogaung area and troop billets and warehouses at Mohnyin.

On 14 February alone, P-51As and A-36As of the 10th AF carried out more than 70 sorties against a variety of targets in Burma. These included supply dumps at Shingban, a motor transport convoy north of Maingkwan, a supply dump and motor transports in the Kamaing area, a troop bivouac near Mogaung, troop and vehicle concentrations between Mogaung and Kamaing, artillery positions at La-awn Ga, and a rail station and warehouses at Lundaung.

In February and March, however, the Mustangs would be utilised as interceptors, for perhaps the only time, when Japanese aircraft started to attack Allied airfields. The next month, 18 Nakajima Ki-49 bombers escorted by a similar number of fighters attempted to bomb airfields near Ledo – 23 Allied fighters, including some Mustangs from the 311th FBG, intercepted the formation and destroyed or damaged most of the attacking bombers.

Throughout the early months of 1944, the P-51As and A-36As would continue to prove themselves to be superb fighter-bombers. There were few targets that the aircraft did not strike over this period – missions included attacks on military command posts, troop concentrations and encampments, bridges, warehouses and storage dumps, road and rail junctions, river transport, radio stations, artillery and anti-aircraft positions all over Burma. The bridge at Tantabin was rendered completely unusable while the approaches of the Ye-u and Bawgyo bridges were damaged. Many coastal and river vessels were destroyed or damaged, as were locomotives and motor transports. Meanwhile, the Allied air forces in the theatre were finally becoming better equipped and prepared. The island of Akyab (now Sittwe) in the Arakan was successfully seized, thanks in part to the availability of RAF and US transport aircraft with five squadrons of RAF Hurricanes and two of Spitfires to protect the air drops.

The 1st Air Commando in Action

On 3 February 1944, Colonel Cochran led the first combat mission for the P-51As of the 1st Air Commando. The fighters, in concert with B-25H 'gunships', concentrated on building their air-to-ground skills with a series of attacks on bridges; warehouses; and road, river and rail transport. The 1st Air Commando's aircraft were painted with five white diagonal stripes on the rear fuselage. These distinctive markings were an instant identification for the Chindits, and were also allegedly added 'to let the Japanese know who was dominating the skies of Burma'.[16] Each stripe apparently represented one of the five 'arms' of the Air Commando – fighters, bombers, light aircraft, transports and gliders.[17]

Well-known image of two Air Commando P-51As, including one named 'Mrs Virginia', flying over the jungles of Burma.

Despite the efforts of the Allies to hold down Japanese forces in Burma, the Japanese 15th Army invaded India through northern Burma on 10 March 1944. The attack benefited from surprise and advanced almost as far as Kohima and Imphal. RAF and Indian Air Force Vultee Vengeance dive-bombers and Hawker Hurricane fighter-bombers helped to maintain the Allied perimeter before a coherent counter-attack was formed. It took until June for the two cities to be relieved and for the Allies to begin to advance towards Mogaung, the objective since December.

However, five days before the Japanese invasion, the second major Chindit operation had begun. This had initially been considered as part of the Allied invasion of Burma. With the Japanese pre-empting the Allies, the Chindits would instead use their ability to disrupt and confuse the enemy invasion behind the lines.

Operation *Thursday* was the second-largest airborne operation of the war. On 5 March 1944, the first of 20,000 British and Commonwealth soldiers were landed in remote locations in Burma where temporary airstrips were rapidly created to help bring in the remainder of the troops and equipment and act as a base for air support operations. The plan was for two landing sites, dubbed 'Broadway' and 'Piccadilly'. At the time, these bases were some 160 miles behind Japanese lines.

In the lead-up to the operation, the 1st Air Commando relentlessly attacked any enemy airfields in range of the landing sites. For several days, the Japanese failed to locate Broadway, though it seemed that forces were being assembled to repel the assault. On 8 March, a fighter sweep comprising over 20 P-51As[ix] discovered concentrations of enemy aircraft building up at Anisakan, which they strafed and bombed – Lieutenant Colonel Mahoney, leading the mission, had decided that each aircraft would carry a single 500lb bomb and a drop tank on the sweep. Strafing attacks were also made on Shwebo and Onbauk airfields; General Arnold wrote: 'The Air Commando discovered that the Japanese were bringing more airplanes into Burma. Twenty P-51 Mustangs promptly raided enemy airfields and destroyed 34 planes, with a loss of two.'[18]

---

ix Van Wagner states there were 21 aircraft in this sweep, while Carter & Mueller state 23. Edward Young in *Air Commando Fighters of World War II*, Specialty Press (2000) states there were 22 Mustangs, while General Arnold, writing in *The National Geographic*, put the number at 20.

Most of these aircraft were reported destroyed on the ground, but one 'kill' was claimed in aerial combat.[19]

The P-51As had also provided vital tactical reconnaissance in the weeks leading up to Operation *Thursday*: '... intrusion of P-51s for three days in succession over Mandalay revealed heavy concentrations on certain routes and constant photographing and strafing on the railway from Shwebo to Mohnyin revealed numerous locomotives and stocks,' reported Lord Mountbatten, the Supreme Commander in SEAC, in a note to Churchill.[20] 'Again it was photographs by this Commando which revealed the blocking of Piccadilly by the enemy in time to prevent a disaster.'

On the eve of the mission, Piccadilly had been discovered to have been blocked with logs, posts and trenches, and was abandoned. This was in fact even luckier than Mountbatten had indicated. While extensive reconnaissance of enemy forces and movements had been conducted, Wingate had discouraged aerial reconnaissance of the landing sites out of a desire to avoid tipping the enemy off to their locations.[21] Without authorisation, Cochran ordered the last minute reconnaissance, which was just in time to forestall the glider tugs.[22] Ironically, the disruption of Piccadilly was later found to have been caused by teakwood farmers, rather than Japanese forces deliberately sabotaging the site.

Two P-51As later escorted a second attack on Shwebo by B-25s, in which further damage to the runway and dispersal area was caused and more aircraft damaged. The 1st Air Commando was in fact so devoted to close air support and strike missions that few of its pilots scored air-to-air victories and the vast majority of aircraft it destroyed were on the ground.

Nevertheless, the Air Commando Mustang pilots' flexibility was demonstrated after Japanese forces located Broadway on 13 March. Some RAF Spitfires had been flown in by then to assist with air defence, but even so, the P-51As were required to help fend off enemy air attacks. Fortunately, the Allies held Broadway and damage was limited to radar and radio equipment and some of the light aircraft used for evacuating the wounded.

The Chindit LRPGs, having been landed successfully, dispersed to strike at rail, road and river communications, hamstringing the Japanese Army's response to General Stillwell's Chinese–American forces, which were pushing down into Burma from the north.

In the thick Burmese jungle, targets were identified first by the Chindit unit releasing mortar smoke. Once the P-51As had found the 'friendly' unit, RAF officers attached to the Chindits would act as forward air controllers, calling the strike over the radio. On occasion, Chindits flying in Stinson L-5s would mark a target with smoke so the P-51As could accurately strike enemy assets that would not have been visible from the faster-flying aircraft.

Using this method, considerable accuracy was possible. At first, the Mustangs bombed and strafed. Later, underwing rocket projectile launchers similar to 'bazookas' were introduced.[x]

At times when they were not specifically required for support of Chindit forces, the Air Commando's strike components employed themselves by looking for and attacking targets of opportunity. Then, in the third week of March, Brigadier Calvert called on the Air Commando to repel Japanese forces for three days while his troops established a fortified position outside Mawlu, which prevented the Japanese using the road or railway. This stronghold was named 'White City' and, as with Broadway, included a rapidly prepared airstrip for resupply and forward operations. The accuracy of the Air Commando's fighter-bombers was such that Calvert was able to call in strikes 50 yards or less from his own positions. White City was under almost daily attack, but dedicated air support helped to maintain the outpost.

Meanwhile, the Chindits had continued to strike at enemy communications and supply routes. Towards the end of March 1944, one of Wingate's columns was pinned down as it attempted to sever communication routes near Indaw, and called in support from the Air Commando P-51As. The Mustangs attacked the Japanese forces with a shallow dive-bombing attack, using napalm incendiary fluid, and strafing. Under cover of this attack, the Chindits were able to withdraw to safety.[23]

One of the most unconventional tasks the Air Commando Mustangs undertook at the behest of the LRPGs was cutting telegraph wires with a jury-rigged device. A 450ft cable was attached at each end to the Mustang's

---

x These devices, using the M-8 rocket projectile, were made up of three launch tubes mounted under each wing. NAA tested the installation on a P-51A, and the rockets were used for the first time by the Air Commando's Mustangs in April 1944.

bomb racks with a weight in the middle. The cable, suspended beneath the aircraft as it flew, would be dragged across telegraph lines in such a way that the weight wrapped around them. As the aircraft flew on, the cables would break or even uproot the telegraph poles. The pilot could then jettison the cable.

On 4 April, the 1st Air Commando Mustangs caught a group of Japanese fighters that had just returned to Aungban after being scrambled to intercept a sweep by the 459th Squadron's P-38s; 24 aircraft were destroyed on the ground and one in the air, and an enemy bomber was shot up on the way home for good measure.

By any measure, the 1st Air Commando's striking force of P-51As and B-25Hs had proved remarkably successful during the period they were active in support of *Thursday* and the fighting that followed. While their support to Wingate's Chindits was immeasurable, they were estimated to have destroyed over 40% of the enemy aircraft destroyed in Burma in March 1944 and over 30% in April – remarkable results for so small a force. The 1st Air Commando with other air forces had temporarily decimated Japanese air strength – in fact it was estimated that in the first few missions, the force had destroyed a fifth of known Japanese air forces in Burma.[24]

The Japanese invasion was to prove the high-water mark of Japanese success in the theatre, and thereafter their tired, hungry and overstretched forces would be pushed back through Burma. The Allied armies had not fallen back as they had in the face of previous assaults, but had stood their ground – enabled by air supply and air support. Furthermore, Operation *Thursday* had landed three brigades of troops in the Japanese rear in northern Burma, which had harried the enemy's supply lines constantly, contributing to the failure of the invasion and the subsequent Allied advance into Burma.

The 'Air Commando' Mustangs operated from Broadway until May 1944, when the onset of the monsoon season rendered the temporary airfields unusable. Late in April, it had been decided to move the Chindit force further north. In support of the 77th Brigade moving to the Mogaung area, nearly 150 aircraft including P-51As and A-36As attacked troops, fuel dumps, gun positions and rail yards at locations across the Mogaung Valley.

On 5 and 6 May, more large-scale attacks took place, with 80–90 fighter-bombers and tactical bombers carrying out support of ground forces throughout the valley each day. The aircraft hit gun positions and supply dumps and attacked troop concentrations. Attacks continued in force until Mogaung was finally captured in June.

The Air Commando Mustangs had also been called upon to support the establishment of another base behind enemy lines, 'Blackpool'. This was far less successful than Broadway and White City, and the Allies were forced off it in two weeks. Nevertheless, the P-51As fended off an attack on Blackpool by 16 Japanese warplanes on 19 May, in which one bomber and two fighters were shot down with no loss to the Air Commando.

Towards China – the End for the Allison Mustang in CBI

Following the end of Operation *Thursday*, the 1st Air Commando withdrew to India, and while the group continued to exist, the force would not be used in the same way again.[xi] Wingate had been killed when his B-25 crashed near Imphal on 24 March. Wingate's replacement was a much more orthodox officer, General Walter Lentaigne. Despite having been the commander of the 111th Indian Brigade, a long-range penetration (LRP) formation, Lentaigne reportedly did not believe in the LRP model, and the momentum went out of the Chindits.[25] From April, the force began to operate much more like a conventional army.

In the absence of any distinct operation for the 1st Air Commando Group – and the 2nd Air Commando Group, which had recently arrived in theatre – their units were deployed to forward bases and employed conventionally. Arnold was keen to see the LRPG-Air Commando model pursued and attempted to persuade the Allied commanders in theatre to accept five of the units, two of which he offered to Stilwell. The General declined to take on the Air Commando units on the basis that he did not have suitable ground units for them to support. Stillwell did have an LRP group under his command, having successfully fought to ensure that

---

xi Further Air Commando units were constituted in April 1944 but were used in a largely conventional fashion. The 2nd Air Commando was employed in support of conventional Army forces crossing the Irrawaddy in February 1945, escorting bombers and carrying out strike missions in support of the Allied advance. The 3rd Air Commando was posted to the Philippines, where it had little opportunity to support commando operations and its elements were used individually.

the American LRPG, the 5307th Composite Unit (known as 'Merrill's Marauders') did not operate under British control in Wingate's Chindit force. However, the 5307th had sustained crippling losses by the time Arnold's offer was made, and the unit was disbanded in August.

SEAC attempted to have Arnold supply the aircraft and personnel he had earmarked for Air Commandos directly to the tactical air forces in the CBI. To help persuade Arnold, SEAC suggested it could form temporary Air Commandos when necessary to support special operations.[26] Arnold was, however, determined that the Air Commandos would be provided as discrete units or not at all. Ultimately, though the model had been thoroughly proved, it would see no more use before the war's end.

Meanwhile, the existing fighter-bomber groups operating Mustangs in theatre continued to support the Allied advance, particularly as the Chinese attacked the Japanese occupying the east of China. On 28 April, ten Mustangs of the 23rd FG, led by Colonel 'Tex' Hill, escorted B-24s in an attack on bridges on the Yellow River in Zhengzhou province. The raid caused 'slight damage' to the bridges, which the Japanese forces were able to repair relatively easily.

On the same day, more P-51As of the 14th AF strafed and bombed Nanchang barracks. The day after that, ten Mustangs escorted bombers attempting to knock out a bridge north-east of Chungmow, joined for the first time by P-47s. The flight was forced to return due to bad weather.

The A-36A and P-51A units in CBI began to give up their aircraft from May 1944, as supplies grew thin and aircraft lost to attrition could not be replaced. The 311th FBG and 23rd FG swapped their Allison Mustangs for Merlin-engined P-51Cs, while the 1st Air Commando switched to P-47s and, later, Merlin-engined P-51 marks. The 311th, who moved to China, and the 14th AF in August, were the last to give up their Allison-engined Mustangs.

Chapter 9

'Fortress Europe'

New threats led to new missions in Northern Europe as 1944 began – this period saw the first Mustang involvement in *Noball*[i] operations, attacking launch sites for V-1 (Fieseler Fi 103) flying bombs, even before they had begun to fall on London and the South East. Mustang squadrons were to become closely associated with reconnaissance of V-1 sites (and later those of the much more potent V-2 ballistic rockets) – 268 Squadron was an early exponent of these missions towards the end of 1943 and obtained some of the first clear photographs of the long ramps used to accelerate the flying bombs as they were dispatched towards England.

In the early part of the year, most of 400 Squadron RCAF's work was devoted to *Noball* operations. These were mainly two-ship missions, with the odd four-ship, across northern France. Some of the targets were on or near aerodromes, such as Amiens and Glicy, but most were in wooded areas and heavily defended. This created problems in itself.

Although most of the operations were flown at several thousand feet altitude for vertical photography, the approaches tended to be at low level for the purpose of evading detection for as long as possible. A four-aircraft flight of Mustang Mk Is on 20 February 1944 hit trouble when intense light flak was encountered near the target areas six miles south-west of Abbeville and four miles south-east of Cayeux. So intense that the operation report remarks, 'Camera in F/L A.S. Collins' aircraft [AP202 'N'] carried away by flak!'[1] Flying Officer McKiggan, flying as low as he dared in AM158 'L', struck the treetops and damaged his aircraft. Despite the damage, both pilots were able to continue. As well as taking the photographs as planned, the Mustangs shot up a gun position near Cayeux and strafed a train north of Abbeville.

---

i The codename was derived from the cricket term 'no-ball', an illegal delivery to a batsman.

Mustang Mk I AM186 'K' of 414 Squadron RCAF in March 1944. (Adrian Balch)

The newest of the RCAF Mustang operators, 430 Squadron, was also involved in *Noball* operations in the spring of 1944. Flying Officer Richard Rohmer (later a Major General and Canada's most decorated citizen) recalled that pilots did not know what the reconnaissance missions were photographing, despite the danger and difficulty:

> 430 Squadron went out on any number of Noball site photographic operations without anyone telling us what it was that we were photographing. We could see that the Noball sites were always in wooded areas. In the centre was a structure like a hockey stick with the long handle of the hockey stick pointing West toward England and the blade of the stick pointing either South or North.
>
> We went in and did the Noball tasks assigned to us. We flew through tons of flak from the German anti-aircraft guns firing at us as we did our straight and level photographic runs.

One such mission took place on 13 May 1944, described by Rohmer in his memoir. Two Mustangs from 430 Squadron went to photograph a *Noball* site after it had been bombed by RAF Douglas Bostons. Like most such sites, this one was in the Pas-de-Calais area near the coast. There were three launch ramps (as the pilots would later find them out to be) in the

AM214 'C' of 309 'Ziema Czerwienska' Polish Squadron in flight. (via Wojtek Matusiak)

vicinity of St Omer. Rohmer and Flight Lieutenant Prendergast were the pilots, with Prendergast taking the main series of photographs with his 8in vertical camera – Rohmer would act as the weaver and then take a series of pictures with his 14in oblique camera as Prendergast finished his run. [2]

The Mustangs skimmed across the Channel at minimum height to avoid detection by radar, before climbing to cross the French coast. It was a clear day – dangerously so in the context of these missions where cloud cover could be a distinct advantage. Prendergast lined up on the target with a mile to go, aligning his aircraft using landmarks either side of the target (which would have disappeared under the Mustang's nose by the time the photography had to start). As the run came to an end, mercifully flak-free, Rohmer banked over and used the aiming marks on the trailing edge of the port wing to take some 'backup' images.

A second run was made, still with no flak, and the two Mustangs set a course for home, 'rubbernecking for enemy fighters', and landed back at RAF Odiham around an hour and a half after take-off. However, Prendergast's camera had failed, and his two perfectly straight and level passes of the target were wasted.[ii] Fortunately, Rohmer's pictures were satisfactory.

---

ii An assessment of tactical reconnaissance after D-Day indicated that vertical photography with the Mustang was often problematic: 'Vertical photography in the Mustang I and IA has never been a success due to unavoidable oiling which tends to occur on the camera lens.' – National Archives document, '2nd Tactical Air Force: Tactical Reconnaissance, 1944–1945: report' under AIR 37/54.

The *Noball* missions were mainly flown by the RCAF Mustang Squadrons, although others took part on occasion – II (AC) Squadron RAF ran four *Noball* operations in April 1944.

Preparing for Invasion

The Mustang's strengths as a tactical reconnaissance aircraft, and the high ability of the RAF squadrons to carry out a range of specialised tasks, had attracted the attention of the US Army. The P-51s kept by the AAF saw extensive use in North Africa and the Mediterranean (see Chapters 6 and 7) but a similar conversion was carried out on a small number of P-51A fighters as the F-6B – these became the only Allison Mustangs used operationally by the US in North-West Europe.

In December 1943, the 67th Reconnaissance Group (RG)[iii] was equipped with 24 F-6B Mustangs in addition to other aircraft. These were assembled at Renfrew, Scotland in October 1943, by Lockheed, which had overseen the modification of the RAF's fighter-reconnaissance Mustangs. The 67th RG was transferred to the 9th Air Force and moved to Middle Wallop.

The F-6B was equivalent to the RAF's Mustang Mk II, and was fitted out in a very similar manner. Like its RAF counterpart, the F-6B had a vertical camera in the rear fuselage and an oblique camera fitted on a tray behind the pilot's head, photographing through a plate-glass panel let into the rear plexiglass.

USAAF tactical reconnaissance Mustang operations based in England were closely modelled on those of their RAF counterparts. The first mission carried out by the 67th RG, later renamed the 67th Tactical Reconnaissance Group (TRG), was a popular on 20 December 1943.

Like their RAF counterparts, the air and groundcrews of the 67th TRG would spend the first months of 1944 helping to build up the vast store of knowledge and understanding of German defences in northern France to help plan the forthcoming invasion and subsequent operations.

In February 1944, the USAAF's 67th TRG at Middle Wallop received momentous information and a critical task – photographing the French coast

---

iii In September 1942, the 67th TRG had moved to England, learning its trade on Spitfires at Membury where it was based as part of the 8th Air Force, and from where it had the chance to study RAF practices in detail.

in detail. This was to enable military planners to design the most significant operation of the war so far – the Allied landings on the coast of Normandy. The 67th TRG's official history recorded that Colonel Peck revealed that month that: 'This is to be one of the most secret missions of the war. This information... cannot be divulged to anyone. You will not only endanger your own lives but will endanger the lives of millions of soldiers.'[3] The 107th Tactical Reconnaissance Squadron of the 67th TRG was equipped with F-6B Mustangs at this point – the 109th had the newer Merlin-powered F-6C.

Complete and unbroken photographic coverage of the invasion areas was required, and the American, British and Canadian tactical reconnaissance squadrons played a crucial role in building up this record of the territory on which the battle for 'Fortress Europe' would be fought.

The squadrons carefully planned how the pilots would conduct these missions. 'Strips' of coastal and inland territory were marked out. At the 67th TRG, a strip of coast 160-miles long and two inland strips 120-miles long and 20-miles deep were identified. These areas would be painstakingly photographed between 15 February and 20 March 1944.

Fifteen of the two-Mustang teams were charged with carrying out the many sorties that would build up to a complete picture of the coast. As with

Three F-6Bs of the 67th TRG at a crowded Middle Wallop in 1944 during the preparations for the D-Day landings.

the RAF squadrons, each pair was made up of a flight leader carrying out the main objective, and a weaver designated to cover the leader and keep watch for enemy fighters.

For consistency, all the sorties had to be carried out at similar states of the tide and in similar light conditions. Each photographic mission was preceded by a meteorological sortie to ensure that the conditions were suitable for photography. It was dangerous work – the second sortie failed to return, and during the third one of the aircraft took a seagull strike to the windscreen (an occupational hazard of flying low over beaches).

The 67th TRG's work was so effective that the group earned the first Distinguished Unit Citation awarded to a 9th Air Force unit based in the UK 'for operations along the coast of France, 15 Feb–20 Mar 1944, when the group flew at low altitude in the face of intense flak to obtain photographs that aided the invasion of the Continent'.[4]

In a similar manner to the 67th TRG, from February 1944 several of the remaining British and Canadian AC Mustang squadrons undertook a series of missions to photograph targets in France. The pitch of activity

F-6B s/n 43-6174 'Jeanie' of the 107th Squadron, 67th TRG 1944 flown by Captain McAllister. Note the mission markings on the nose. (Selfridge Military Air Museum)

increased steadily between February and May, with vast numbers of targets for reconnaissance required. This included swathes of the Normandy coast, allocated to 430 Squadron RCAF, which several of its pilots dismissed as a decoy, thinking it too far from England to be the site of a seaborne invasion.

It was a small, but hardened group of RAF, RCAF and USAAF Mustang Squadrons that geared up for the long-awaited invasion of Fortress Europe. Only a handful of RAF and RCAF units were still flying the Allison-engined Mustang on AC missions during the invasion of France, three British and two Canadian, though another two squadrons would partially re-equip with the fighter later on, and one more would briefly operate the Mustang Mk I for the first time. Nos. 2 and 268 Squadrons RAF were incorporated into 84 Group, 35 Reconnaissance Wing while 168 Squadron RAF and 414 and 430 Squadrons RCAF became part of 83 Group, 39 Reconnaissance Wing.

Directing the Naval Bombardment

A number of AC Mustang squadrons decamped to Dundonald in Scotland in early 1944 for training with 516 Squadron RAF. This unit was a 'development' squadron of Combined Operations Command (COC), set up with the aim of developing expertise and tactics in air aspects of combined operations. Operational squadrons were periodically affiliated to COC for exercises with the Army and Navy in the Dundonald area, run by 516 Squadron. Most of the unit's flying was concentrated around Loch Fyne and along the Firth of Clyde from Barassie to Largs. (This unit actually had a few Mustangs on its own strength but gave them up when supplies of the Allison-engined sub-types started to run short.)

The Mustang squadrons were principally attached to 516 to train in spotting for naval guns during shore bombardment. In February, 414 Squadron RCAF spent two weeks at Dundonald, followed by II (AC) Squadron RAF in March and 268 Squadron in April.

The detachments to 516 Squadron began with lectures on naval gunnery, then some flying in the local area to identify the bombardment targets on the Mull of Kintyre. The crews visited the ships they would be spotting for during training to help build up the bonds of mutual understanding.

Bombardment practice started with army 25-pounder artillery before moving on to proper naval guns. Once the pilots had found their feet, Royal Navy ships would open fire with their main guns, their shells directed onto the target by the Mustang pilots in the air. Some of the ships involved in the training were the 6in cruisers HMS *Belfast*, HMS *Enterprise*, HMS *Sheffield* and HMS *Glasgow* and the 5.25in cruiser HMS *Diadem*. In fact, most of the ships assisting with the training took part in the D-Day bombardments. The aircrews then made further visits to the ships to discuss the training operations, iron out any problems and suggest improvements.

Shortly before the invasion, ten varied squadrons combined at Royal Naval Air Station Lee-On-Solent. Four Royal Navy Fleet Air Arm Seafire squadrons and the US Navy's VCS-7 (swapping its Seagulls and Kingfishers for Spitfires) joined two RAF Spitfire Squadrons, and the two RAF and one RCAF Mustang Squadrons that had trained in naval gunnery. (One of the Spitfire units was in fact 26 Squadron, which had exchanged its Mustangs for the Supermarine type in March.)

These ten squadrons were to perform gunnery spotting for the Western and Eastern Naval Task Forces during Operation *Overlord*. The Western Task Force was charged with supporting the landings of the US 1st Army on Omaha and Utah beaches, while the Eastern Task Force would support British and Canadian troops landing on Gold, Sword and Juno beaches.[5]

In theory, the squadrons that would be engaged in gunnery spotting pooled their aircraft so any pilot could fly any machine. In reality, pilots were restricted to the types they were cleared on, so the Mustang pilots stuck with Mustangs and the Seafire/Spitfire pilots did likewise. Furthermore, the British and Canadian Mustang pilots would start the day of the invasion spotting for naval guns, but switch to tactical reconnaissance sorties later in the day as troops gained a foothold and, if all went well, started to move inland. It was also imperative that the landing forces were aware of any reinforcements arriving from the German rear. The mission would then be similar to those carried out during Operation *Jubilee* two long years before.

The ORB for 414 Squadron records that 'there was no complaining... and every man was keen for the momentous day which was about to begin'.[6]

The Mustangs launched for their first bombardment spotting at 5.00am. At II (AC) Squadron, for example, three two-aircraft flights made up of a mixture of Mustang Mk IAs and Mk IIs left Lee-on-Solent at intervals of 2–3 minutes. One of the Mustangs went unserviceable before take-off, so Flying Officer McElwain continued alone. His target was neutralised, as was that of Flight Lieutenant Percival and Flying Officer Broderick, while Flight Lieutenant Weighill and Flying Officer Shute directed the bombardment successfully onto their target – though it may not have been knocked out completely. On this occasion they were able to carry out their task with no more interruption than a little light flak.

Four more flights left at around 6.00am, three of which successfully engaged targets but Flying Officers Burt and Crane experienced intense flak. Crane's Mustang took a hit to its mainplane, and he had to return to Lee. Burt attempted to carry on, but his radio failed. The next four pairs went up between 9.00am and 10.00am, putting the training to good use – some improvisation was necessary as some objectives were found to be decoys and other tasks were thrown up on the spur of the moment when the Mustang pilots spotted a likely target that had not previously been identified. Squadron Leader Gray and Flight Lieutenant Furneaux turned the ships' fire onto a concentration of approximately 100 motor transports spotted in the south-west corner of the wood at Bois de Calette, while Burt and Flying Officer Hope also found an impromptu target. Flight Lieutenant Corrigan's wireless failed on his second mission so his weaver Flight Lieutenant Black controlled the shoot instead.

The other squadrons had similar experiences – 414 Squadron's aircraft also left for their first sorties at 5.00am. Targets typically included coastal batteries and other first-line defences, as well as concentrations of forces such as tanks and motor vehicles. Each squadron covered targets from Le Havre to the Cherbourg peninsula, the extent of the invasion front.

Flying Officer Rohmer was flying over the beaches at H-Hour on a reconnaissance flight and was able to witness the handiwork of the gunnery-spotting Mustangs at first hand. 'Below us the terrain was crater-pocked from the thousands of bombs that had rained down during the night,' he later wrote: 'New craters were being made before our eyes as shell after shell from the battleships, cruisers and destroyers standing offshore smashed down under us. The devastating barrage was now lifting from the shore, working inland in an attempt to destroy any enemy forces that might impede the imminent beaching of the first landing craft.'[7]

Tactical Reconnaissance on D-Day and Beyond

The three British and Canadian Mustang Squadrons switched roles as planned later in the day, to tactical reconnaissance in support of the invading forces. In particular, the 1st Canadian Army was served by the Mustangs of 39 Wing. After the morning's spotting, 414 Squadron flew back to Odiham to conduct the remaining operations from there. The Canadian squadron was rested until going back into action at 6.00pm. The other two Mustang squadrons flew throughout the afternoon.

When the Mustang squadrons' D-Day duties changed to tactical reconnaissance, the two-aircraft flights began to search railways, marshalling yards and roads beyond the beachhead for signs of reinforcements. Most missions were successful, reporting the locations of railway and river traffic including a tug towing pontoons near Quevillon. Flying Officers Haworth and Varley reported back that there was extensive flooding in the area of Carentan and Sainte-Mère-Église caused by the Germans destroying canal locks.

The weather closed in later in the day though, and some missions were aborted – the landings had proved lucky with the weather from a reconnaissance perspective, gaining a toehold before the visibility deteriorated.

The F-6Bs of the 107th TRS continued to undertake tactical reconnaissance throughout the landings, in support of the US 1st Army. The TRS, with the other units of the 67th TRG, was required to act as the 'eyes' of the invasion force, quickly spotting potential difficulties or defences that could not be identified from the ground and passing their observations on.

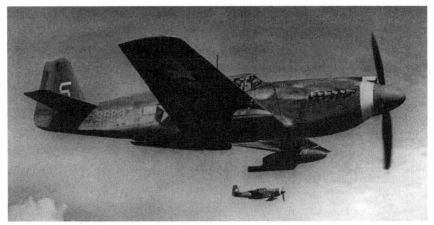

P-51A Mustang, 43-6237 ' S' and another aircraft, 'P' carrying smoke-curtain equipment during an exercise. Smoke laying by aircraft did take place during the D-Day landings but not, it is thought, by Mustangs.

The following day, Tac/R missions continued for all the Allison Mustang units in the campaign – the focus was often on bridges, and whether they remained intact or had been destroyed by retreating German forces – if intact, the pilots had to report if the bridges were likely to be able to bear the weight of motor transports or tanks. The Mustangs also reported where anti-glider defences had been installed in fields and movements of troops or transports, as well as attacking any targets of opportunity that presented themselves. The experience in attacking trains before the invasion was put to good use, and helped to hamper German forces' response to the invasion in bringing troops forward by rail. Squadrons generally flew between 10 and 25 sorties a day following the invasion, depending on the weather and the serviceability of aircraft.

The Canadian unit, 414 Squadron, patrolled the Chartres and Caen areas and reported columns of motor transports and a concentration of goods trains. Flight Lieutenant Burroughs and Flying Officer Bromley surprised a Ju 52 and shot it down, the squadron's first aerial victory of the second front.

The Allies had secured air superiority over the beachhead, so losses to enemy aircraft were relatively light for the RAF Mustang squadrons. Even so, roaming groups of enemy fighters could still cause trouble. On 10 June, Flight Lieutenant Hutchinson and Flying Officer Mossing of 414 Squadron, after photographing gun positions, were attacked by eight Fw 190s – Mossing damaged one before the Fw 190s themselves were bounced by Spitfires and three of the German fighters were shot down. A week later, a flight of II (AC) Squadron was set upon by 24 Fw 190s. Flying Officers Tasker and Williams were separated during the dogfight, and Tasker was posted missing.

Every few days, it seemed, each of the squadrons would lose a man or two, believed killed or simply missing. Flak, as a rule, was intense and accurate, and the elderly Mustang Mk Is were not always as reliable as they had been. Flying Officer Gent of II (AC) Squadron had a lucky escape when his engine failed on returning from a sortie – he bailed out and was picked up by an ASR launch.

The fighting continued on the ground, and the AC-trained squadrons were being worked hard in support of ground forces. 'Arty/R' (artillery reconnaissance) missions were particularly in demand for Allied forces held up in their advance by German artillery. Tactical and photographic reconnaissance also went on throughout daylight hours, with Mustangs adopting a constantly undulating 'rollercoaster' pattern of flight in an attempt to confound the dense, deadly 88mm flak, fired from batteries that peppered the countryside. Army liaison officers and wing staff would discuss the Army's needs and the wing's ability to meet them, and plan missions on that basis. These missions would then be passed to the squadrons to carry out.

Several units, including II (AC) and 268 Squadrons joined 414 Squadron at Odiham in Hampshire on 27 June 1944. During this period, it was common for the Mustangs to fly a short hop from England to a forward airstrip in France to top up with fuel. Soon afterwards, squadrons began to move to France to operate from the forward bases permanently – 430 Squadron RCAF moved to 'B8' battle airstrip near Bayeux on 29 June. By 6 July, the 107th TRS had moved to Le Molay, some 10 miles behind the front line.

In early July, the RAF and RCAF Mustang squadrons ceased their offensive activities and concentrated purely on reconnaissance. It appeared that Air Marshal Sir Arthur Coningham, the CO of 2 TAF, ruled that allowing the specialised tactical reconnaissance aircrews to attack targets of opportunity represented too great a risk.[8] At least, this is what the pilots were told the reasons were – it was just as possible that the decision was made to husband vital aircraft. That month, 268 Squadron re-equipped with Hawker Typhoons, which had been mooted as a replacement for the Mustang in fighter-reconnaissance squadrons. The experience of 268 Squadron with this type would suggest that the experiment was not a success.

On 17 July, a couple of weeks after the decision forbidding attacks on targets of opportunity, Flying Officer Rohmer of 430 Squadron was leading a flight of four Mustangs on a reconnaissance near Livarot. They spotted a large Horch staff car on a road west of the village with its top down, revealing that the vehicle was carrying several senior military personnel, suggested by the glint of gold from their uniforms. Rohmer lost no time in reporting the vehicle's position to Group Control Centre, frustrated that his flight could not attack the target themselves. Nevertheless, the value of the report was immediately apparent – two Spitfires were directed to the target and found it as it turned onto the main road between Livarot and Vimoutiers.

It later emerged that that the staff car was, in all probability, that of Field Marshal Erwin Rommel. The illustrious commander was on his way back from a meeting with a panzer corps commander to direct defences against an attack on St Lô in person.[9] His car was strafed by Spitfires near Livarot and he suffered a fractured skull when the car crashed. He was taken to a hospital in Évreux and was out of the battle for months. Arguably, he never fully regained his health, and his loss to the German defences was undoubtedly significant.

At the end of July, part of 35 Wing including II (AC) Squadron moved to France. The pilots and groundcrews quickly had to get used to living in tents instead of barracks and operating their aircraft from temporary 'perforated steel plate' (PSP) airstrips instead of concrete runways and aprons. The crews also had to get used to a change from the relative safety of a home base. German bombers could often be heard overhead during the night, and while the bombing was patchy, it kept everyone on their toes. On occasion, German fighters risked the Allied fighter umbrella to strafe the forward airfields. Each man had to dig his own slit trench, an activity embraced with enthusiasm after the first raids.

After Cherbourg was taken at the end of June, the fighting moved on to Caen and Falaise. A great deal of artillery spotting took place as the Allies grappled with the stronghold of Caen, which had been one of the objectives of D-Day itself but was still in German hands a month later.

The Mustangs would begin each artillery shoot by identifying the target and establishing the range with a single battery. When that had been achieved a full artillery division would open fire. Bridges to the south of Caen were destroyed in this way, preventing reinforcements from being moved west to counter American forces breaking out of the bridgehead. Finally, after a massive bombing and artillery attack, Caen was taken, 34 days behind schedule.

Tactical reconnaissance beyond the 'bomb line' continued apace as the Allied armies advanced. This could sometimes prove difficult as the 'bomb line' changed continually with Allied gains and German counter-attacks. Mustang reconnaissance aircraft worked closely with rocket-equipped Typhoon squadrons to identify and attack large concentrations of German tanks. The effect these attacks had soon restricted German armour to moving only at night, when tactical reconnaissance aircraft could not spot them.

Mustang Mk Is of 26 Squadron at Château-Bernard in France in December 1944, supporting Operation *Venerable* **– gunnery spotting for French warships.**

The remaining Mustang squadrons were once again in heavy demand in August 1944 during the battle in the 'Falaise Pocket', the decisive battle of the Normandy campaign in which four German armoured divisions were encircled and destroyed. Unfortunately, many of the myriad reports of German forces in retreat made by the tactical reconnaissance Mustangs and other aircraft could not be acted upon. The fast-moving front line had led to a number of Allied air attacks on friendly ground forces in error, so air attacks were restricted.

In September 1944, 309 'Ziema Czerwienska' Polish Squadron regained some Mustang Mk Is before converting to the Merlin-engined Mustang Mk III the following month when they became an escort fighter squadron (302 'Poznan' Squadron would do the same in April 1945). The two Polish units would not become operational until they had fully converted to the newer Mustangs, and the Allison-engined variants were mainly used for training. In October 1944, 168 Squadron gave up its Mustangs in exchange for Typhoons, while in November 268 Squadron went the opposite way and returned to the Mustang, adopting the newer Mk II variant (equivalent to the USAAF's F-6B). This made 268 Squadron one of only two RAF units to operate all three Allison-powered variants of the Mustang, the other being II (AC) Squadron.

In October and November 1944, the 107th TRS gave up its F-6Bs for newer Mustang variants. Again, this was not down to the unsuitability of the F-6B but unavailability – only 35 P-51As had been converted to F-6B specification. It is little short of a miracle that enough lasted to be able to maintain the type in an operational role almost to the end of 1944.

As the Allies pushed into Belgium and Holland, the remaining British and Canadian Mustang AC squadrons went with them. The RCAF unit 430 Squadron undertook tactical reconnaissance during Operation *Market Garden*, the ill-fated attempt to take Arnhem.

The RAF's Mustangs were now, for the most part, suffering from years of hard use. They had stood up very well to the stresses and strains of constant operations, many of them at extreme low level and exposed to light and medium flak wherever they went. All but a few squadrons gave up their Allison-engined Mustangs during 1944. A comment stemming from a late October 1944 meeting sums it up well: 'The amount of evidence put forward in favour of the Mustang ruled out any hint that the desire for

AM214 'C' of 309 'Ziema Czerwienska' Polish Squadron with an accumulator trolley to start the engine. (via Wojtek Matusiak)

its retention as a tactical reconnaissance aircraft was mere conservatism. The clearer this became, however, the clearer became the impossibility of the supply situation.'[10]

In November 1944, II (AC) Squadron and 430 Squadron had begun to re-equip with Spitfires, but both units still had a number of Mustangs on strength as the new year began. The main role for II (AC) Squadron during this period was tactical reconnaissance over Holland, as the Allies advanced in a series of battles for individual regions. The most common formation was the well-established pair of flight leader and weaver. Reconnaissance was carried out over the zone between the Rhine and Maas rivers, around Arnhem, and even into Germany around the Wesel–Bocholt area.

The vast majority of this work was tracking German communications, very like the missions carried out in the developmental days of AC Command's Mustang units. The prohibition on attacking targets of opportunity had been lifted by this time. On 23 December, Group Captain Anderson flying FR900 and Flight Lieutenant McElwain flying FR898,[iv] along with two Spitfires, strafed a convoy of tugs and barges on the Zuider Zee, leaving the boats severely damaged. Several motor transports were attacked and destroyed during the same mission.

As New Year's Day approached, 268 Squadron was based at Gilze-Rijen in the Netherlands. There the unit became caught up in Operation *Bodenplatte*, a vast air attack on Allied air forces in Holland and Belgium. *Bodenplatte* was aimed at fatally damaging the ability of the Allies to conduct air operations and winning back air superiority. It failed, after every possible fighter that could get into the air helped to beat back the assault. The 'reconnaissance' Mustangs joined the counter-attack, and Flight Lieutenant Mercer brought down a Junkers Ju 88. In addition, Flight Lieutenant Lyke claimed a Focke-Wulf Fw 190 damaged. These claims were to be the last air combat victories of Allison-engined Mustangs in the European Theatre of Operations (ETO).

Big Ben and 'The Last Shall be First'

In December of that year, the veteran Mustang unit 26 Squadron began to convert, partially, back to the Mustang Mk I. The squadron had continued in the tactical reconnaissance role after converting to Spitfires in March 1944, but a detachment of the unit was formed using the Allison-engined aircraft for special operations. The long-range and low-level abilities of the Mustang Mk I was required again. Initially, the Mustangs were intended

---

iv Some sources, such as Halley, J., *Royal Air Force Aircraft FA100-FZ999*, Air Britain, 1989, state that FR898 had been lost over the English Channel on 27 July – it could be that the aircraft flown by McElwain was FR896, which was also operated by the squadron at this time, and FR898 was recorded in error.

to take part in Operation *Independence*, a combined campaign to unseat German forces from the mouth of the Gironde. However, this was cancelled and other uses found for the Mustangs for the time being.

Three Mustangs, flown by Flight Lieutenants Sheppard and Mallorie and Flying Officer Hughes flew from the squadron's base at Exeter to Coltishall in Norfolk on 5 December 1944. The aircraft were to fly reconnaissance missions over the Netherlands as part of *Bigben* operations. *Big Ben* was the codename for the V-2 rockets, and operations with the *Bigben* label were aimed at intelligence and countermeasures concerning the rockets.

V.I. SITE IN PAS DE CALAIS.

A reconnaissance photo relating to a *Noball* mission against V-1 'Doodlebug' launch sites (with the target circled). (RAF Harrowbeer Interest Group)

A V2 TRAIL AND THE MOON – TAKEN BY KEN SNELL OVER HOLLAND.

Mustangs took part in *Big Ben* anti-V-2 rocket reconnaissance missions in 1944 – one pilot, Ken Snell, snapped the trail of this rocket over Holland as it flew. (RAF Harrowbeer Interest Group)

Generally, reports of rocket launch sites being set up were passed to the RAF's ADGB forces, which quickly dispatched aircraft to bomb the target. Sometimes these were tactical bombers, but most often were Spitfires from Coltishall, dive-bombing with 250lb or 500lb bombs. A call would simultaneously go to the Mustang detachment for photographic reconnaissance of the site immediately after the attack – and sometimes before and even during it – to assess the damage. On other occasions, areas suspected to conceal launch sites were photographed in an attempt to locate hidden missiles and facilities. Reports could be received from troops on the ground, aircraft spotting launches taking place, or the Resistance. However, the V-2 launch sites were highly mobile and much harder to spot than the large V-1 'hockey sticks', and good photographic reconnaissance was essential.

The Mustangs were no longer in the best condition. By 24 December, one had had to be replaced because it was unserviceable. On that day, Flight Lieutenant Hughes' Mustang developed engine trouble while on the way to the target and had to turn back – Flight Lieutenant Mallorie, flying AP167, continued alone, with an escort of two Spitfires from 303 (Polish) Squadron. This mission was the significant *Big Ben Ramrod 16*. Unlike most *Big Ben* operations, this was not aimed at the launch sites themselves, but at a large block of flats at Marlot in The Hague, which was being used as an operations centre and billet for the troops associated with the V-2 launches. On this occasion, three Spitfire squadrons converged on the target to paste it with bombs. Mallorie arrived overhead at 10.45am, about 15 minutes before the attack began, and was able to take a series of vertical photographs from 5,000ft as it took place. Mallorie made two more passes, one at 5,000ft and another at 3,000ft, by which time there was

A Mustang of 400 Squadron RCAF undergoing maintenance at its Dunsfold base in late 1943 or early 1944.

considerable light and medium flak in the air, though not too accurate. Mallorie flew direct to North Weald so the photographs could be developed straight away, before returning to Coltishall. Three V-2s fell on England that Christmas Eve.

It was a similar story with regard to serviceability four days later, when Mallorie himself had to turn back because of high oil temperature and Flight Lieutenant Hughes carried on to complete a successful solo operation with excellent photographs of bombed launch sites. Once again, an escort was provided by two Spitfires of 303 Squadron. Seven 'pinpoints' were covered from 4,500ft, despite intense medium flak over the target and the coast. In fact, Hughes' Mustang was hit three times, causing deep gouges in the fuselage behind the cockpit and on the starboard wing. He was able to fly back to North Weald without difficulty though, and the photographs revealed six V-2s 'in a previously unknown situation'.[11] This won the squadron plaudits from the group's CO.

Flight Lieutenant McGrady joined the original three members of the Coltishall detachment on New Year's Eve 1944, and on the same day Sheppard obtained some good photographs despite his Mustang being damaged by flak. One target was covered adequately, but others could not be photographed satisfactorily due to thick cloud and high winds. The flak blew a large hole and two smaller holes in the starboard wing of Mustang AP167, and a fragment grazed the propeller.

Flak over the targets was commonplace, and the Mustangs often came away with some damage. On 19 January 1945, during a *Big Ben* mission over The Hague, Mallorie's aircraft was hit in the tailplane by a cannon shell from a light flak gun, and although Mallorie made it back to Coltishall, AM164 had been rendered 'Cat AC' – beyond the capability of the unit to repair.

On 3 February, Flight Lieutenants McGrady and Gordon flew a reconnaissance to Loosduinen to photograph the effects of a precision dive-bombing attack in progress. This mission was an attempt to completely knock out a factory which was believed to be producing liquid oxygen[12] for the V-2s' rocket motor. The target was well bombed (which had to be done carefully as civilian houses were nearby) and the photographs successfully captured the damage inflicted. Other *Big Ben* sites were photographed during the sortie, and both aircraft returned to North Weald unscathed

Mustang Mk I AG425 of 26 Squadron being refuelled and rearmed at Gatwick in 1944.

despite the now-expected flak. Further missions were made throughout February, including other liquid oxygen production sites and woods believed to be hiding missiles.

While the *Big Ben* operations had been taking place from Coltishall and North Weald, the main part of 26 Squadron moved to Harrowbeer in Devon, having divested itself of its Spitfires and re-equipped fully on Mustangs. Here, the squadron refreshed its training in spotting for naval bombardment.

In April, the squadron moved to Chateau Bernard in France in support of Operation *Venerable*. This operation was a resurrection of the cancelled Operation *Independence* – a combined army, naval and air effort to neutralise dug-in German garrisons at the mouth of the Gironde, which were preventing the Allies from capturing the important port of Bordeaux. The fortress garrison at Royan was to be bombed by the US 8th Air Force, and the Pointe de Grave on the opposite bank to be shelled by the French Navy battleship *Lorraine* and cruiser *Duquesne*. The Mustangs were required to spot the fall of shot for the French warships.

The squadron's ORB noted that, 'All aircraft are being got into top form for the forthcoming "Ops".' Sorties started at dawn on 15 April and continued the whole day while the light lasted. The squadron carried out 56 sorties, directing gunfire onto batteries and reinforced shelters. The operation continued the next day until midday. The targets had been pounded mercilessly for a day and a half, but by the middle of the second

Mustang Mk I (NA-83) AM251 of 414 Squadron RCAF at RAF Harrowbeer, May–June 1943. This was the regular aircraft of Flying Officer G. W. Burroughs, one of the squadron's highest scoring pilots. (RAF Harrowbeer Interest Group)

day, the 26 Squadron ORB remarked, 'Royan was taken and the fighting on the Pointe de Grave is virtually finished.'

The partnership between 26 Squadron and the French Navy units had proved a success, so was repeated for attacks on Île d'Oléron. The island was another pocket of resistance holding out along the Atlantic coast. On 30 April, 26 Squadron flew 32 sorties in support of the cruiser *Duquesne*'s bombardment of targets on the island. Radio problems experienced early in the day were quickly resolved and, in the words of the squadron's ORB, 'some very good shoots were carried out despite the usual erratic gunnery of the French ships'. Gunnery spotting continued until early evening, when *Duquesne* blew out a barrel on one of her 203mm guns. By this time, ground forces were well established and the need for gunnery support had lessened.

By May 1945, it was increasingly apparent that the war in Europe was all but won. On 1 May, 26 Squadron returned to Harrowbeer via Cherbourg. On 10 May, reconnaissance sweeps of the Channel Islands were carried out, which revealed white flags flying and Allied insignia displayed. The following month, the unit gave up its Mustangs for the second and last time, switching to Spitfire FR XIVs and moving back to the continent. Fittingly, this squadron had been both the first and the last in RAF service to operate the Allison-engined Mustang.

Chapter 10

Loose Ends

The total replacement of Allison-engined Mustangs on the production line with Merlin-engined variants, and the introduction of an additional line at a second factory, spoke volumes for the quality of the Mustang with the Rolls-Royce/Packard engine. However, this was not the whole story. Even as the preparations for full-scale production of Merlin Mustangs commenced, it was suggested that a certain proportion of production could continue to be fitted with Allison engines – and indeed, that this was desirable.

In November 1942, a month after the first flight of the Merlin-powered Mustang Mk X, the Minister of Production suggested to US planners that, 'for certain... theatres, the Mustang should be fitted with the Allison engine, leaving the remaining Merlin output from the Packard plant for other United Kingdom types.'[1] This admittedly had as much to say about uncertainty over the production volume of Merlin engines and the Mustang generally as it did about the esteem felt for the existing Allison versions. Nevertheless, the fact that some continuing Allison production was advocated at all confirms that there was still value seen in the type with this engine.

Richard Fairey of the British Supply Mission (formerly the BPC) reported in the same month that the US authorities were not prepared to continue with an Allison Mustang production line as this would potentially have delayed the introduction of what they then regarded as the 'definitive' Mustang (which eventually became the P-51D, or Mustang Mk IV in RAF service).[2] In the event, there were too many difficulties involved to make production with two engine types practicable, added to which the anticipated immediate shortage of Merlin engines was averted.

However, as seen in Chapter 5, there were those who later saw certain advantages in the Allison-engined types over the much-prized Merlin-powered variants. Colonel Clare W. Bunch, Operational Engineering, NAAF, identified in June 1943 that the V-1710-engined Mustang had benefits compared with its Merlin-engined sibling:

'It is suggested that the Allison-engined P-51A may lend itself better to a combination of low-altitude fighter-intruder and a medium bombardment escorter than will the Merlin powered P-51B due to the inherent difficulty of operating the Merlin engine at the low RPMs necessary for a low fuel consumption,' wrote Bunch.[3] Equally, 2 TAF regarded the Allison Mustang as 'ideal' for the fighter-reconnaissance role as late as October 1944 and that replacing these aircraft with newer types had been 'a retrograde step'.[4]

Nevertheless, there were initially few really pressing reasons for the US authorities to reconsider the use of the Merlin as the Mustang's primary powerplant. The Merlin had turned the Mustang into what promised to be a superlative escort fighter, which at the time was more important than a low-altitude fighter-bomber, intruder or tactical fighter. Further developments in the Merlin family offered potential of over 2,000hp war emergency power ratings. While Allison tried to engineer improvements in its own two-stage supercharger to keep up with the Merlin's performance, there was little impetus to change from the winning combination of the Mustang and the Merlin. Despite this, the selection of the Merlin for all production models of the Mustang after the P-51A did not represent the end of the aircraft's association with the Allison V-1710.

As 1943 progressed, fears about Packard's capacity remained. Furthermore, while Allison's production was holding up (it would start to fall in the second half of 1944 due to lower demand for types powered by the V-1710), the company was reporting considerable excess capacity. Allison reported that the company could have produced an additional 10,000 engines between March and December that year.[5] In August 1943, crippling losses to USAAF bomber forces led to General Arnold commissioning a study into fitting two-stage supercharged Allison engines into the Mustang. The need for as many escort fighters as possible that could shepherd the bombers all the way to the target provided further impetus for the authorities to encourage an additional engine, which it was hoped would be competitive with the Merlin.

Allison had invested considerable work into an auxiliary-stage mechanical supercharger, which attached to the engine-stage supercharger of the existing engines. The existing two-stage supercharged V-1710, the -93 model, was some nine inches longer than the Merlin 61 and could not have been fitted without a substantial redesign of the existing airframe.

The Air Force commissioned NACA to look into improving the efficiency of the auxiliary stage of the supercharger. The work consisted of increasing the auxiliary-stage gear ratio from 6.85:1 to 8.08:1, changing to interstage carburetion, introducing aftercooling and examining methods for injecting coolant internally. Further work replaced the existing flat supercharger guide vanes with parabolic vanes and redesigning the ducting to reduce pressure losses. Allison incorporated several of the NACA-suggested improvements in the further development of the V-1710, with several improved versions following including the -109 and -117 which increased the power available. This process eventually resulted in the -119 (F32R) model. This included water injection and an aftercooler, which lowered the temperature of the air-fuel mixture before it entered the cylinders to prevent premature detonation of the fuel.[6] These developments, on paper at least, promised to make the V-1710 competitive with the latest projected Merlin, the RM14SM or 100-series.

Problems remained – the necessity of redesigning the forward fuselage would have entailed not-insignificant work, while reintroducing an Allison Mustang production line would have presented considerable practical problems, just as Merlin Mustangs were needed in large numbers. As a result, little serious work was done on creating a 'second generation' Allison Mustang with the existing airframe.

The XP-51J

While considerable difficulties had been identified to adapt the existing Mustang design to the 2-stage V-1710, an extensive redesign of the basic Mustang, which began in early 1943, presented an opportunity to incorporate an uprated Allison. The 'lightweight' NA-105 programme involved a series of experimental aircraft. These aircraft, designated XP-51F and XP-51G, using two different types of Merlin, had significantly redesigned structure and aerodynamic form and were in many respects a totally new aircraft based on Mustang 'DNA'. In November 1943, two aircraft were added to the NA-105 programme, to be fitted with the V-1710-119.

The XP-51F first flew in February 1944 and the XP-51G in August of that year. They did not go on to enter production directly, but led to the NA-126, which entered service as the P-51H.

On the same day that the USAAF placed a production order for the P-51H, 30 June 1944, a formal contract was agreed with NAA to cover the two further NA-105 experimental 'lightweights'. These were designated NA-105B by NAA, and XP-51J by the Army, and received the serials 44-76027 and 44-76028. By now, it was unlikely that the AAF was interested in the aircraft as a potential production machine, so the two Js were probably given the go-ahead as engine testbeds, to help with the Twin Mustang programme (see page 212), or simply for comparative purposes.

Due to the experimental, hand-built nature of these aircraft, it was possible to relocate the firewall without going to the trouble of developing new production tooling. The XP-51J was otherwise similar to the four preceding Merlin-powered 'lightweights', though all had detail differences.

The XP-51J could be distinguished from its near-sisters by the different exhaust-stub arrangement and the completely fair cowling with no carburettor intake, as well as other smaller variations.[i] The carburettor intake was relocated to the ventral intake scoop, feeding rammed air forwards along the fuselage to the new updraft carburettor (previous Allisons had used a downdraft carburettor). This feature entailed cutting a further hole in the firewall to route the ducting, which was not popular with pilots, especially considering the problems later experienced with the engine, who were concerned about safety.

The 'J' first flew on 23 April 1945, piloted by Joe Barton. The first of the two NA-105Bs was handed over to the Army on 15 February 1946, after only seven flights had been made by NAA pilots. The second was handed over after only two flights.

The engine was projected to be able to drive the XP-51J to 491mph at 20,700ft. Unfortunately, the new version of the engine experienced myriad problems. These included backfiring throughout the power range, potentially damaging the auxiliary supercharger, which was itself subject to numerous failures. The engines' tendency to expel oil could not be resolved, and the engines ran roughly. The dash 119's potential power

---

i The J's were fitted with the taller fin and rudder similar to that of the H-model and may have been from the outset, unlike the P-51G which was retrofitted with the taller tail.

The sole XP-51J, an unsuccessful lightweight Mustang development with a two-stage Allison V-1710-119.

could never be realised, and it is doubtful that the XP-51J ever reached anywhere near its potential maximum speed.

The XP-51J would not serve as the basis for a production variant, but acted as a test bed for further development of the V-1710 to assist the final Mustang development – the F-82 Twin Mustang. The Twin Mustang, which was recognisably developed from the single-seat type but was substantially a new aircraft, was, in service, mainly powered by Allison V-1710-143/145(G6R/L) engines, despite having been designed with Merlins in mind. The F-82's engine lacked the aftercooling of the -119 and was less powerful. Furthermore, the continuing problems with the engine meant that it had to be de-rated and never performed as it might have. Nevertheless, there is a certain symmetry to this, the final version of the aircraft, being developed for Merlin power before switching to a variant of the V-1710 – the opposite path to that taken by its single-engined forebear.

After the War

Even after the end of hostilities, a small number of Allison Mustangs still had a career. The burgeoning air-racing scene was a natural place for surviving Allison Mustangs, as they were still among the fastest aircraft at low level, where pylon racing took place. Models such as the A-36A and P-51A boasted better high-speed, low-altitude handling than Merlin-

A-36A s/n 42-83721, was scrapped at Buckley Field and struck off on 18 February 1945. The 'winged bullet' emblem on the nose indicates it had served at a gunnery training school.

engined variants and were in some respects aerodynamically superior for high-speed flight, especially when compared to the low-back P-51D.

After the war, 41-37426/BuNo 57987, the Navy's first P-51, was given the civilian experimental registration NX1204V. It was apparently prepared for racing, as it was photographed with the race number '97' painted on the rear fuselage. It was then sold to the Dominican Republic's Air Corps (Cuerpo de Aviación Militar Dominicana) where it was issued with the serial FAD-1705 and probably written off in 1948.

Several A-36As and P-51As, and at least one P-51, took part in postwar events such as the National Air Races in Cleveland.[7] The aircraft mostly underwent small modifications to help improve their speed. These could include widening the carburettor air scoop, fairing over the dive brakes (in the case of A-36As) and adding four-bladed propellers.

The 1947 National Air Races, the second year that the races had run after stopping for the Second World War, featured two A-36As which were flown by Woody Edmondson and Kendall Everson. Both aircraft took part in the Kendall Trophy, a race for Mustang variants. Everson, in 'Race 44' (NX39502) sponsored by the Essex Wire Corporation, came second to Steve Beville's P-51D, with a speed of 377.926mph. Edmondson came third in 'Race 15' (NX4E, not to be confused with his later P-51D of the same registration), with a speed of 372.392mph.

That year, Edmondson also qualified his A-36A for the prestigious Thompson Trophy race. Unfortunately, Edmondson's engine blew on

Kendall Everson's racing A-36A NX39502 (originally 42-83665) in 1947.

Hand-inscribed photograph of Woody Edmondson's racing A-36A NX4E, 'City of Lynchburg' at Cleveland in 1947.

lap 11, and he was forced to crash-land (some versions indicate that he bailed out). Spectators reportedly found him showing more interest in finding his lost wristwatch than in his own injuries or wrecked aircraft.

The following year, Charles Bing flew an aircraft listed as a P-51A to fifth place in the Sohio Trophy handicap race. This year there were no Allison Mustangs in the Thompson race – Edmondson raced another P-51D. However, the V-1710 continued to contribute to the racing scene, and to the success of Mustangs – certain aspects of the Allison were seen as superior to the standard Merlin components, such as con-rods, and many race-tuned Merlins were later adapted with these Allison parts.

1949 was the last year the Cleveland races were held. That year, James Hannon entered Everson's former A-36A, NX39502 (sometimes mistakenly identified as a P-51A), as 'Race 2'. He retired from the Tinnerman Trophy race and finished eighth in the Thompson Trophy 'R' Division race. By this time, some later designs of aircraft had begun to sport some radical speed-boosting modifications such as wing tip radiators, drastically clipped wings and ever more heavily boosted engines. These eroded the natural advantage of the low-level specialising Allison Mustangs. In any case, the withdrawal of US military support for the races due to the Korean War, building on the land where the grandstands had been sited and increasing concern over safety spelled the end of the Cleveland National Air Races.

The racing aircraft later contributed to the preservation and warbird movement – NX39502, for example, was acquired by the USAF Museum in the 1970s and is now displayed as 'Margie H' from the Mediterranean Theatre of Operations (MTO). Even Edmondson's NX4E, which was written off in its accident in 1947, may have contributed parts to later restorations.

Kendall Everson's A-36A NX39502 as it appeared in the 1949 Cleveland races as Race #2.

NX39502 in around 1953–4, towards the end of its flying career.

Survivors

The vast majority of Allison-engined Mustangs were disposed of during or shortly after the Second World War. Most were scrapped. The RAF considered its Mustang Mk Is obsolete, and those few remaining having had a very long and hard life, were likely scrapped very soon after VE Day. Its Mustang Mk IAs and IIs were provided under Lend-Lease and therefore had to be either returned or disposed of. The latter was their fate.

USAAF Allison Mustangs overseas appear to have been disposed of in theatre, if the example of the A-36A is representative. The number of A-36As recorded in the US does not show a significant increase when the type was withdrawn from frontline service, but by subtracting this number from the 'All AAF' figure, the number 'elsewhere' shows a significant fall: in August 1944, it was recorded that there was one more A-36A 'Stateside' than in July but 48 fewer overseas (from a total of 58).

In the US, unlike the UK, a handful of Allison Mustangs survived military service to enter civilian hands – mostly for racing, as noted above. The immediate postwar race scene seems to have allowed surplus A-36As and P-51As to survive long enough to interest the preservation movement, notably A-36A 42-83665. Nevertheless, there was a period, while the general interest in warbirds was gradually developing, during which the early form of the Mustang had fallen into such obscurity that it was considered virtually extinct.

The oldest surviving Allison Mustang did not emerge through the racing route. The first of the two XP-51s, 41-038, having been operated by NACA throughout the war, was passed to the National Air and Space Museum (NASM) in 1949. There it languished in storage, its significance both to the US and the UK seemingly unrecognised. (It was, after all, not just the first USAAF test aircraft, it was essentially the only surviving example of a Mustang Mk I, having been fourth on the production line.)

In 1975, with the NASM having little use for 41-038, it was acquired by the Experimental Aircraft Association (EAA). It underwent a somewhat regrettable 'restoration' to flight, eradicating a certain amount of the aircraft's originality. (For example, its original guns, which were still in situ, had their breeches sawn off to save weight, and the airframe was stripped of its wartime finish and repainted in silver in an effort to evoke its original bare metal.) Mercifully, in 1982 the aircraft was retired from flight and it now resides permanently in the EAA Aviation Museum. The aircraft remains the closest thing on display to the Mustang Mk I that served the RAF so faithfully, retaining some of the features from the earliest aircraft such as the fairings for the chin guns.

The A-36A 42-83665 was delivered by NAA in October 1942 and spent most of its life with training units at Eglin Field, Florida, where it received minor damage on a couple of occasions in accidents but was repaired and put back into service. In February 1945, it was put up for disposal and the following year acquired by Kendall Everson and the Essex Wire Corporation for racing, registered N39502. It changed hands a few times over the succeeding years but probably did not fly after 1954, when it was stripped and dismantled. In 1971 the then-owner, Charles Doyle, donated it to the USAF Museum. The museum restored it over the next two years, and it was put on display in 1973, painted as the aircraft flown by Captain Lawrence Dye of the 522nd FBS in the Mediterranean in 1943–44, with the name 'Margie H', albeit with its own serial.

Little is known about another A-36A, 42-83731, other than that it spent its career in the US, almost certainly in training. It was transferred to the 'Reconstruction Finance Corporation' for disposal in May 1945, purchased in the early 1950s and placed on the civil register as N50452. Little seems to have happened with this aircraft until 1988 when it was acquired by Chino Warbirds of Houston, restored to flying condition and re-registered N251A. In the 1980s this aircraft was painted and 'dressed' to resemble a tactical reconnaissance

P-51 with dummy cannon on its wings, Normandy invasion stripes and a yellow nose – something of a melange of a colour scheme, not representing any real aircraft. It then gained another spurious colour scheme with broad black bands over aluminium paint, and 'boxing eagle' nose art. In 2002, the A-36A crossed the Atlantic and displayed at the 'Flying Legends' airshow at Duxford, thus becoming, in all probability, the first Allison-engined Mustang variant to fly in the UK since shortly after the end of the Second World War.

The aircraft was then acquired for the Comanche Fighters stable of Tom and Dan Friedkin in Texas. Throughout the 2000s, 42-83731 was painstakingly restored, flying once again in 2010 in bare metal, before being painted in an authentic colour scheme representing 42-83947 of the 524th Squadron in Italy in 1944, notable for its many mission markings extending down the fuselage all the way to the tail.

For an aircraft with a production run of only 500, a fair number of A-36As have survived. Moreover, of the four known in existence, three are airworthy. Aircraft 42-83738, however, has followed a rather unconventional route. The aircraft was another one probably used largely for training and disposed of after the war. It was flown under the registration NL4607V from 1955, and then sold to Sid Smith in 1962 and registered N4607V. At some point, Smith modified the aircraft with a P-51D 'dog house' scoop and radiator – no doubt original radiators were becoming scarce by this time. He also fitted a flat-sided sliding canopy and P-51D undercarriage, and had the aircraft painted yellow with red lightning bolt motifs. In 1975, the A-36A was retired to a museum in Santa Fe, New Mexico, before being acquired by John R. Paul, under whose ownership a most bizarre 'restoration' took place, aimed at converting this most rare of Mustang variants into a Merlin-engined approximation of a P-51B.

Fortunately, 42-83738 was acquired by a new owner and meticulously restored to factory A-36A specifications by American Aero Services, taking to the air once again in July 2012. The aircraft is now operated by the Collings Foundation in the colours of 'Baby Carmen', an aircraft of the 86th FBG in Italy in 1943.

Currently the oldest surviving P-51A is the dash 10 model 43-6006, although it is something of a hybrid like 42-83738. This aircraft was delivered to the USAAF in April 1943 and spent time at Mines Field, Los Angeles before being transferred the following month to Ladd Field,

Alaska, for cold weather trials. On 14 February 1944, 43-6006 was caught in a snowstorm and crashed near Summit, killing the pilot Edward Getter. There the wreck of the aircraft remained until 1977 when it was recovered by Waldon Spillers. From 1978 to 1985, 43-6006 underwent reconstruction, utilising parts of other Mustang variants to expedite the process, most visually obvious being a P-51D 'dog house' radiator scoop and A-36A cowling panels. Its first post-restoration flight took place in 1985. It was later acquired by Jerry Gabe, who applied the name 'Polar Bear' to it, under which it became well known on the display circuit and racing at Reno.

The discovery of corrosion and other issues in the airframe led to the decision to carry out a ground-up restoration, which commenced at Pacific Fighters in 2015. Here, some of 43-6006's original P-51A features were restored, such as the correct radiator scoop. However, instead of applying an authentic P-51A scheme the owner decided to restore 43-6006 to approximate the appearance of the second XP-51, 41-039. Here, 43-6006's A-36A nose layout was helpful, as it provided the correct nose cowling arrangement and allowed the installation of nose guns (albeit lacking the distinctive fairings present on the original XP-51s). However, the mix of A-36A, P-51A and P-51D features (the aircraft retains the newer variant's wing, with its larger root extensions) makes 43-6006 as much of a mishmash as when it was 'Polar Bear', albeit slightly more cohesive visually – and it undeniably looks beautiful in polished aluminium and pre-1942 USAAC markings with the Wright Field emblem on the fuselage.

P-51A 43-6178 was delivered to the USAAF in 1943 and sold after the war. It changed hands various times, remaining mostly in storage from 1963 until acquired by Kermit Weeks' Fantasy of Flight in 1981. Since then it has been stored dismantled and stripped down, awaiting restoration.

P-51A 43-6251 spent the immediate postwar period, from 1946 to 1953, as an instructional airframe at Cal Aero Technical Institute, Glendale, California, painted in a distinctive black and yellow colour scheme. It was then acquired by Edward T. Maloney, moving around several times before ending up at the Planes of Fame museum in Chino, California, where it was restored to flight. For many years the aircraft was flown and displayed in RAF colours, either as a generic Mustang Mk I or with specific markings such as AG470/RU-M of 414 Squadron RCAF, the aircraft flown by Flying Officer Hollis Hills when he scored the Mustang's first aerial combat victory. It is currently (as of 2020) operating in the colours of 'Mrs Virginia', an aircraft of the 1st Air Commando.

P-51A 43-6274 was another aircraft retained in the US, and had evidently been rendered non-airworthy after around a year in service, as some time in 1944 it was loaned to the Frederick School in Frederick, Oklahoma as a 'gate guardian', mounted in flying attitude on posts. In 1978 it went to the Yanks Air Museum, Chino, California for restoration and display. In 1993 the aircraft was restored again, now wearing the colours of AX-H, an F-6B of the 67th TRG in England in 1944, complete with a K-24 camera mounted behind the pilot's seat.

Those eight aircraft represent the total of all the surviving Allison Mustangs, out of the 1,581 built. There exists an additional P-51A – '311', a replica built by expert warbird restorer Gerry Beck, which was built from original drawings to be identical to production aircraft, and first flew in 2006, with the registration N8082U. The aircraft was painted to resemble the modified racer 'Precious Metal' in order to play that aircraft in the 2008 film *Thunder Over Reno*. N8082U crashed in 2007 when it collided with a P-51D at Oshkosh, resulting in Beck's death. The replica P-51A is currently undergoing restoration.

What's in a Name? Reprise

At around the time that 42-83665 was first displayed at the USAF Museum, the myth that the aircraft was known as Apache in service was gaining ground, and for many years it was displayed with signage repeating the erroneous name. Only through the persistence of Tom Griffiths was the error finally corrected, in 2019.

This is a bizarre case of a myth becoming so prevalent that it gained enough 'critical mass' that even institutions and historians who knew it to be untrue found it almost impossible to challenge, and the name gained something of an 'official' stamp of approval. Fortunately, historians – most notably Griffiths and the late Michael Vorrasi[ii] – have done much recent work to challenge the myth and dispel the idea that the A-36A was ever, officially or unofficially, given the name 'Apache' in service.

---

ii   The National Museum of the USAAF placed signage by its A-36A referring to it as the Apache – Griffiths demonstrated over a lengthy correspondence with the museum that the name Apache was erroneous and A-36As had always been considered Mustangs by the USAAF. In 2019, the museum changed its signage to reflect this.

Michael Vorrasi established beyond reasonable doubt that the application of 'Apache' to the A-36A originated in publications no earlier than the 1970s, and appears to have arisen from confusion with NAA's preference for the name Apache relating to early Mustang variants in the US, from roughly the start of 1941 to July 1942. (To add to the confusion, the type gained an informal name in the Mediterranean, 'Invader', which became so widespread that at one point it could arguably be regarded as semi-official. See Chapter 6.) In fact, official US Army sources including the A-36A parts catalogue and the USAAF's list of approved aircraft names[8] indicate that the A-36A was always 'officially' named Mustang, even though the name was rarely used.

Appreciation

It is hoped that the preceding pages will indicate all that can currently be said about the Allison Mustang, and whether this 'untold story' was worth expending years of research, writing and the best part of 100,000 words on. Nevertheless, a brief summary of the Allison Mustang's contribution feels appropriate here.

The RAF, having the Allison Mustang as its primary tactical reconnaissance type, was arguably able to complete more operations over greater distance, more effectively, and with greater survivability, than any other type would have been capable of. Furthermore, the range, performance and striking power of the Allison Mustangs allowed the RAF's AC squadrons to carve out their own offensive role over occupied Europe that realised a low-level but persistent degradation of enemy communications.

The USAAF also employed their Allison Mustangs to great effect. The tiny number of P-51s and even tinier number of P-51As fitted as tactical reconnaissance aircraft realised achievements out of all proportion to the size of their ranks. As with the RAF aircraft, it is hard to imagine another type with the performance, endurance and survivability against enemy fighters that could have been available at the time.

In the attack role, the groups of A-36s in the Mediterranean and CBI theatres enabled a versatility and precision that other types apparently struggled to match. There is little doubt that they were among the most effective fighter-bombers of the Sicilian and Italian campaigns, if not the most effective. In the early days of the invasions, their ability to carry out pin-point strikes demonstrably aided the Allied advance and helped prevent it from getting bogged down. Later on, the switch to more of an interdiction role frustrated Axis counter-attacks and hampered the reinforcement of defences. It is reasonable to conclude that P-40s would not have been able to achieve the same level of accuracy or survivability against either enemy fighters or ground fire. Neither would they have been as successful in short-term switches to bomber escort. The A-36A was a genuine 'swing role' aircraft 70 years before the term existed.

In the Far East, the P-51As of the 1st Air Commando further proved both the air-to-ground and air-to-air prowess of the Allison Mustang. The 311th Group, meanwhile, not only reinforced the lessons of the Mediterranean, but proved that the P-51A could just as easily provide close escort to strategic bombers as its Merlin-engined counterparts could in Europe, when missions were flown at medium altitudes.

In fact, at its optimum altitude, the Allison Mustang's air-to-air abilities were not inferior to the Merlin Mustang's – arguably better in some cases, due to the lower stick forces experienced in manoeuvres and lack of tendency to depart from controlled flight in certain circumstances. The V-1710's restriction of the Allison Mustang to low and medium altitudes has led to a sense in some quarters that the aircraft was no good as a fighter in the European theatre (or at all). In fact, by the end of the war in Europe, there was just as much of a role for low–medium-altitude fighters as high-altitude ones (arguably even more of a role) and it should be noted that the RAF had considerable success with the Hawker Tempest, a dedicated low–medium-altitude fighter, in the air-to-air role. There is no reason to doubt that a large force of P-51As in 2 TAF could have been very effective. Perhaps opinions of the aircraft have been coloured excessively by the fact that at the time the RAF was first assessing the Mustang, the need was for high-altitude fighters. By the end of the war, air combat altitudes and the 'full throttle' height of the Allison Mustang had converged.

Ultimately, considering the total of fewer than 1,600 aircraft built, the Allison Mustang made a considerable mark. It did so in its own right, not simply as a 'proof of concept' for the much more numerous Merlin Mustang. The Allison Mustang and the people who created it, believed in it and made it what it was – designers, engineers, pilots, military leaders, bureaucrats and groundcrews – deserve their story to be told more often, and understood better.

Appendix 1

Technical Details

The NAA Mustang, P-51 and A-36 series of aircraft are described in the type's structural repair instructions manual as 'single-seat, low wing fighters designed for light attack bombing and high-speed combat service'. This reflects the roles the Mustang had evolved into, rather

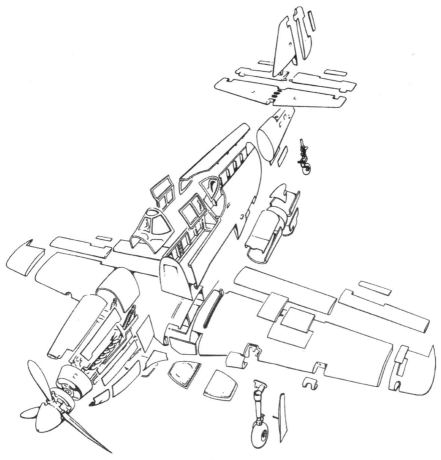

Exploded diagram of the Mustang Mk I's major assemblies from the type's repair instructions.

than been specifically designed for. The design was originally for a 'pure' fighter, though as seen in the main narrative, the aircraft's role began to broaden almost as soon as it first flew.

The evolution of the series was, briefly, as follows:

- NA-73X – the first aircraft in the series ('X' denoting an experimental example of the manufacturer's model number 73).
- NA-73 – the production version derived from the prototype, known as the Mustang Mk I in RAF service.
- NA-83 – a slightly improved version, which nevertheless retained the Mustang Mk I designation in RAF service.
- NA-91 – a variant similar to the NA-83 in many respects, but modified to carry an armament of four 20mm cannon. It was known as the P-51 by the US Army and Mustang Mk IA by the RAF and was the last model originating specifically from a British order.
  (These models, in both RAF and US service, were mainly used in the tactical reconnaissance role, with modifications and additional equipment to reflect this.)
- NA-97 – the first model specifically developed for the US Army, a dedicated dive-bomber and attack aircraft, with dive brakes and bomb racks, as well as revised gun armament. This type was officially known as the A-36A in US service.
- NA-99 – a development of the NA-97 for the US Army, retaining the NA-97's bomb racks, though the dive brakes were deleted. This aircraft, known as the P-51A by the US and Mustang Mk II by the RAF, had an engine optimised for slightly higher altitudes, moderate structural and aerodynamic refinements, and the gun armament was revised once again. (The RAF continued to use the type as a tactical reconnaissance fighter, though the US Army tended to use it as a fighter-bomber and escort fighter.)

A description is given below of the Mustang's major features, followed by the detail differences from the initial type introduced in each successive model. (NB unless otherwise stated, reference to 'all models' or 'all Mustangs' will relate only to early, Allison-engined variants. The XP-51J is considered in Chapter 10.)

Fuselage

The Mustang's fuselage was composed of a front section, from the firewall back to Frame Station 248, and a rear section to which the empennage was attached. A bulkhead of solid 0.032in-thick Alclad sheet formed the rear face of the forward fuselage section.

The fuselage structure was built around four longerons, which were constructed from H-shaped extrusions in 24ST aluminium. The longerons were tapered towards the rear of the fuselage as the loads decreased, by

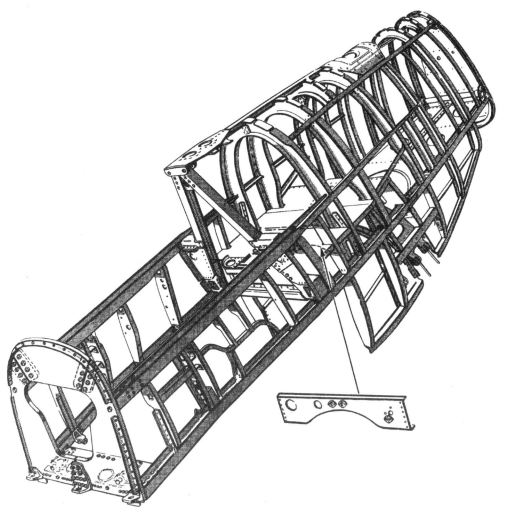

The rear fuselage structure of the Mustang Mk I, which would remain similar through the Allison-engined variants.

progressively grinding away the flanges on one end of the 'H' until it became a 'U' section. The upper longerons extended aft from the firewall and terminated at station 216, while the lower longerons extended aft to the tail joint at station 248.[i]

The shape of the fuselage was formed by pressed-aluminium frames. These were mostly inverted U-shaped formers in 24SO or 24ST aluminium alloy, in thicknesses varying from 0.032in to 0.064in. Generally, the frames were formed with flanges to stiffen the structure and provide a location for skin attachment, although a small number of frames carried extruded angles and stiffeners for these purposes. The width of each frame depended on the stress borne by that area of the fuselage.

A number of shelves and supporting beams were installed within the fuselage to enable the necessary equipment to be mounted therein. The fuselage shelves also acted as webs, adding extra stiffening to the fuselage.

From the NA-73X through to the P-51A, the radiator intake housing was an integral part of the fuselage structure, with the frames extending below the lower longeron. (On the Merlin-powered variants, the radiator scoop housing would become a separate sub-assembly, and the main fuselage structure would terminate at the lower longeron.)

From the firewall to the rear of the cockpit, there were no full frames, but the upper and lower longerons were braced by quarter frame structures.

The aft end of the cockpit was surmounted by an inverted-V shaped 'nose-over structure' which was mounted to the lower longerons and triangulated by a beam across its base. The sides of the nose-over structure were braced against the upper longerons.

Compared to other contemporary fighters, there was a relatively small number of fuselage stringers, which carried the loads from the outer skin to the frames. The stringers were all located on the upper deck, and on the NA-73X to P-51A (and indeed P-51B/C) were T-angle bulb extrusions in 24ST aluminium alloy.

The fuselage skin was constructed of 24ST Alclad ranging from 0.040in to 0.081in thickness. All the skin exposed to the airflow was flush-riveted

---

i 'Stations' refer to the location of frames, ribs and other components measured in inches from a particular (datum) location. For fuselage stations, the measuring point is just aft of the propeller spinner. Wing stations are measured from the centre rib, while tailplane stations are measured from the fuselage centreline and fin stations are measured from the root.

with AN426-AD-type rivets. Most rivet locations were countersunk. The Mustang was considered unusual in this respect, especially compared to British practice, in that the skin was relatively thick. This meant the internal structure could be reduced and a smoother surface achieved.

Powerplant and Related

Prior to the switch to the Packard Merlin in the P-51B/C, the Mustang was powered by models of the Allison V-1710 'F' series. This version of the 1710 cubic inch liquid-cooled inline engine introduced various improvements over the previous 'C' series (the 'D' and 'E' were extended-shaft versions that evolved in parallel). Most notably, the epicyclic (planetary) reduction gear, which necessitated a long, tapered casing, was replaced with a much shorter spur reduction gear. This allowed a more compact installation and had the effect of raising the thrust line compared to the 'C' model.

The V-1710 was a relatively 'modular' design, and it was straightforward to produce engines rated at different altitudes by fitting supercharger impellers of different ratios. Like the 'C' model, the 'F's used in the early Mustangs had a single-stage, single-speed engine-driven supercharger. All ran on 100 octane fuel and drove the propeller in a right-hand direction, as denoted by the R suffix applied by Allison. The engine could be started by internal battery, external battery or by hand. It used a Bendix-Stromberg ejection-type carburettor.

The NA-73X, (along with the NA-73, NA-83 and NA-91) was powered by an Allison V-1710-39 (F3R) with a supercharger ratio of 8.8:1.

The Allison V-1710-87 (F21R) was developed to power the A-36A. This engine was optimised for low-altitude operations, with the supercharger gear ratio lowered to 7.48:1 from the standard 8.8:1, and offered 1,325hp for five minutes at take-off or maximum military power, between sea level and 3,200ft altitude. The -87 engine required a larger oil pump than the F3R.

The P-51A was powered by an Allison V-1710-81 (F20R), which had a supercharger ratio of 9.60:1, giving a critical altitude for military-rated power of 17,500ft, compared with 12,000ft for the Mustang Mk I's V-1710-39 (F3R) and 3,200ft for the A-36's -87 (F21R). It also had a slightly higher boost at full throttle – 57.0inHg compared with 56.0inHg. This increased the Mustang's performance markedly at medium altitudes.

The V-1710-81 was not fitted with synchronisation drives, so chin guns could not be included. The -81 engine required a larger oil pump than the F3R and was fitted with an automatic manifold pressure regulator.

The carburettor intake trunking was revised again from the P-51A-2, so that now the pilot could select the filter, or bypass it, from the cockpit. The filter could be brought into the airstream through a system of levers and bellcranks. Selecting unfiltered ram air provided slightly greater performance. The pilot could also still select warm air from the engine bay, via the small door just upstream of the carburettor.

Engine	Condition	Power (hp)	RPM	Manifold pressure	Altitude
V-1710-39	Take-off	1,150	3,000	45.5inHg	Sea level
	War emergency[ii]	1,470	3,000	56.0inHg	Sea level
	Rated military	1,150	3,000	42.0inHg	12,000ft
V-1710-87	Take-off	1,325	3,000	47.0inHg	Sea level
	War emergency	1,500	3,000	52.0inHg	2,500ft
	Rated military	1,325	3,000	47.0inHg	3,000ft
V-1710-81	Take-off	1,200	3,000	51.5inHg	Sea level
	War emergency	1,360	3,000	57.0inHg	Sea level
	Rated military	1,125	3,000	44.5inHg	17,500ft

The engine was attached to the firewall using two Y-shaped horizontal cantilever bearers, built up from 24ST sheet webs and extruded section top and bottom members riveted into a box-section. The design was largely the same from the NA-73 to NA-99, although a number of individual components were replaced with improved versions from sub-type to sub-type. There were no cross-bearing members, unlike on later Mustang variants. The engine mount was attached to the airframe by four bolts only. The firewall itself was made of steel armour plate.

Engine cowling formers were pressed from stainless steel sheet in a variety of thicknesses, and formed a base onto which the cowling panels were attached with Dzus fasteners. Many cowling panels were removable,

---

ii This category of measurement was introduced in August 1943.

including four lower and two side panels, and the single-piece upper cowling section complete with carburettor air scoop. These were formed from 24ST and 24SUT Alclad.

The oil tank was constructed from two drawn half-hemispheres of 2SO and 52SO aluminium, welded around their common

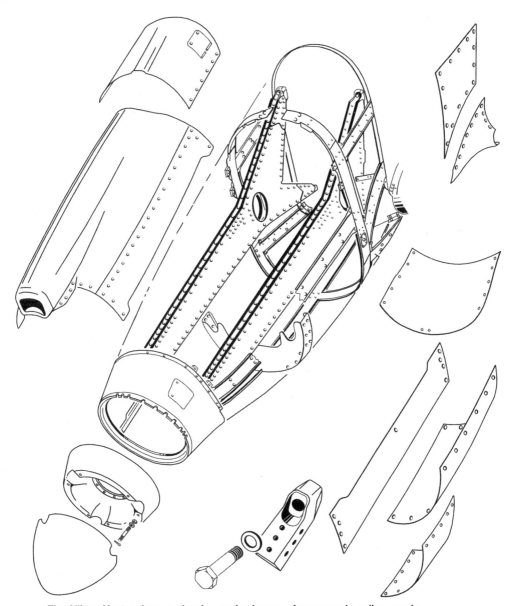

The Allison Mustang's nose showing engine bearers, formers and cowling panels.

circumference. The coolant tank was a cylinder, bent into a 'U' to conform to the contour of cowling. It was formed of drawn half-tubes of 2SO aluminium. In each case, the same type of tank was used in all models of Allison Mustang.

The oil and coolant radiators went through a process of evolution – this took the form of minor changes to improve the function of the devices, until a more radical change was introduced in the P-51A.

Propeller

A Curtiss Electric three-blade, electrically controlled, constant-speed propeller was used, though the exact model varied from type to type. The propeller could be operated as a fully constant-speed unit, or with pitch manually-controlled by the pilot. Aircraft were fitted with a 2:1 reduction gear.

The spinner was a two-piece unit constructed from 0.081in 3SO aluminium alloy, supported by bulkheads spot-welded to the spinner shell.

The propeller mode – constant-speed or manual – could be selected by way of a four-position selector on the forward switch panel. When in constant-speed mode, engine RPM was maintained by an engine-driven propeller governor, which automatically adjusted blade angle (pitch) to meet the load. The desired speed (RPM) was selected by the pitch control mounted near the throttle, on the cockpit port sidewall – selecting fine pitch gave maximum RPM, while moving the control back, towards coarse pitch, gave progressively lower RPM. When not in constant-speed mode, the selector on the switch panel also allowed manual adjustment of propeller pitch, and a circuit breaker protected the circuit from electrical overload.

The first 33 Mustang Mk Is (except for AG368) were delivered with a 10ft 6in-diameter C5315S-D8 model propeller, with blades of hollow steel construction and a pitch range of 30°, with coarse pitch at 58° and fine pitch at 23°. AG368 and aircraft from AG378 onwards were fitted with a 10ft 9in-diameter propeller model C532D-F32 with duralumin blades. This required a modified spinner with a larger and differently shaped blade cut-out.

The P-51A used a Curtiss Electric C.532-F32/50700 propeller, of 10.75ft diameter.

Cockpit

All Allison Mustang variants were of the 'high back' type, apart from the experimental XP-51J. The cockpit was reportedly designed around a pilot 5ft 10in tall.

The canopy enclosure was a three-panel structure. Each side panel had a sliding window in the forward section. The left-hand panel was hinged along its lower edge, while the top panel was hinged at its right-hand edge. The windscreen panels were secured by screw-fastened retaining strips, allowing damaged panels to be removed and replaced with relative ease.

An improved, bulged 'blown' hood, eliminating the canopy frames and allowing greater visibility, was introduced relatively late in the Allison Mustang's career (Merlin-engined P-51Bs and Cs were appearing in theatre by the time the design was finalised). The new hood was manufactured to NAA designs by R. Malcolm and Co. Fitting it involved structural alterations to the fuselage and cockpit, the attachment of external rails and

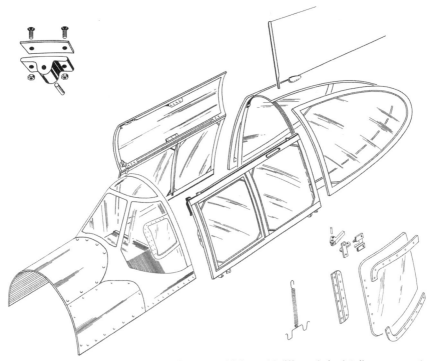

The cockpit enclosure of the Allison Mustang, which would differ only in detail across most variants. Note the 'clear vision' panel in the left windscreen, enlarged in detail, which was unique to the P-51A.

the relocation of the radio aerial mast. The canopy was not introduced on the production line – conversion sets were issued to frontline squadrons and maintenance units. Some Allison Mustangs in the ETO received the canopy modification before Allison variants were retired, as they were particularly useful for tactical reconnaissance pilots.

The floor of the pilot's cockpit was formed by the upper surface of the wing centre-section.[iii] The pilot's seat could accommodate either a seat-type or a back-pack parachute. The seat back was padded by a kapok cushion that could double as a float for the pilot in the event of a ditching. A US-standard safety belt and shoulder harness was fitted on US aircraft, and British aircraft were fitted with a Sutton harness. The seat could be adjusted up-and-down but not fore-and-aft.

Two-piece rear seat armour was added to most aircraft in frontline roles.

A 'shroud', which was integral to the windshield, extended into the cockpit and acted as a housing for the gunsight, defrosting unit and the auxiliary ring-and-bead sight. The back edge was covered in a circular rubberised extrusion.

The cockpit could be heated and ventilated if required. Cold air could be drawn into the cockpit via a tube led from the radiator scoop intake, while warm air was fed from just behind the radiator. This warm-air supply could be used to heat the cockpit and, on early NA-73 aircraft, to defrost the windscreen.

The control stick was non-removable and operated the elevators and ailerons. The control column was a plain stick-type with rubber pistol grip and could be locked with spring-loaded plungers when on the ground.

The rudder was controlled by individual 'pendulum' type pedals, which had a travel of 6.5in. The position of the rudder pedals could be adjusted fore-and-aft to accommodate pilots of different heights. The wheel brakes were operated by applying toe pressure on the respective rudder pedals.

Fore-and-aft trim was adjusted by a wheel on the left-hand side of the cockpit. Rudder and aileron trimmers were operated by moulded knobs placed on a ledge on the left-hand side of the cockpit.

---

iii On V-1650-engined variants, the wing was lowered three inches, so a non-structural plywood floor was installed.

Wings

The wings were a one-piece, single-spar structure (although there were auxiliary spars front and rear) that attached to the fuselage by four bolts. The wings were built in two main sections, joined at the centre line by means of a heavy-gauge rib serving as an assembling surface. The wing was set at an angle of incidence of 1° and a dihedral of 5° measured at 25% chord line. The mainplanes were tapered at a tip/root ratio of 0.449.

The structure of the wings was described as, 'typical all-aluminium design'. Each mainplane was assembled around a front spar, set around the point of maximum depth, as well as a rear spar and a short leading-edge spar in the location of the wheel well. The rest of the structure was formed from extruded stringers, ribs pressed from sheet metal and 24ST Alclad sheet skin. Ribs and formers were spaced on average 12.5in apart.

The main spar was fabricated from two sections of 24ST aluminium alloy sheet, spliced at Station 108.8215. The inboard section of the spar was built up from a single flat sheet of 0.129in thick 24ST, and the outer section from 0.102in sheet. The sheets were folded at the top and bottom to form upper and lower flanges, or spar caps, running the length of the spar. The rear spar was of similar construction, 0.064in-thick inboard and 0.051in-thick outboard. Lightening holes were drilled into the outboard section. The nose spar was formed from a single 0.064in sheet, and the tip spar from 0.051in sheet, with bent-over cap strips as with the other spars. The tip spar had lightening holes let into the web. Vertical spanwise webs reinforced the area aft of the ammunition trays.

Stringers were mostly 24ST aluminium alloy extrusions, although a small number of rolled 24ST Alclad sheet and 24ST alloy sheet shapes were also used. The stringers were generally identified by the NA-standard die that was used to extrude them – for example 1E110T, which was the most common type in the Mustang wing.

Ribs were pressed 24ST or 24SO Alclad sheet items, provided with flanges through which they could be riveted to the outer wing skin. Areas where full-depth ribs could not be accommodated – such as where the fuel tanks were located – were generally reinforced with formers, made from lengths of Alclad 'hat' section sheet stock.

The leading edge of the wing was 'surfaced to a glass like smoothness to reduce drag to a minimum'[1] with naphtha aerofoil smoother. Around six coats were recommended.

The wing tips were constructed of ribs, stringers and a short rear spar, and were removable. The tip fairing was constructed of 52SO aluminium alloy, while the rest of the tip was skinned in 24ST Alclad.

The mainplanes had a gross area of 233 square feet, leading to a gross wing loading of 37lb/ft in the Mustang Mk I.

Conventional navigation lights were mounted on the upper and lower surfaces of the wing tips and at the trailing edge of the rudder.

Flaps and Ailerons

The wing flaps formed the entire trailing edge of the wing from the root fairing to the inboard end of the ailerons, and were of the 'plain flap' type.

They were constructed entirely of 24ST sheet, and were 116in in length, with a mean chord of 20.258in and a total flap area of 32.6ft. The flaps were supported at three points along their length by ball-bearing hinges. Construction consisted of two spars with pressed, flanged ribs and rolled stringers.

The Allison Mustang's ailerons were, like the flaps, supported by three ball-bearing hinges. The ailerons were balanced both statically and dynamically, but not aerodynamically sealed as with the P-51B and later Mustangs. Although experiments to improve roll rate took place during the aircraft's life (the XP-51 41-038 still carries the modified ailerons from these experiments), the design remained similar on all production Allison-engined variants.

Maximum movement was an unusually small 10° up and down.[iv] Construction was almost entirely from 24ST sheet, built up into spars and ribs, and also forming the skin. They were fitted with booster tabs, one of which could be used to trim the aeroplane laterally. The trim/booster tabs were of plywood construction on all Allison-engined variants. The ailerons were each hinged at three points with ball-bearing

---

iv Confusingly, the repair instructions state that the ailerons were 'controlled differentially', when in fact there was no differential in their operation – i.e. travel was the same both up and down. Many contemporary aircraft employed ailerons with a smaller degree of travel down relative to up in order to mitigate the tendency of the down aileron to induce adverse yaw.

hinges. Counterweights mounted forward of the hinge line on forged brackets ensured aerodynamic stability.

All control surfaces were moved by means of flexible cables (being a 'pull-pull' system).

Empennage

Construction of the tail surfaces remained the same from the NA-73X across all Allison-powered production models. They were fully cantilever structures, and were not adjustable.

The fin was constructed around a forward and aft spar and flanged ribs, covered in Alclad sheet skin. The tailplane was similar, with the addition of four extruded stringers, two above and two beneath. The tailplane was set at 2° incidence. As with the wings, the tips were detachable, self-contained structures.

The rudder and elevators were fabric covered. Grade A mercerised cotton fabric was machine-stitched to shape on three sides then slipped over the framework like an envelope, and the open side hand-sewn. The cover was secured to the framework with countersunk screws through dimpled washers. It was then doped (which shrunk and thus tightened the covering), and finishing tape was applied over the screw heads to ensure a smooth surface. A counterbalance weight was attached to the leading edge of the rudder, near the top, which projected forward of the hinge line into a square recess cut into the rear of the fin. Similar counterweights were fitted near the outer end of the elevators.

As with the ailerons, the rudder and elevator trim tabs were of plywood construction.

Armament

The armament of Allison-engined Mustangs evolved throughout the aircraft's career, encompassing machine guns, cannon, bombs and more unorthodox weapons. Armament layouts for each sub-type will be discussed below.

Undercarriage

The undercarriage remained similar throughout all models, and indeed most components remained the same from the NA-73/Mustang Mk I to the NA-106/109 P-51D/K.

The main landing gear comprised single-leg, half-fork full cantilever legs that were fully retractable. The tailwheel was also of the half-fork, cantilever design and was also fully retractable. When retracted, the undercarriage was fully enclosed.

Each main gear leg included a shock strut of the Bendix 'pneudraulic' type, made up of a cylinder and piston, which absorbed shocks through the compression of oil and air reservoirs. A forged, chrome-molybdenum 'scissor' torsion link connected the piston and cylinder. The main leg pivoted on a magnesium alloy support casting, which also transmitted landing loads to the wing rib at station 75.

The main wheels were made up of aluminium alloy hubs, which were single castings, connected to the legs with hardened steel axles and shod with 27in tyres, with a maximum pressure of 45psi. Tyres provided for Mustangs included nylon moulded Goodyear items. Worn out tyres could be remoulded and returned to active service. Brakes were hydraulic.

The tail wheel was connected to an oil shock-absorber unit, which was mounted within a magnesium alloy casting. It was fully castoring and could be steered using the rudder pedals or left free to swivel.

Gear retraction and operation of fairings was hydraulic or by means of cables connected to hydraulically actuated components. For example, the retraction of the tail wheel leg automatically pulled the tail wheel fairing doors closed.

Equipment

Equipment varied by type and by user, with most equipment either specified or supplied by the customer. North American built the Mustangs to either British or US specifications, so appropriate equipment would be installed during manufacture. For example, a first-aid kit, water containers and rations were common to all variants (unless otherwise stated) and were stored in the radio compartment.

More specialised equipment was fitted by the customers themselves – in the case of the UK, in maintenance units or via subcontractors like Lockheed, which assembled the aircraft upon arrival and modified most to AC standards.

For US aircraft, installation of equipment such as reconnaissance cameras and the associated modifications to the airframe were dealt with by government modification centres. (Once production bedded in later in the war, more theatre or role-specific changes were incorporated on the assembly line.)

The most significant items of equipment, and areas of difference between the various sub-types, will be considered below.

Systems

Allison Mustangs essentially had two hydraulic systems – the wheel-brake system and an engine-pump operated hydraulic system. Both of these drew from the same reservoir, which was located on the firewall, but otherwise had totally separate pipelines. The engine-driven hydraulic pump operated undercarriage and fairing doors and flaps, as well as other systems specific to certain models. A handpump was available for when the engine-driven pump was not running. The NA-73 had an arrangement unique to Allison Mustangs, which will be discussed below.

An engine-driven pneumatic pump supplied a vacuum for operating gyro instruments. If this failed, the turn-and-bank indicator could be driven off air from the carburettor intake.

An engine-driven generator and an accumulator supplied electrical current for operating all lighting, gun firing and heating, cameras, radio, propeller controls, fuel booster pump and various other systems and devices.

NA-73X

Although a prototype Mustang, the NA-73X, was built and undertook early testing, the BPC had already purchased the NA-73 design 'off the drawing board'. For this reason, the single NA-73X (which bore the US civil experimental registration 'NX19998') was relatively lightly used and was quickly retired. The aircraft essentially served to satisfy the manufacturer and customer that the design was sound. When the first production-specification machines arrived and could begin service testing in earnest, its usefulness was largely at an end. (In fact, the NA-73X was originally considered one of the 320 machines ordered, but later, another production-specification airframe was added to the line and provided to the British.)

The NA-73X appears to have had two phases of modification. It is possible that the process of modification was more gradual, but most photographs show the aircraft either in rollout condition (up to the November 1940 crash) or after it had been returned to flight in January, with slight but distinct differences between the two phases.

The underside nose cowling panel had two fairings for the chin-mounted machine guns, although these were smaller and of a different design to those used on the early production models. The wings were not pierced for guns (and in fact, leading-edge apertures were painted on). It is believed that no armament was ever fitted to the NA-73X. The windscreen had an armoured glass panel mounted inside it.

After the aircraft was returned to flight early in 1941, the chin-gun fairings were not present, their apertures faired over. A tube was apparently fitted to the foremost exhaust stub during this phase, which seems to be an air intake, possibly for cooling purposes.[v] This did not appear on any other Mustang variant.

Finally, photographs of the repaired NA-73X in flight seem to show a slight 'bump' in the lines of the cowling underside where it met the wing. It is not clear what this might be for.

Fuselage

The basic structure of the NA-73X was similar to that of the production NA-73 model, although there were some differences to the final standardised aircraft. The engine was repositioned and the nose reshaped on production aircraft. More obviously, the radiator scoop was of a markedly different shape.

In profile, the radiator scoop was somewhat shorter and more curved along its underside than on the production NA-73, giving the appearance of a distinctly deeper 'belly'.

The intake utilised the wing underside as its upper surface, unlike all later models which had a gutter or lip to separate the boundary layer. The intake featured a hinged flap that allowed it to widen the mouth of the scoop, in addition to the similar flap at the exit of the radiator tunnel.

As the engine was positioned differently than in production aircraft, the NA-73X had a shorter overall length and a different shape to the cowling. In addition, the upper portion of the firewall was vertical on the NA-73X

---

v   Earlier versions of the V-1710 needed a tube to direct cooling air onto the spark plugs on the exhaust side, and it is possible that the tube was associated with this. The removal of the nose gun fairings and apertures could be one reason for the additional intake.

(visible from the external panel lines), and the lower portion angled forward from the upper section. On all subsequent aircraft, the firewall maintained a constant slope from top to bottom.

The intake scoop for the engine's carburettor was set back from the nose and swept slightly back from the lower edge. This design was proven to starve the engine of air in certain conditions, and it was extended to slightly overlap the spinner backplate on later aircraft. However, by the time the flaw had been discovered, the NA-73X was more or less at the end of its useful life, and it was almost certainly never modified with the new scoop design.

Cockpit

The NA-73X had a unique cockpit enclosure with a single-piece bulged aerodynamic windscreen with significant compound curvature. This was found to be detrimental to visibility and was replaced on production aircraft with a more conventional, multi-piece, framed windscreen.

Undercarriage

The main landing gear doors were a unique shape, with a 'step' on the trailing edge that was not present on any production aircraft.

Some sources indicate that from its rollout, the NA-73X was fitted with wheels from a T-6 trainer, and photographs are consistent with this, showing an eight-spoke wheel. The same wheels can be seen in photographs of the NA-73X following its crash in November 1940. The wheels had been changed for ten-spoke items by the time the prototype was returned to flight after its crash, which more closely resemble the production items.

A lever in the cockpit allowed the pilot to actuate the steerable tailwheel or leave it free to castor.

Powerplant and Related

The engine installed in the NA-73X was an Allison V-1710-39 (F3R) – the exact powerplant initially fitted was one of the first few built. Although the engine itself did not differ from that used in the subsequent production versions (NA-73, 83 and 91), it differed in its installation – most notably it was 8in further aft with less of a downward tilt compared with production aircraft – and some associated details.

The coolant radiator was a cylindrical, copper-tubed device with a space in the middle where the cylindrical oil radiator was mounted. The two radiators were separate structures, and the oil radiator could be removed from the coolant radiator.

Mustang Mk I (NA-73)

The production of the Mustang began with a short series of hand-built NA-73 aircraft that were constructed before the full production line was established. The full series-production NA-73 was introduced after around the tenth machine.

Fuselage

Compared with the NA-73X, the production radiator intake mouth was extended forward. It was also lowered slightly and formed a fully enclosed 'tunnel'. This enabled a 'gutter' to be interposed between the intake and the centre-section undersurface, which helped prevent ingestion of turbulent boundary-layer airflow, improving radiator efficiency. As a result, the shape of the radiator scoop fairing section differed markedly from that of the prototype.

The NA-73 radiator intake scoop was hinged, as the NA-73X's had been, for increased cooling. Unlike on the prototype where the entire front part of the scoop opened, the production NA-73's radiator intake was composed of upper fixed and lower hinged 'jaws'. There was also an adjustable exit flap, which enabled air supply to the radiator to be increased when required.

A radiator air scoop deflector was also fitted to NA-73s, to block some of the air from the radiator in certain conditions when the engine was at low power and help prevent the oil over-cooling. This took the form of a flap in front of the scoop intake, which hinged downwards when actuated. The deflector was hydraulically controlled, being deployed when a separate latch was pulled and the adjacent radiator air scoop selector was pushed fully forward (into the position marked 'SHUT').

A formation light was mounted on each side of the fuselage, to illuminate the wings and help with station-keeping in low-light conditions.

Cockpit

Unlike the NA-73X, production NA-73s had a three-part windshield with side panels made of laminated glass. The centre panel sloped aft at around

40° and was backed with 1.5in-thick bulletproof glass. The armoured glass panel was hinged to allow easy cleaning of both sides, and the gunsight also hinged in order to allow the glass to swing freely. A rear-view mirror was installed inside the canopy.

The windscreen could be de-iced using exhaust-heated air on aircraft up to AG615. Subsequently a glycol spray was adopted; with this system, pilots had to take care to drain the de-icing tubes before take-off, or inertia could drive the fluid onto the screen, hampering visibility.

A steel armour plate behind the pilot was supposed to be fitted to the first 100 aircraft, although the first few examples may have arrived without this. (As of July 1941, only the first hundred machines were allocated to ACC which, as it operated in Northern Europe, needed its aircraft to be fitted with armour – at this point, the remaining aircraft were being considered for overseas theatres.) The armour plate comprised two, slightly overlapping, pieces.

Warm and cold air could be directed into the cockpit as required. On aircraft up to AG366, cold air was controlled by a knob on the floor to the left of the pilot's seat. On subsequent aircraft, the pilot simply opened a door in the ventilation shaft to the extent required. Hot air was admitted by turning a knob on the floor to the right of the pilot's seat. (In fact, the Mustang Mk I tended to suffer from an over-hot cockpit due to the radiator casing emerging into the fuselage behind the pilot, particularly in early aircraft.)

Mustang Mk I aircraft were fitted with a welded aluminium alloy seat. The cockpit was illuminated by two swivel lamps, one on each side. All instruments were individually lighted. Controls for all lighting, internal and external, were on switch panels in the cockpit.

Equipment

A P.8 compass was fitted in the UK, as part of the modifications for ACC use, though at least some aircraft were also equipped with the US B.16 compass. (From the 50th aircraft, AG394, a compass was provided under the US Defense Aid Programme.) Early tests remarked that both were 'very inaccurate', but that modification by the Compass Laboratory was in hand.

Radio equipment consisted of an R.3003 IFF set, with either an Army radio or a fighter VHF set. It was originally the RAF's intention that the TR9D VHF set would be fitted, and consequently wiring and junction boxes related to this radio were initially installed. However, in AC aeroplanes, army radio sets were installed instead. These were the '19' sets developed by Pye, the same as those fitted to armoured vehicles and variously described as the WS19, A19 or 19D. (Although described in the plural, they were effectively combined into a single unit.)

Richard Howes of the Pye Telecommunications Historic Collection describes the WS19 sets thus:

> The correct equipment title is 'Sets' not set, as it actually consists of three separate systems. This example is a USA manufactured Mk II model made as part of the Lend-Lease program and includes dual English/Cyrillic legend so that it could be supplied to our new Russian Allies if needed. It consists of power supply, radio transmitter/receiver, aerial tuning variometer, and one control box. A separate microphone and headset would have been used plugged into the control box on top of the set.

A special control unit, the Type 180, allowed the army radio to interface with the pilot's controller.[vi] The WS19 weighed 95lb, only 1lb heavier than the TR1133A VHF set. (The R.3003 set weighed 31lb.)

If the WS19 was not fitted, it could be replaced with a TR9D or TR1133A fighter VHF. On aircraft with the oblique camera fitted behind the rear cockpit glazings, the radios were relocated to a tray in the rear fuselage, beneath the camera.

With the initial set-up fitted to Mustang Mk Is, the IFF aerials extended from the tailplane tips to the side of the fuselage, while the W/T aerial stretched between a mast aft of the cockpit and the tip of the fin. Later, the IFF was replaced on many aircraft with the Mk III, which was indicated by the wire aerials being supplanted by a short dipole beneath the port wing. The wire aerial for the radio was also replaced later in the war by an aerial buried in the mast. (Some of the last aircraft in service may also have had a whip aerial as fitted to all Mustangs with the Malcolm Hood modification.)

ACC aircraft were modified for the tactical reconnaissance role and consequently had a single F.24 camera installed on a shelf behind the pilot's

---

vi According to the Pye Telecom Historic Collection.

head ('Mod 319'). A special mounting enabled the camera's aiming point to be adjusted on the ground. A hole was cut in the glazing on one side or both sides of the rear glazing and a 'cowl' formed a seal between the lens of the camera and the glazing, so the lens was exposed to the air, but airflow could not penetrate into the aircraft.

When the vertical camera in the rear fuselage was developed for US Army aircraft, details of the installation were shared with the RAF, and some Mustang Mk Is and Mk IAs were eventually fitted with this as well. However, in British service there were complaints that the vertical installation was a failure because of 'unavoidable oiling', though plenty of vertical photography seemed to have been carried out with Mustangs.

Wings

The NA-73's wings were similar to those of the NA-73X in most details apart from the installation of armament. An inspection door of 0.040in aluminium alloy sheet was set into the upper surface of the wing tip, for access to the gun camera.

The fuel capacity of early Mustang Mk Is as stated in the pilot's notes was 130 (imperial) gallons, 10 gallons less than the stated capacity.[2] (When AG351 was assessed at the A&AEE, both its fuel tanks were found to be marked 70gal, but the starboard tank was measured as containing only 60) – a standpipe in the port tank provided an emergency reserve supply in the event of leaks or damage to the fuel system.

Navigation lamps were provided on the upper and lower surface of the main plane tips. Landing lamps were mounted at the leading edge of each main plane.

Undercarriage

Photographs of AG345 show a dust cover fitted over the outer face of the wheel hub resembling a plain hub. Most NA-73s had uncovered ten-spoked alloy wheels.

A separate 'emergency' knob opened a bypass valve which allowed the undercarriage and fairing doors to open under their own weight. The undercarriage lever had an 'emergency down' position which pushed the lockpins home if selecting 'down' had not locked the undercarriage.

Armament

The Mustang Mk I was armed with eight guns. These consisted of four 0.30in MG40 Colt Browning machine guns in the wings and four 0.50in Colt Browning MG53-2 machine guns, two of which were mounted in the chin position, and two in the wings (the inboard gun).

Early aircraft had fairings fitted to the nose guns where the barrels emerged from the cowling, but these were found to be unnecessary and were deleted. Aircraft up to at least AG422 were delivered with fairings, but by the end of NA-73 production they were no longer included.

There were numerous combinations of both standard and overload condition listed in contemporary documentation, and recommended loads varied considerably:

Condition	Rounds per gun			
	Chin 0.50in	Wing 0.50in	Inboard 0.30in	Outboard 0.30in
Standard (pilot's notes early)[3]	300 rounds (Correct 200 rounds)[vii]	300 rounds	932 rounds	814 rounds
Standard (pilot's notes late)[4]	200 rounds	200 rounds	1,000 rounds	1,000 rounds
Standard 'Load A' (A&AEE)[5]	200 rounds	200 rounds	1,000 rounds	1,000 rounds
Overload 'Load B' (A&AEE)	200 rounds	306 rounds	1,432 rounds	1,314 rounds
Standard (AFDU)[6]	200 rounds	300 rounds	900 rounds	800 rounds
Standard (Mustang Mk I data card F3R engine)[7]	200 rounds	300 rounds	500 rounds	500 rounds

---

vii This earlier version of AP2025 suggests 300 rounds for each nose gun, but it is believed this was a typographical error, as all other sources and photographs of the ammunition boxes indicate that no more than 200 rounds per nose gun could be carried.

Naturally, operational squadrons may have found their own ideal ammunition load. A report by Northwest African Tactical Air Forces suggested that ACC Mustangs were typically equipped with 'a total of 1000 rounds for the .50 cal. guns and a total of 3492 rounds for the .30 cal. guns'.[8] This is consistent with 200 rounds for the nose 0.50in guns, 300 rounds for the wing 0.50in guns and an average of 873 rounds for each of the 0.30in guns (932 for outboard guns and 814 for inboard, as per the earlier pilot's notes).

All guns could be harmonised by armourers to a set pattern in a period of 30 minutes.

A selector, on the port side of the instrument panel, enabled selection of all the guns to be fired at once, or just the fuselage or wing guns, through a system of electrical solenoids.

The guns could be heated by means of Stewart-Warner 789F heater units, via a controller on the port instrument panel.

The fuselage guns could be charged by the pilot, using handles on either side of the instrument panel. The charging handles could be used to safety-lock, load and even cool the guns.

Gun aiming was achieved with the aid of a standard ST-IA pilot's reflector gunsight (the British export version of the US N-3A gunsight), although the Mustang Mk I pilot's notes remark that some aircraft had been fitted with a periscopic sight (for 'over the nose' deflection firing). The factory-fitted gunsight glasses were generally replaced with improved items in British service.

An auxiliary ring-and-bead gunsight could be installed by the pilot if the reflector sight failed – the ring part of the sight was secured by clips under the instrument panel shield, and could be fitted into a bracket on the underside of the upper windscreen frame when required. Photographs of some USAAF F-6 Mustangs suggest that this may have been left permanently in place by some pilots, at least in reconnaissance squadrons.

A Fairchild W7B or G45 cine gun camera was mounted in the outer port wing. The Fairchild camera worked by clockwork.

Powerplant and Related
The production NA-73 had the same engine model as the NA-73X, but as it had been repositioned slightly, led to a longer nose with a subtly

different shape to that of the prototype. This set the 'definitive' shape for all production Allison Mustangs.

Some aircraft had a Claudel Hobson automatic boost control fitted. When this was the case, all-out level boost was obtained with the throttle lever fully forward. Despite the name, the control was not fully automatic – when climbing, the pilot was required to advance the throttle with increasing height to maintain boost. Essentially, the device was intended to prevent the boost from increasing beyond permissible levels, though in fact ACC disconnected the boost control at some point during 1942 to provide greater power at low altitude. It was claimed that this did not adversely affect the engine's reliability (see Chapter 4).

The engine was supplied with fuel-air mixture via a Bendix-Stromberg injection carburettor. The pilot's control was a four-position selector with automatic rich and automatic lean settings, a manual full-rich setting for emergencies if the automatic control failed to work and an idle cut-off setting to stop the engine.

A fuel booster pump was provided for situations when a greater supply of fuel was required. Initially this was fully manual, but Mod 344 linked the booster pump's operation to the propeller pitch control, although it could still be switched on manually if required.

In common with American practice, exhaust stubs were supplied by the airframe manufacturer rather than the engine manufacturer. ACC required flame-damping exhaust stubs to be fitted, though early aircraft were fitted with plain, round ejector-style stubs. Subsequent NA-73s were fitted with a fishtail stub of NAA design, although this type of stub was found to have insufficient flame-damping qualities for night flying, and Kittyhawk stubs were preferred (see Chapter 2). Where Kittyhawk stubs were not available, the NAA stubs were sometimes flattened by hand to improve their flame-damping qualities. As a result, NA-73s carried a range of different exhaust stubs and there does not appear to have been a 'standard' item, in early service at least.

The short scoop design of the NA-73X and early production NA-73s was found to starve the engine of air under certain circumstances, so these aircraft were later rebuilt with a longer scoop which extended forward to the spinner backplate. (All subsequent Mustangs up to the introduction of the Merlin engine were fitted with the longer scoop, though detail design of the intake and the upper cowling fairing changed between sub-types.)

No dust/sand filter could be fitted to the NA-73's air intake, as delivered (although NA-83-standard cowling panels with provision for filters may have later been available as an aftermarket accessory to enable the RAF to modify NA-73s if required). The NA-73 intake featured a spring-loaded door to admit warm air from the engine exhaust to the carburettor if the intake began to ice up.

Systems

The NA-73's hydraulic system operated in an unusual fashion. A knob on the port side of the cockpit had to be depressed to call on the hydraulic system for pressure. The hydraulic pump operated continually, under normal circumstances simply circulating the fluid around the system without pressure. When the knob was depressed, however, a valve closed, stopping the flow and allowing hydraulic pressure to build up. This provided around two minutes of pressure with which to operate any of the systems which used hydraulic power (undercarriage and fairing doors, flaps, radiator air scoop and air scoop deflector). The pressure would continue to build until 1,000lb per square inch was reached, after around two minutes, at which point the relief valve would open, the knob would have returned to its original position, and the fluid would begin to circulate again. The hydraulic pressure gauge only registered when the hydraulic system was in use.[9]

Electrical systems were powered by an Eclipse 30 volt 50 amp engine-driven generator, with a control unit, which limited the supply to 28.5 volts.

XP-51 (NA-73)

The fourth and tenth production airframes[viii] were earmarked for evaluation by the US Army, and designated XP-51. As such, they were similar in most respects to the RAF's Mustang Mk I aircraft. They were, however, fitted with American GFE – US radios and other items.

---

viii The place in the production line occupied by the two XP-51s is well known, but there has been considerable confusion among Mustang historians over whether they were allocated the fourth and tenth RAF serials, some other RAF serials, or no serials at all before they were pulled from the production line. AG348, the fourth aircraft in the RAF's sequence, was prepared in RAF colours and shipped to the UK, later being one of the aircraft issued to the Soviet Union, so this cannot be the same aircraft as 41-038. It is the opinion of the author that no RAF serials were ever applied to the two XP-51s, as it was known from the beginning both by the RAF and NAA that they would be issued to the USAAF, though evidence is hazy around this issue.

Armament

The second XP-51 was fitted with experimental Bendix automatic-hydraulic gun-charging apparatus, which was of interest to the AAF at the time. (The first aircraft was delivered only with provision for gun charging to be installed.) The two XP-51s were among the few aircraft to have nose gun fairings.

Powerplant and Related

The engine and propeller were provided as GFE – in fact, the engine installed in the first XP-51 was the same one that had been in the NA-73X until removed for repair following the accident.[10]

In common with RAF NA-73s, the XP-51s had round ejector exhaust stubs when delivered.

The propeller fitted was a government-furnished Curtiss Electric C-5315S-D8, as with early NA-73s.

Equipment

As delivered, at least the first XP-51 lacked certain items of equipment that had been specified by the Army. This included the radio. An SCR-283 command set, with pilot controls and throat microphone had been specified and was probably later fitted. A hook for a T-17 radio microphone was added to the specification before delivery. According to the specification, no antenna for the radio was installed, though photographs of 41-038 and 41-039 shortly after delivery show a mast and aerial installed.

The gunsight installed was an N-2A optical gunsight, though the specification had originally called for an N3 sight.

Standard Air Corps switches were fitted, except where specified.

The pilot's seat could accommodate a seat-type parachute, and was fitted with the standard US B-11 safety belt (apparently no shoulder harness was specified).

Desert equipment and provision for a hatchet to damage the aircraft in the event of capture were removed from the specification.

Wings

One landing light was placed in each outer panel leading edge, and standard US running lights were fitted in the wing tips. In most respects, lighting was similar to production NA-73s.

New aileron and flap bracket bolts were installed before the first aircraft was flown by the Army, as NAA had discovered defects in the original kind used. (This modification was being applied to production aircraft.)

Upon completion of the AAF evaluation, the first XP-51 (41-038) was allocated to NACA for aerodynamic research (41-039 also eventually went to NACA). Part of this was to assess different forms of aileron to improve roll rate. NACA modified the ailerons with a 'bevelled' surface over the original 'cusped' items (which had concave outer surfaces), and the aircraft retained non-standard ailerons for the rest of its active career.

The XP-51s carried a variety of aerodynamic testing equipment such as large pitot probes and a 'wake rake' during their lengthy careers at NACA.

Mustang Mk I (NA-83)

The NA-83 was originally intended to be a continuation of the original 320 Mustang Mk Is, for a follow-on order of 300 aircraft. This would incorporate a number of the improvements either desired by the RAF or put forward by NAA. As mentioned in Chapter 1, NA numbers were used as both designations for models and as 'charge numbers' to relate a particular specification for an aircraft to the reality on the production line. It made sense to introduce modifications and improvements when a new order was placed for administrative and practical reasons, and consequently it made sense to introduce a new NA number to cover the revised specification.

The RAF originally hoped that for the follow-on order, the Mustang's armament could be changed to four 20mm cannon. In the end, though, the cannon were not available due to delays in the US manufacturing programme, and the armament remained the same as the NA-73. Consequently the NA-83 was essentially a slight refinement of the earlier version, and after some discussion (see Chapter 2), the Air Ministry decided that the NA-83 would receive no change of designation in RAF service.

Perhaps the most substantial refinement of the NA-83 was the 'tropicalisation' of the aircraft, with provision for equipment that would allow use in hot and dusty climates such as North Africa or the Middle East. This reflected changing priorities in Britain; though ultimately the NA-83s would be used in the same manner as the NA-73s.

In other respects, minor improvements were made to the wing, cockpit and equipment to improve performance or make the aircraft more 'user friendly'.

Wings

A revised stringer layout was introduced on the lower surface of the main planes. The inspection door and leading-edge window in the port wing tip was retained on at least some aircraft even though the camera was no longer installed there (see page 251). An additional fairing at the wing flap root was introduced (Mod 42).

Powerplant and Related

The NA-83 used the same V-1710-39 that the NA-73 did, although some refinements to the installation were made.

Arguably the most significant of these was the redesigned carburettor scoop, with provision for fitting a Vokes filter. The new cowling can be recognised by the trunking, when viewed from above, having an elongated rhomboid shape, wider in the middle, compared with that of the NA-73, which was parallel-sided for most of its length. If the filter was required it had to be installed on the ground, and there was no bypass other than the automatic de-icing intake (if the main intake scoop choked, a spring-loaded door behind the exhaust stubs would open by suction ensuring the air supply was maintained). Baffles could be installed in place of the filter if the latter was not required. This arrangement would remain the same for the Mustang Mk IA/P-51 and the A-36A.

The radiator scoop was also redesigned slightly, and a combined oil and coolant radiator from a different manufacturer, Harrison, was fitted in place of the NA-73's Air Research radiator. The new radiator was similar in most respects to the previously used item and retained the same part number (73-46050 – note that the part number retained the '73' prefix indicating that it effectively replaced the earlier type and could be fitted to the NA-73 and NA-83 alike). The oil radiator was thermostatically controlled, unlike that of the NA-73, shutting off some areas of the radiator when the oil fell below a certain temperature. As cooling was now adequate, with no difficulties with over cooling, the radiator intake deflector flap was deleted. However, the coolant radiator was evidently unsatisfactory in some respects, as some NA-83s had their radiators re-tubed on arrival in the UK. Indeed, ACC requested that all its NA-83s receive this modification, while stating that it was unnecessary in the case of NA-73s.[11]

A baffle was introduced in the interior of the aircraft to prevent warmth from the radiator casing overheating the cockpit.

Systems

The hydraulic system worked in a more straightforward manner on NA-83 and subsequent aircraft – a hydraulic accumulator was installed which meant that pressure was immediately available on selecting any of the required functions.

The formation lights (also referred to as 'wing flood lights') were deleted (Mod 50).

Undercarriage

The procedure for emergency lowering of the undercarriage was slightly different on NA-83 aircraft, which did not have an 'emergency down' position on the undercarriage lever. The handpump had to be used if the wheels failed to lower under their own weight, and the manual actuation of the lockpins was deleted.

Armament

The gun camera was changed to an N-1 type, and was moved from the wing to the lower cowling beneath the propeller, behind a clear window ('Mod 38').

Mustang Mk IA (NA-91)

The NA-91 introduced further changes adding to the general, ongoing refinement of the type, the most substantial of which was in the armament.

Armament

Four 20mm Hispano cannon (licensed in the US by Colt as the M1 and later the AN/M2) supplanted the mixed-calibre machine guns in the wing gun bays. Nose guns were deleted, though the F3R engine continued to include synchronisation gears. The previous four-piece lower cowling was consequently changed to a two-piece item, which was not pierced for machine guns.

As with earlier aircraft, it was possible for the pilot to select the guns he intended to fire. The control column had both a button and a trigger – the trigger alone operated the inboard cannon only, while depressing both the button and the trigger fired both sets at once. (Depressing the button by itself did not fire any of the guns, but if the inboard guns' ammunition had been used up, the outer guns could be fired by the same procedure as for firing all four guns). In order to fire any of the guns, the 'safety' switch on the forward switch panel had to be on.

Wings

The wings of the NA-91 were reinforced with auxiliary beams at the aft end of the cannon bay and in the leading edge, forward of the cannon bay. The arrangement of ribs differed from preceding (and succeeding) aircraft. A number of ribs in the central portion of each mainplane were divided between the front spar and the additional beam assembly to make space for the cannon bay and significantly deeper ammunition tray required by the 20mm cannon shell belts.

In addition, the wing tip inspection door was deleted (as the gun camera was no longer located there), and the wing tip was reinforced with an additional two stringers on the lower surface.

Powerplant and Related

The basic engine was the same V-1710-39 as fitted to the Mustang Mk I. However, the Claudel Hobson boost control was replaced with a slightly more sophisticated Delco Remy unit. This was fully automatic and could maintain any selected boost up to full throttle.

A stop was provided at the take-off position, which was held in place by a wire. When war emergency power was required, the pilot pushed the throttle lever against the stop until the wire broke. The stop remained in the 'war emergency' setting until reset by groundcrew, although the boost control would still regulate the boost selected by throttle position.

The engine also gained a manually operated warm-air intake to supplement the automatic intake that had been in place on earlier aircraft. A control twist-handle was located on the top-left corner of the instrument panel.

A new kind of flared, semi-fishtail exhaust stub was introduced on the NA-91, replacing the round ejector stubs fitted to earlier models. This type of stub was fitted as standard to all subsequent Allison Mustangs, though they were sometimes modified or replaced with Kittyhawk stubs to improve flame-damping qualities (see Chapter 2).

P-51/F-6A (NA-91)

Although all NA-91s were technically designated P-51s, only the US Army routinely referred to its aircraft as such. Most were converted to P-51-2 (reconnaissance) standard, which was later given the designation F-6A though in use they were generally referred to as 'P-51s'.[ix]

The US Army retained 57 of the 200 NA-91s ordered by the RAF and converted most of those aircraft to tactical reconnaissance (P-51-2/F-6A) specification. A few were retained for experimental and evaluation purposes – for example, NAA retained the second production machine, 41-37321, to help develop the P-51A, and 41-37426 was transferred to the US Navy for evaluation. Two aircraft were later modified by NAA as XP-51Bs. The decision to retain the 57 aircraft was made relatively early in the manufacturing of that series, to the extent that US aircraft had American equipment and colour schemes applied as they were produced, rather than being converted from RAF specification after completion, as happened with some other types.

Nevertheless, in most respects, the US P-51s were similar to their RAF counterparts. Equipment and some systems were the main areas of difference.

Armament

There were minor changes to the armament compared to the RAF version of the aircraft. The most significant was that the system for selective firing was deleted and the trigger simply fired all four guns simultaneously. The now redundant stick top button was repurposed to operate the camera on aircraft modified to reconnaissance status.

The gunsight was an ST-1A unit as on RAF aircraft, with an auxiliary ring-and-bead sight. It was generally fitted with a pad to protect the pilot's head in the event of a crash landing.

Equipment

US Army P-51s/F-6As were fitted either with the SCR-274 or SCR-522 'command' radio sets. The SCR 274N (Signal Corps Radio 274 Navy) was

---

ix The repair instructions manual does not refer to the F-6A (the F-6B, C, D and K are covered) but does refer to the P-51, and logbooks from tactical reconnaissance pilots tend to use the designation P-51 rather than F-6A.

required by the Close Air Support Directorate, so it was likely that most F-6As in theatre were fitted with this type of equipment.

The SCR-274N system was based on a Navy unit and was unusual in being a set of modular radios, rather than a single radio set using complicated band-switching. It was a short-range set consisting of two transmitters and three receivers, along with the necessary accessories. (Unlike the RAF's ACC, which needed a special army radio, US Army aircraft could use their standard aircraft units for communicating with army units. This was of great use for close support and tactical reconnaissance.)

The SCR-522 was essentially a US-produced version of the British TR1143 VHF wireless set. Although, in common with most licence-built equipment, the American version differed in numerous respects from its British counterpart. However, the unit was introduced specifically to allow interoperability and interchangeability with British forces and equipment, so the plugs and connectors matched British standards, and the major units were interchangeable with British-built equivalents, even though the internals differed.

The oblique camera installation trialled at Wright Field in 1942. A later version was developed that did not project outside the line of the fuselage and therefore did not require a bulged glazing. (Dana Bell)

The SCR-522 consisted of a transmitter and receiver housed in a single box, with a power supply and control box. The SCR-522 had four crystal-controlled channels, and was rather more compact than the SCR-274N. The unit was located on a stationary shelf aft of the battery, and the control box was mounted on a bracket aft of the right-hand switch panel in the cockpit.

Those P-51s converted to reconnaissance status had provision for two K-24 cameras – one variable-position vertical or oblique camera in the lower rear fuselage behind the radiator scoop, and one oblique camera behind the pilot's head.

For the latter camera, a different arrangement to RAF aircraft was developed. The version adopted for operational use required the camera to be installed offset to port, as the larger SCR-274N radio did not allow room in the centre of the shelf. In fact, the camera projected some way outside the normal line of the exterior glazing. For this reason, a clear plexiglass blister replaced the usual glazing. Unlike the RAF arrangement, the camera did not penetrate to the exterior of the aircraft, but shot its photographs through a plate glass insert in the glazing.

P-51 rear camera installation. (Dana Bell)

P-51 rear camera mount, demonstrating how it could be angled to change from vertical orientation to inclined aft. (Dana Bell)

The rear fuselage camera was mounted in a remotely adjustable frame, and shot through a plate-glass insert in the outer skin. It could photograph directly downwards, or angle to the rear. (The camera's angle in the lateral plane was fixed.) If the rear camera was operating in the oblique mode, its photographs would overlap with those of the front camera by approximately 3°. Either camera could be operated alone, or both together.

A camera switch box was fitted on the upper right corner of the pilot's instrument panel. The period of time between photographs could be adjusted using an 'intervalometer' dial on the floor of the cockpit. The pilot took photographs by pressing or holding down a thumb button on the top of the control stick.

A door was cut into the rear fuselage to allow camera cartridges to be installed, removed and replaced.

Cockpit
Windscreen de-icing reverted to a warm-air supply, unlike RAF aircraft which retained a glycol spray.

The pilot's seat was fitted with a B-11 safety belt and 'standard AAF shoulder harness'.

A-36A (NA-97)
The A-36A was a dedicated dive-bomber variant of the basic Mustang, which nevertheless retained much of the earlier aircraft's air-to-air and tactical reconnaissance capability. Indeed, the pilot's flight operating instructions

noted that the 'acrobatic qualities of this airplane are exceptional, and the lateral control is excellent at all speeds.'

Fuselage

Three recognition lights of red, green and amber, which could be operated separately, were installed in the underside of the belly scoop.

Powerplant and Related

The radiator was revised, though largely similar to the item used on the NA-73 to NA-91. It remained a cylindrical structure, but with a gap in the top of the coolant radiator to provide space for the oil cooler valve on the oil radiator. The frontal area of the oil radiator was reduced to 176 square inches, and the structure was divided into four compartments by way of hollow baffles.

The radiator intake scoop was redesigned significantly from earlier aircraft, having a non-adjustable opening, which was shown in tests in England to be worth about 8mph. The exit scoop could still be opened to draw more cooling air through the radiator tunnel. This was moved by a hydraulic strut, controlled manually by the pilot with a control handle at the aft end of the control pedestal, left of the pilot's seat.

A-36A   P-51A

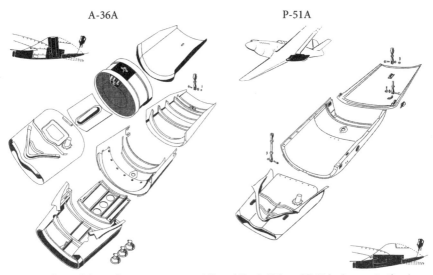

A comparison of the radiator scoop assemblies of the A-36A and P-51A, demonstrating how the latter's was simplified and streamlined.

An automatic relief valve was fitted to permit the oil to bypass the oil cooler if it reached excessive pressure from over cooling.

On aircraft from 42-83663 to 42-83857, carburettor anti-icing was provided from a reservoir located behind and below the pilot's seat and operated with a handpump to the left of the pilot's seat. On 42-83804 and subsequent aircraft, the tank was a temporary unit located in the right wing ammunition box, and powered by an electric pump.[x]

The A-36A could be fitted with either the V-1710-39 (from the P-51) or the V-1710-81 (from the P-51A) if required, though various changes to components and systems were necessary to effect the change. These were set out in the aircraft's erection and maintenance manual.[12]

Wings

Dive brakes were installed outboard of the gun bays, immediately aft of the ammunition feed trays. These were slatted flaps of built-up sheet-metal construction which folded out from the upper and lower surface of each wing to create drag without lift. The upper brake was hinged aft while the lower flap was hinged forward, so as to cancel out air loads during actuation. Both upper and lower brakes were 35in long and had a 90° range of movement. When folded they formed part of the wing surface.

The A-36's wing derived more from that of the Mustang Mk I (NA-83) rather than the preceding Mk IA/P-51 (NA-91). The internal structure and external skinning returned to a form more closely resembling that of the earlier aircraft. Differences chiefly centred around the middle of each plane where the armament bays and dive brakes were located. The arrangement of ammunition compartment reinforcement webs was altered from that of the Mustang Mk I by replacing the two intermediate half-webs with a single full-height web perforated with square lightening holes. The dive brakes folded partially over the ammunition trays, and consequently they had to be opened to gain access to the tray. (For this reason, the suggestion that A-36s often had their dive brakes wired shut in service cannot be correct.)

---

x The serial range is as set out in the A-36 pilot's notes, which does not make clear why there is an apparent overlap.

There were less substantial changes to the arrangement of stringers in the outer panels, setting a pattern that would not be altered until the P-51D was introduced. The wing tips reverted to the earlier design with just a single stringer in the lower surface. (This was retained until the P-51D, which introduced four stringers in the lower surface.)

Two landing lights were located in the leading edge of the left wing.

The pitot tube was relocated from the underside of the starboard wing to a long probe mounted on the wing tip leading edge.

Armament

The A-36A's gun armament consisted entirely of 0.50in Brownings, with four in the wings and a further two in the nose. (An all-0.50in arrangement may have been considered by NAA before the US Army had ordered any Mustangs.) The guns were aligned, the nose guns vertically and the wing guns vertically and laterally, to converge with the line of the gunsight at 300 yards distance.

Unlike the earlier RAF-commissioned versions of the aircraft, there were no means to select which guns could be fired – all six would fire simultaneously when the trigger on the control column was depressed. The nose guns could be manually charged by the pilot, while the wing guns were charged on the ground and could not be recharged in the air. It was recommended that the fuselage guns were not operated when the engine was running at less than 1,000rpm or more than 3,000rpm.

The N-1 gun camera was mounted between the fuselage guns in the chin position, sighting through a small plastic window.

Detachable aerodynamic bomb racks were fitted beneath each wing, which enabled the A-36A to carry two 100lb, 250lb, 300lb or 500lb bombs.[xi] A 75-gallon (62.5-imperial gallon) external drop tank for long-range scouting or combat missions could be carried in place of a bomb. Alternatively, a 150-gallon (125-imperial gallon) ferry tank beneath each wing extended the ferry range to over 2,940 miles. (It is

---

xi Oddly, official documentation varies with regard to the stated bomb-load of the A-36A. The maintenance and erection manual (October 1944 edition) refers to '100-, 300- or 500-pound bombs, depth charges or chemical tanks' while the pilot's notes (June 1944 edition) refers to 'one 250-, 300-, or 500-pound demolition bomb'.

unclear whether these ferry tanks were ever used operationally.) Both types of tank could be jettisoned.

The bomb shackles introduced on the A-36A, part number 97-63002, would be retained for the P-51A, B and C, and in modified form – part number 97-63002-5 – the P-51D.

Equipment

Radio equipment consisted of a command set, for communication with other aircraft or a ground station, and a so-called 'radar set' might also be fitted – actually an IFF transponder.[xii]

The standard command set was as per the P-51. IFF sets SCR-695, SCR-515 or SCR-535 could also be fitted, though the latter two were somewhat secret pieces of equipment in 1943–44, and very little information was provided for their use and installation in the standard documentation.

The radio equipment was mounted on shelves behind the pilot's cockpit (similar to the F-6A but without the modifications to include camera equipment). The top shelf could slide out for removal and adjustment. The antenna differed from that of earlier aircraft. It incorporated a mast, which was insulated within a fairing for use with the SCR-522. It could not be used with the SCR-274N, so an additional wire antenna was installed and electrically separated by an insulating device on the fuselage. A third aerial antenna could be installed for radar (IFF) equipment. This could take the form of wires extending from the fuselage to the tailplane tips if the SCR 535 was fitted, an AN-95 dipole beneath the starboard wing outer section if the SCR 695 was fitted, or an AN-40 dipole beneath each wing near the root if the SCR 515 was fitted.

Photographs of A-36As in service indicate that on some aircraft, the fairing for the SCR-522 mast was removed.

A pyrotechnic signal recognition device was located aft of the radio compartment with a control to the pilot's right enabling him to select flares of any desired colour.

---

xii It appears that IFF transponders were regarded as 'radar' equipment because ground-based radar could 'interrogate' the aircraft-based transponder to ascertain if it was friendly.

Cockpit

The cockpit canopy was the same as previous variants, although photographs indicate that some aircraft received 'clear view' panels in the left-forward glazing. These were not fitted at the factory, and appear to be field modifications. On some aircraft, they resemble the type fitted as standard to P-51A aircraft, while others were of a somewhat different shape.

The pilot's seat was made of plywood and accommodated a seat-type parachute. It was fitted with a type B-11 safety belt and type 41G8725 shoulder harness

A 'relief tube' was fitted for the pilot, exiting through an aluminium scoop beneath the rudder.

P-51A/F-6B (NA-99)

The P-51A once again incorporated a number of improvements over its predecessors. In fact, it had some of the most substantial changes of any aircraft in the Allison Mustang family, notwithstanding the dive brakes fitted to the A-36A. For the first time, the structure of the fuselage was revised, and more substantive alterations took place to the radiator and fairing than the minor tinkering carried out with previous variants.

The aircraft was produced in three blocks – the P-51A-1, A-5 and A-10. There were slight differences between aircraft of different blocks and even some dispute as to what constituted a 'block'; some documents refer to an additional A-2 block (see Chapter 4), which would have been field-upgraded A-1 aircraft.

Fuselage

The P-51A had moderate redesigns to its structure and skinning. For example, the stringer on the spine was extended further aft to frame station 232, a channel section extended the upper longeron back to the same point, and the radio shelf was longer. The small fuselage access hatch was moved from the spine to the fuselage side. The framing that supported the radiator scoop housing was also revised and reinforced.

A change of radiator (see page 262) was accompanied by a redesign of the lower radiator air scoop and exit flap. The structure was simplified, and the number of parts was reduced from earlier aircraft. It also resulted in an aerodynamically cleaner, shallower scoop fairing. As with the A-36A, the intake was non-adjustable but a rear flap could be opened to draw more air through. This flap was wider than that of previous aircraft, and incorporated a section of the outer skin almost to the full width of the housing.

Other changes were minor, such as a slightly thinner armour and a thinner gauge of aluminium being used for the fuselage shelves – 0.064in rather than 0.081in, possibly reflecting a drive to shave as much weight off as possible.

Wings

The wing structure was largely identical to that of the A-36A. The dive brakes were deleted, and front ammunition compartment web removed, leaving just two webs to support this space.

One landing light was deleted, leaving one sealed-beam lamp in the leading edge of the left wing.

The pitot tube was restored to a position beneath the starboard wing where it had been on the NA-73 to 91. The pitot used was a Kollsman D-2 pitot static head.

Powerplant and Related

The P-51A used a unique radiator design in the Mustang series. Instead of the cylindrical item used on earlier models, the P-51A radiator was a truncated U-shape, shallower and wider than previous radiators. It fitted, horseshoe-fashion, around the oil cooler (which remained cylindrical). A shutter assembly was attached to the oil radiator.[xiii]

The P-51A had the capacity for propeller de-icing, albeit only during ferry flights. An electric pump supplied fluid from a tank temporarily installed in the left-rear ammunition box to feed shoes on the propeller.

Armament

The armament changed again, by deletion of the nose guns. The wing guns were similar to those of the A-36A: four free-firing belt-fed 0.50in machine

---

xiii The new radiator was not a requirement of the V-1710-81, as this engine could be fitted to the A-36 (according to the *Erection and Maintenance Instructions for Army Model A-36A Airplane*, pp. 142–3). It was most likely introduced for aerodynamic benefits, though may have been developed with the single-stage Merlin in mind.

guns, two in each wing, with a normal load of 275 rounds per gun. (The maximum ammunition load was 280 rounds in each rear ammunition compartment and 350 rounds in the front compartments.) Like the P-51, the P-51A's guns could only be charged on the ground.

The guns were aimed by an improved N3B optical electric type gunsight with ring and dot reticule, and the gun camera changed yet again. On the P-51A this was an N1 or AN-N4 gunsight aiming-point camera fitted in the left wing leading-edge inboard of the gun bay, and harmonised at 300 yards according to the pilot's instruction manual (the USAAF School of Applied Tactics, Orlando, Florida, indicated the camera on the P-51A-10 tested there was harmonised at 400 yards). Unlike previous installations, this finally allowed clear gun camera pictures without excessive vibration or the likelihood of the lens being obscured by oil from the propeller. The camera could be operated with the guns, or independently. A switch panel on the lower left side of the instrument panel allowed the pilot to select guns, gun camera and gun heating as required.

Detachable bomb shackles were fitted under each wing, of the same type as the A-36A, and could carry the same range of stores.

Equipment

The P-51A could be fitted with the same two command radio sets as the P-51 and A-36A, but unlike those aircraft, the standard set was the SCR-522 rather than the SCR-274N, which became the alternative set. The IFF could be an SCR-535 unit, an SCR 515 or an SCR 695 – initially, the former of these was listed as standard, but the September 1944 edition of the pilot's operating instructions indicated that by that time the usual combination was for an SCR-522 radio and SCR-695 IFF.

The SCR-522 aerial was a short post above the radio compartment. An aerodynamically profiled, insulated mast fitted over this to carry the wire antenna of the SCR-274N. The SCR-695 IFF aerial was an AN-95 dipole beneath the port wing, unlike the wire aerial used for the SCR-535. If the SCR-515 was fitted, an AN-80 dipole was fitted beneath each wing.

To improve the operational efficiency of the SCR-522, a programme of replacing the factory-installed antenna (NAA part 99-71028) with the AN-104A mast was undertaken from June 1944. The existing masts were only replaced when they were found to be defective, so it is not apparent how many aircraft's masts were replaced before the P-51A was retired.

The internal installation of both radio sets varied slightly from those of the A-36A.

The pyrotechnic system varied from that of the A-36A. Instead of the flare launcher in the rear fuselage, the P-51A's was an M-8 flare pistol located in the cockpit. The pilot loaded and fired this manually, fitting it into a mount on the side of the fuselage to the left of the pilot's seat.

Thirty-five P-51As were converted to F-6B standard. This was a similar tactical reconnaissance conversion to the F-6A, with installation for two K-24 cameras. The installation was the same as that developed for the F-6A, with a moveable vertical/oblique camera in the rear fuselage and an oblique camera mounted behind the pilot's head.

Cockpit

A slight improvement was added to the P-51A's canopy in the form of a clear vision panel for aiding visibility while flying in rain, sleet or snow. It took the form of a hinged section in the left-hand glazing of the windscreen. This was made possible by an area of negative pressure at that point of the canopy, which prevented the elements from entering the cockpit when the panel was opened.

A number of F-6Bs were modified with the 'Malcolm Hood' blown, sliding canopy.

Undercarriage

Tailwheel steering was actuated not via a lever, as in earlier aircraft, but by holding the control column back – the column was connected to the tail wheel by means of a cable. If the control column was held forward, the tailwheel was free to castor.

Mustang Mk II

The RAF's Mustang Mk IIs were P-51A aircraft received under Lend-Lease. Because the P-51A was developed to US specifications, and because of the means by which it was acquired, it differed relatively little from its American counterpart.

As opposed to the USAAF, which used the P-51A as a fighter-bomber and escort as well as in the reconnaissance role, the Mustang Mk II was employed exactly as the Mk I was: solely in tactical reconnaissance. Differences from American aircraft chiefly related to equipment.

Equipment

For the most part, the Mustang Mk II used the same radio equipment as the P-51A, such as the SCR-522 command set, which was equivalent to the British TR1143 VHF, and an SCR-695 IFF, which was equivalent to the British Mk III.

This included a BC-966-A (British Type R.3090) receiver and related control panel. The receiver was installed on the upper shelf behind the pilot's seat. A Mk IIIG set could also be fitted.

The Mustang Mk II could be fitted with bomb racks, but although it was tested with bombs and 150-gallon (125-imperial gallon) ferry tanks, it appears never to have used either device operationally, and the bomb racks were never fitted in ACC service.

One or two F.24 cameras were generally fitted to operational aircraft. All AC aircraft had the oblique camera behind the pilot's seat, installed in the UK, while some also had the vertical installation as developed by NAA.

Cockpit

The pilot's seat was the same plywood item fitted to the P-51A and introduced on the A-36A. Although, as with all British Mustangs, it was fitted with a Sutton harness rather than the US belt and shoulder harness.

Wings

A US AN-95 aerial was mounted beneath the starboard wing, 5.17ft from the tip and 1.7ft from the leading edge, for the IFF.

The US underwing recognition lights were deleted on RAF aircraft and the holes in the skin plated over.

Dimensions (Mk I)

	Imperial	Metric
Span	37.03ft (37' 5/16")	11.29m
Length (total)	32.192ft (32' 25/16")	9.81m
Length (not including spinner)	30.026ft (30' 5/16")	9.15m
Root chord	8.666 ft (8' 8")	2.64m
Tip chord	4.166ft (4' 2")	1.27m
Mean aerodynamic chord	6.633ft (6' 73/5")	2.02m
Aileron travel	10°	
Undercarriage track	11.833ft (11' 10")	3.61m
Main wheel diameter	2.25 ft/27in (2' 3")	0.69m
Tail wheel diameter	12.416in (125/8")	0.32m
Elevator travel up	30°	
Elevator travel down	20°	
Rudder travel	60°	
Flap travel	50°	
Propeller diameter NA-73	10.5ft (10' 6")	3.2m
NA-83/91/97/99	10.75ft (10' 9")	3.28m
Height (at rest)	12.666ft (12' 8")	3.86m
Wing incidence	1°	
Wing dihedral	5°	
Wing area	233.19ft^2	71.08m^2
Tailplane span	13.177ft (13' 21/8")	4.02m
Tailplane incidence	2°	

Appendix 2

Mustang Colours

Camouflage Colours and Patterns

RAF

RAF Mustangs were initially camouflaged at the factory, though AG345 was rolled out in an unpainted condition before receiving its proper finish. NAA applied the camouflage, national markings and serial. Codes and other markings were applied locally.

The camouflage pattern applied by NAA was the RAF's Temperate Land Scheme in American paints, which were equivalent to the British colours, as follows:

Du Pont 71-013 Dark Green
Du Pont 71-021 Sky Type S Gray
Du Pont 71-035 Dark Earth

(These colours each differed slightly from the approved British colours but represented the closest match.) The camouflage pattern was a disruptive scheme in MAP-approved variations. This colour scheme was applied to all Mustang Mk Is and Mk IAs. Even though the green and brown camouflage was superseded for UK-based fighters in August 1941, NAA continued to paint Mustangs in these colours until the Mk IV appeared (meaning most had to be repainted on arrival in the UK).

After the RAF's scheme for day fighters changed from the Temperate Land Scheme to the Day Fighter Scheme, which was put into effect on 15 August 1941, Mustangs in RAF service were gradually repainted to conform to the new regulations. The new colour scheme was for a Dark Green and Ocean Grey disruptive pattern, over Medium Sea Grey undersides. This process took a long time, and some Mustangs appear to have retained the green/brown/Sky camouflage for some time after the new scheme was introduced.

When Mustangs arrived in the UK, it was generally the case that they would be passed to a modification centre to be brought up to the required standard. This included modifications to fit the aircraft for AC work and rectification of any unsatisfactory features. For the most part, aircraft were also repainted in the appropriate British colours at this time, although this was not necessarily the case for NA-73s. Furthermore, in early 1942 a number of aircraft were passed to squadrons and 41 OTU in an unmodified state. This may account for the relatively high number of Mustangs retaining the Temperate Land Scheme after August 1941.

Over a period of time, aircraft already in service were repainted in the Day Fighter Scheme. An approximation of Ocean Grey for application by squadrons and maintenance units was developed as a mix of Medium Sea Grey and Night (black) paints, and in some cases units had to improvise. Naturally, there is considerable variation in the tone of the grey applied to Mustangs repainted during this period, in many cases seeming somewhat darker than Ocean Grey 'proper'. Where paint was created at a local level, particularly where it does not match the approved tone, it has become retrospectively referred to as 'Mixed Grey'. (Several photographs of II (AC) Squadron aircraft in 1942 show distinctly dark shades of grey, for example.) After this period, colours generally became more standardised.

While the process of repainting NA-73 Mk I aircraft in service was gradual, NA-83 Mk Is, Mk IAs and Mk IIs were generally stripped and repainted before being issued to operational units.

US Army

The P-51s taken over from British orders were painted in US colours at the NAA factory. These consisted of Olive Drab upper surfaces and Neutral Gray undersides. All subsequent A-36s and P-51As were painted in a similar scheme.

Aircraft based in the US were in some cases stripped of their camouflage paint and appeared in a natural metal/silver livery.

National Identification Markings

RAF

Initially, roundels applied at the factory were of the pre-1942 type. On the Mustang, these comprised an approximately 30in Type A1[i] roundel on the fuselage, an approximately 48in Type B roundel on the upper wing surface and an approximately 40in Type A roundel on the lower wing surface, using the 'Dull' blue and red shades introduced in the late 1930s. A 24in x 24in Type A fin flash was applied to the fin. All Mustang Mk I and Mk IA aircraft were delivered with these markings applied. As applied at the factory, paint colours were as follows:

DuPont 71-001 White
DuPont 71-007 Dull Red
DuPont 71-010 Yellow
DuPont 71-012 Dull Blue

When aircraft were repainted after arrival in the UK, the fin flash was altered to the standard 24in x 27in, in British colours.

Later, these markings were changed to the 'Type C' roundels first introduced in July 1942. Mustang Mk IIs left the factory with the new national markings, while Mk Is and Mk IAs only received them in the UK. The markings consisted of a 36in Type C1 roundel on the fuselage, 40in Type B on the upper wings and 32in Type C roundels on the lower wings, with a 24in Type C fin flash. Where re-applied in the UK, markings were painted in British MAP colours:

Identification Blue (Dull)
Identification Red (Dull)
Identification Yellow
White

---

i The use of lettered and numbered roundels was an unofficial system devised by Bruce Robertson and introduced in *Aircraft Camouflage & Markings 1907–1954*, Harleyford, 1954. It is used here for convenience.

While in the US, British roundels were generally replaced with American cocardes. Photographs of stateside Mustangs bound for the RAF tend to show American national markings, apart from those photographed specifically for publicity purposes related to the aircraft's RAF service – for example, the sequence of air-to-air photographs of AG345 taken in November 1941. There are variations in individual cases, and it is not clear if there was a concrete policy to follow. For example, the well-known image of Mk I NA-83 AL958 in flight shows the aircraft with its RAF serial and camouflage, pre-May 1942 US cocardes with red centre and no fin flash. Another well-known image, showing NA-91s in the final stages of preparation, depicts Mk IA FD553 wearing RAF camouflage, RAF fin flash and US cocardes of the post-May 1942 type.

US Army

Contemporary national markings were added to the US Army's P-51s at the factory – these consisted of a white star on an Insignia Blue disc on the fuselage and the upper left and lower right wings. Those on the wings were 35in diameter and placed 55.5in from the wing tip, at an eighth span, the star pointing forwards. The fuselage insignia was 40in diameter and centred 48in from the tail joint, the star aligned with the skin panels in that region.

A-36As differed in some respects. National markings on the fuselage were 5in smaller in diameter, at 30in, and were 11in further forward, at 57in from the tail section joint.

In June 1943, a modified markings scheme added a white bar, half the width of the disc either side of the cocarde, and the whole marking was outlined in Insignia Red. From this time they were added to all US Mustangs in the field, and at the factory for late-production P-51As. The top edge of each bar was continued from the horizontal line across the star, and the bars' depth was equal to one quarter of the disc's diameter.

In August–September 1943, national markings were modified to the Type 4 standard by altering the red border to Insignia Blue, the same colour as the disc itself (though in practice, where fresh paint was applied over a faded marking, the blue disc showed up as a distinctly different tone to that of the blue border).

Squadron/Individual ID Letters

RAF

At the same time as the Sky fuselage band was introduced (December 1940), the colour of code letters was changed to match. As these were applied to Mustangs at squadrons, they were generally of the correct colour and size (as opposed to factory-applied markings and colours). However, the non-standard placement of fuselage roundels sometimes meant the code letters were placed in an unconventional way – for example, with one letter ahead of the cockpit. These letters were generally 24in or 30in in height.

Initially, aircraft wore three-letter codes typical to most operational RAF aircraft with a two-letter squadron identifier and a single-digit individual aircraft letter. From Autumn 1942, however, the squadron code letters on operational aircraft were removed, leaving only a single individual aircraft letter.

US Army

As with RAF aircraft, US P-51s and A-36As had the individual aircraft serial added at the factory. For fighters of the time, this was usually applied to the fin and rudder. However, on the Mustang, serials were applied to the rear fuselage instead, in 10in characters, with their axis aligned with the fuselage star.

On the 111th TRS's P-51s the bars introduced with the 1943 Type 3 Markings obliterated part of the serial, which was in some cases relocated to the fin/rudder in smaller characters. (Because of the A-36A's smaller national markings, the fuselage serial generally remained unscathed when the 1943 Type 3 markings were added.)

US forces did not have a single code format as with the RAF. The two fighter-bomber groups operating A-36As in the MTO, however, introduced their own code and recognition markings. The 27th FBG used one or two code letters on the fuselage (later with a white diagonal stripe on the fin), while the 86th FBG used two letters, one atop the other, on the fin.

Squadron flight and aircraft code letters were added by the 111th TRS (the only unit operating P-51s after the invasion of Sicily) from Autumn 1943.

Some Mustangs in the CBI theatre had coloured spinners or code letters locally applied. In this theatre, aircraft of the 23rd FG were in some cases applied with that unit's famous 'sharkmouth' emblem on the nose between around November 1943 and November 1944.

There were also unit markings in use for 'stateside' aircraft. Third Air Force III Tactical Air Division aircraft carried a three-digit 'buzz number', consisting of an individual aircraft letter, squadron number and field letter. Furthermore, aircraft used for training at Zephyrhills were given a white band at the front of the nose, which was a marking applied to most aircraft at the training school, not unlike the ETO recognition marking, but the spinner remained Olive Drab. A single code letter on the fin was generally applied.

Role-specific Markings
RAF

After December 1940, all RAF day fighters were required to have their spinner painted Sky. As delivered, RAF Mustangs' spinners were painted in Dark Earth. As with the camouflage scheme itself this took time to change on NA-73 aircraft that had been accepted into squadron service without the change having been made. (It has been suggested that pilots disliked the Sky spinner as it made the aircraft easier to spot at low level.) An 18in Sky fuselage band was also introduced in December 1940, but like the newer camouflage colours and the Sky spinner, this was never applied at the NAA factory. It was applied to aircraft in the UK, before delivery for most NA-83 and NA-91 aircraft, and remained until Second 2 TAF aircraft began to remove it in January 1945.

On 1 July 1942, Fighter Command aircraft were required to have a 6in yellow stripe painted on the wing leading edges. Some Mustang squadrons painted these from just inboard of the wing tip to just inboard of the guns, whereas others applied the stripe to the entire leading edge.

RAF aircraft sometimes had a 'sighting mark', a small white line, painted on the trailing edge of the port wing to help them line up the target for oblique photography.

Special Operation and Theatre Markings
RAF

On 1 July 1942, the Air Ministry instructed that additional recognition markings be applied to Mustangs, which had been mistaken for German aircraft on a number of occasions by home defence forces. These markings consisted of a 12in yellow band painted chordwise just inboard of the aileron. (Some squadrons are said to have applied narrower bands, while others took some time to implement the order.) On 1 December 1942, it was ordered that the chordwise bands be deleted.

US Army

Variations on the factory-applied colour scheme were sometimes introduced at unit level and in theatre for recognition or identification.

Additional recognition markings were applied to P-51s and A-36s shortly after arriving in North Africa. The fuselage markings were outlined in Identification Yellow (or British equivalent), and wing bands similar to the short-lived RAF markings were applied in the same colour. These were 15–18in thick and applied between the outer gun and the inboard edge of the aileron. A US flag was painted across the fin and rudder as an additional recognition aid. These markings were discontinued by April 1943. CBI-based aircraft do not appear to have worn the yellow wing bands.

F-6Bs in the ETO were given a white spinner and the front part of the nose, the rear edge probably corresponding with the panel line of the cowling 'ring' at that point. They were applied with a corresponding chordwise white band similar to the yellow bands mentioned above. These aircraft wore RAF-style squadron codes, with a two-letter unit code such as 'AX' for the 107th Squadron, and an individual aircraft letter, arranged either side of the star marking. The codes were applied in yellow and used US-style angled characters.

The most distinctive P-51A recognition marking was the five diagonal white stripes worn on the rear fuselage of 1st Air Commando machines in the CBI theatre. Photographs show that the thickness and angle of the stripes varied from aircraft to aircraft. Additionally, a horizontal white stripe of approximately 12in thickness was painted across the fin and rudder.

One-off Colour Schemes

During its initial 'roll out', the NA-73X appeared in all-over bare polished aluminium. (Photographs of the aircraft in its initial rollout condition have appeared in a number of retouched versions showing variations on AAC markings and one version with RAF roundels.) However, it is unlikely that any markings were added before its November 1940 crash, other than the aircraft's registration applied in large black characters above the starboard wing and below the port wing, which was also worn on the rudder.

Some changes to the aircraft's external appearance were made before it was ready to fly again in January 1941. A tapering, black, anti-glare panel had been painted onto the upper nose cowling, and Army Air Corps stripes were painted on the rudder. Unlike the earlier retouched images, the photographs showing AAC stripes on the repaired NA-73X can be reasonably assumed to be genuine, as the same marks and discoloration on the rudder appear on several different photographs. No other contemporary US national markings are believed to have been added.

RAF

The A-36s of 1437 Strategic Reconnaissance Flight, RAF retained the basic US camouflage of Olive Drab over Neutral Gray. Initially, the aircraft continued to wear their US serial, though later RAF serials were assigned and painted on the rear fuselage. A single white code letter (A–F) was applied behind the cockpit. RAF roundels were applied in the customary six positions on the wings and fuselage. Some sources suggest that these aircraft were painted in RAF desert camouflage but the author has seen no evidence to corroborate this.

The P-51/F-6A aircraft operated by 225 Squadron were given a variation on the RAF desert colour scheme, though photographs are inconclusive as to how extensive the repainting was. The aircraft were evidently painted in a disruptive camouflage scheme, probably at squadron level rather than formally at a maintenance unit, as the fuselage roundel on aircraft 'WU-M' is of non-standard proportions. It is unclear whether the P-51s were fully repainted in Dark Earth, Middle Stone and Azure Blue. The alternatives are that the disruptive pattern was applied in Middle Stone, leaving the existing Olive Drab to form the darker colour. Equally, the underside may have been left in Neutral Gray.

These aircraft were not issued with RAF serials, and the squadron continued to refer to them by their full US serials or the last four digits thereof. It is therefore reasonable to assume that all or part of the US serial number was left on the rear fuselage, though again, photographs do not exist which show whether or not this was the case.

US Army

The two XP-51s were delivered in all-over silver/bare metal, apart from a semi-gloss black anti-glare panel on the upper cowling, which tapered to a point, unlike most USAAF single-seater, anti-glare panels which tended to be straight-sided. National markings were the 1921–42 Type 1 variety, consisting of rudder stripes and wing cocardes. A vertical blue stripe and 13 equally spaced horizontal red and white bars were applied on the rudder, even though this marking was in the process of being phased out. Cocardes with white stars with red centres on an Insignia Blue disc were applied above and below the wings. There were no fuselage national markings.

They later had 'Wright Field' logos applied on each side of the fuselage. This was a black arrowhead with 'WRIGHT' written on a white rectangle within. The serials 1038 and 1039 were painted in dark, possibly black, characters on the tail and below the exhaust stubs. Later, both aircraft were repainted in Olive Drab over Neutral Gray, with the serial rendered in yellow on the tail.

Two P-51s were used for 'confusion camouflage' experiments. The first of these was an F-6A (with full camera modification including clear blister behind the cockpit). It was earmarked for trials of a 'dazzle' style camouflage designed by Captain Paul Hexter. This was a black and white 'splinter' camouflage designed to break up the aircraft's outline and present lines of perspective different to those of its actual shape. It was intended to momentarily confuse an enemy observer as to the speed, distance and direction of the aircraft. Two versions were tried – initially, the dazzle pattern covered the entire surface of the aircraft apart from a narrow strip on the rear fuselage spine and an anti glare panel on the nose, which were both Olive Drab. Later, the upper surfaces of the wings were painted Olive Drab as well.

A second experiment took place with P-51 41-32375, which was painted to represent rounded tips to the wings and tail surfaces, a white 'background' and a heavy black outline. The results of both experiments are not known, but they did not progress further.

A single P-51 was evaluated by the US Navy. This was in very simple colours, consisting of natural metal/silver all over, apart from national markings and a dark, possibly black, anti-glare panel. National markings were Type 4 design with bars, worn on the fuselage and one on each wing, above the left and below the right.

The two XP-51Js, 44-76027 and 44-76028, were overall bare metal/silver, with Type 4 national markings. They wore their serial numbers in black, low across the fin and rudder, and had a black anti-glare panel on the nose. The spinners appear to have been painted white.

Select Bibliography

Atwood, J. L., 'The P-51 The Real Story – Rebuttal', *Journal of the American Aviation Historical Society*, Summer 1997

Craven, W. F. and Cate, J. L., *The Army Air Forces in WW2*, Vol. 1, Office of Air Force History, Washington, D.C. (1949)

Ethell, J. L., *Mustang: a documentary history of the P-51*, Jane's, London (1981)

Futrell, R. F., *Command of Observation Aviation: A study in control of tactical airpower* (USAF Historical Studies No. 24), USAF Historical Division, Research Studies Institute, Air University, Alabama (1956)

Gruenhagen, R. W., *Mustang: The Story of the P-51 Fighter*, Arco, New York (1976)

Hansen, J. R., *The Wind and Beyond: A documentary journey into the history of aerodynamics in America*, NASA, Washington, D.C. (2003)

Horkey, H., 'The P-51 The Real Story', *Journal of the American Aviation Historical Society*, Fall 1996

Ludwig, P. A., *P-51 Mustang: Development of the Long Range Escort Fighter*, Classic Publications, Surrey (2003)

Meekcoms, K. J., *The British Air Commission and Lend-Lease*, Air-Britain (Historians), Kent (2001)

Jacobs, E. N., *Preliminary report on laminar-flow airfoils and new methods adopted for airfoil and new methods adopted for airfoil and boundary-layer investigations*, National Advisory Committee for Aeronautics, (1939)

Smith, P. C., *Straight Down!: The A-36 Dive Bomber in Action*, Crecy Publishing, Cheshire (2000)

Van Wagner, R. D., '1st Air Commando Group: Any Time, Any Place, Any Where', Military History Series 86-1, USAF Air Command and Staff College, 1986

Wagner, R., *Mustang Designer: Edgar Schmued and the P-51*, Smithsonian Institution Press, Washington (1990)

Whitney, D. D., *Vee's for Victory!: The Story of the Allison V-1710 Aircraft Engine 1929–1948*, Schiffer Publishing Ltd, Atglen (1998)

Whitney, D. D. 'Supercharging the Allison: A Presentation to the Aircraft Engine Historical Society', 17 July 2009

Endnotes

Chapter 1: The Path to the Mustang

1. War Cabinet and Cabinet: Memoranda (GT, CP and G War Series). 'Memorandum. Former Reference: CP 316 (37). Defence Expenditure in Future Years. Author: Thomas W. H. Inskip', National Archives under CAB 24/273, December 1937

2. War Cabinet and Cabinet: Memoranda (GT, CP and G War Series). 'Memorandum. Former Reference: CP 109 (38). Title: Anglo-French Conversations. Author: Halifax', National Archives under CAB 24/276/36, 28–29 April 1938

3. War Cabinet and Cabinet: Memoranda (GT, CP and G War Series). 'Memorandum. Former Reference: CP 109 (38). Title: Anglo-French Conversations. Author: Halifax', National Archives under CAB 24/276/36, 28–29 April 1938

4. War Cabinet and Cabinet: Memoranda (GT, CP and G War Series). 'Memorandum. Former Reference: CP 177 (39). Title: Purchasing Commission in the United States of America and Canada. Author: E Leslie Burgin', ('Report on the mission by the Rt Hon Lord Riverdale of Sheffield, K.B.E., LL.D., to Washington, New York and Ottawa, August 1939'), National Archives under CAB 24/288/26, 26 August 1939

5. War Cabinet and Cabinet: Minutes (WM and CM Series). WM Series. Cabinet Conclusions. Record Type: Conclusion. Former Reference: WM (40) 124. ('Conclusions of a meeting of the War Cabinet held at 10 Downing St, SW1, on Thursday May 16, 1940 at 11.30 am'), National Archives under CAB 65/7/19, 16 May 1940

6. Wagner, Ray, *Mustang Designer: Edgar Schmued and the P-51*, Smithsonian Institution Press, Washington (1990), p. 51

7. Atwood, J. L., 'The P-51 The Real Story – Rebuttal', *Journal of the American Aviation Historical Society*, Summer 1997, p. 108

8. Wagner, Ray, *Mustang Designer: Edgar Schmued and the P-51*, Smithsonian Institution Press, Washington (1990), p. 78

9. Atwood, J. L., 'The P-51 The Real Story – Rebuttal', *Journal of the American Aviation Historical Society*, Summer 1997, p. 108

10. National Advisory Committee for Aeronautics, *Preliminary report on Laminar-flow airfoils and new methods adopted for airfoil and boundary-layer investigations*, June 1939

11. Meredith, F. W., Note on the Cooling of Aircraft Engines with Special Reference to Ethylene Glycol Radiators Enclosed in Ducts, R&M No.1683, British ARC, 1936

12. Meekcoms, K. J., *The British Air Commission and Lend-Lease*, Air-Britain (Historians), Kent (2001), p. 24

13. See Atwood, J. L., 'The P-51 The Real Story – Rebuttal', *Journal of the American Aviation Historical Society*, Summer 1997, and Horkey, H., 'The P-51 The Real Story', *Journal of the American Aviation Historical Society*, Fall 1996

14. Dearborn, C. H. and Silverstein, A., Drag Analysis of Single-Engine Military Airplanes Tested In The NACA Full-Scale Wind-Tunnel, Langley Memorial Aeronautical Laboratory Langley Field, Va., NACA October 1940

15. Hansen, James R., 'The Wind and Beyond: A documentary journey into the history of aerodynamics Volume II: Reinventing the Airplane', (Document 4-26 c), NASA, pp. 887–8

16. GALCIT Report #286, 'Wind tunnel tests on a ¼ scale model of the NA-73', (referred to in Wagner, Ray *Mustang Designer: Edgar Schmued and the P-51*, Smithsonian Institution Press (1990) p. 57)

17. Hansen, James R., *The Wind and Beyond: A documentary journey into the history of aerodynamics Volume II: Reinventing the Airplane*, NASA, Washington, D.C. (2003) p. 883

18. Ibid., Document 4-26(a), p. 885

19. Ibid., Document 4-26(b), p. 887

20. Ibid., Document 4-26(c), p. 888

21. Whitney, Daniel D., *Vee's for Victory!: The Story of the Allison V-1710 Aircraft Engine 1929–1948*, Schiffer Publishing Ltd. p. 264

22. Horkey, Edward, 'The P-51 The Real Story', *Journal of the American Aviation Historical Society*, Fall 1996, p. 180

Chapter 2: The Mustang Finds Its Niche

1. War Department AAF Materiel Command, 'Final Report of Inspection Performance and Acceptance of North American Airplane Model XP-51', Dayton Ohio, July 1942

2. Wagner, Ray, *Mustang Designer: Edgar Schmued and the P-51*, Smithsonian Institution Press, Washington (1990) p. 51

3. Ethell, Jeffrey L., *Mustang: a documentary history of the P-51*, Jane's, London (1981) p. 15

4. Army Air Forces Technical Report, 'Final Report of Inspection, Performance and Acceptance of North American Airplane Model XP-51', 15 July 1942

5. White, Maurice D., Hoover, Herbert, H. and Garris, Howard, W., 'Flying qualities and stalling characteristics of North American XP-51 airplane' (AAF No. 41-38), April 1943, p. 4

6. Air Ministry and Ministry of Defence, 'Royal Air Force Overseas Commands: Reports and Correspondence. A.O.C. in C. MIDDLE EAST. British Army co-operation tactical employment of Mustang aircraft: report' National Archives under AIR 23/7323, 31 December 1943

7. Air Ministry, and Ministry of Defence: Papers accumulated by the Air Historical Branch. 'DIRECTORATE OF AIR TACTICS. Air Fighting Development Unit: report on Mustang I aircraft', National Archives under AIR 20/3620, 5 May 1942

8. War Cabinet and Cabinet: Minutes (WM and CM Series). WM Series. Cabinet Conclusions. Record Type: Conclusion. Former Reference: WM (39) 75. ('Conclusions of a Meeting of the War Cabinet held at 10 Downing Street, on Wednesday, November 8, 1939'), National Archives under CAB 65/2/9, 8 November 1939 (see also CAB 66/3/10 and CAB 66/3/11, 'Air Requirements for the Army')

9. Ibid.

10. Futrell, Robert F, *Command of Observation Aviation: A study in control of tactical airpower* (USAF Historical Studies No.24), USAF Historical Division, Research Studies Institute, Air University, Alabama, September 1956, p. 6

11. Hall, David I., *Strategy for Victory: The Development of British Tactical Air Power, 1919–1943*, Praeger Publishers Inc, Weatport (2008) p. 62

12. Ibid.

13. COS(41)89(O) 'Army Air Requirements' War Cabinet and Cabinet: Chiefs of Staff Committee: Memoranda, 30 May 41, National Archives under CAB 80/57

14. Ibid.

Chapter 3: Challenges and Opportunities

1. Cate, J. L., 'Plans, Policies, and Organization', from Craven, W. F. and Cate, J. L., *The Army Air Forces in WW2*, Vol. 1, Office of Air Force History (1949) p. 565

2. Mortensen, Daniel R., *A Pattern for Joint Operations: World War II Close Air Support North Africa* (1987) p. 18

3. Watson, Richard L., 'Pearl Harbor and Clark Field', from Craven, W. F. and Cate, J. L. *The Army Air Forces in WW2*, Vol. 1, Office of Air Force History (1949) p. 198

4. Ibid., p. 284

5. Smith, Peter C., *Vengeance!: The Vultee Vengeance Dive Bomber*, Airlife (1986), p. 41

6. Ludwig, Paul A., *P-51 Mustang: Development of the Long Range Escort Fighter*, p. 130

7. Ibid., p. 74

8. North American Aviation drawing N32000, Inglewood California, 3 May 1942

9. Ludwig, Paul A., *P-51 Mustang: Development of the Long Range Escort Fighter*, p. 75

10. Ibid., pp. 75–6

Chapter 4: Preparing for Service

1. Air Ministry, 'Army Co-operation Command: Registered Files. Re-arming of Squadrons with Mustang aircraft', National Archives under AIR 39/111

2. Air Ministry and Ministry of Defence, 'Royal Air Force Overseas Commands: Reports and Correspondence. A.O.C. in C. MIDDLE EAST. British Army co-operation tactical employment of Mustang aircraft: report' National Archives under AIR 23/7323, 31 December 1943

3. Ibid.

4. Ibid.

5. Air Ministry and successors: Operations Record Books, Squadrons. 'No. 414 SQUADRON (RCAF) Operations Record Books' 1 September 1941–31 December 1943, National Archives under AIR 27/1809

6. Ian Clarke, report of several conversations with his father Freddy (Flt Lt) Clarke, www.acesofww2.com

7. Hollis F. Hills, 'Mustangs at Dieppe', p. 3 (unpublished manuscript reproduced at acesofww2.com/can/aces/Hills.htm)

8. Huston, John W., *American Airpower Comes of Age: General Henry H. "Hap" Arnold's World War II Diaries*, Vol. 1, Air Univ Press Maxwell AFB AL

9. Ministry of Supply: Establishment, Registered Files (Series 1). 'Type biographies and sources. Mustang aircraft' (Fortnightly Mtgs between M.A.P. and A.M. re Mustang with Merlin 61 engines) National Archives under AVIA 46/132

10. Proof Department, Tactical Combat Section Army Air Forces Proving Ground Command Eglin Field, Florida, 'Final Report on Tactical Suitability of the P-51 Type Airplane' 30 December 1942

11. Horkey, H., 'The P-51 The Real Story', *Journal of the American Aviation Historical Society*, Fall 1996, p. 181–2

12. Proof Department, Tactical Combat Section Army Air Forces Proving Ground Command Eglin Field, Florida, 'Final Report on Tactical Suitability of the P-51 Type Airplane' 30 December 1942

13. Photographic Laboratory, Experimental Engineering Section, Material Center, Wright Field 'P-51 equipped with cameras for air support operations' 24 August 1942

14. Futrell, Robert F., *Command of Observation Aviation: A study in control of tactical airpower* (USAF Historical Studies No. 24), USAF Historical Division, Research Studies Institute, Air University, Alabama September 1956, p. 23

15. Proof Department, Army Air Forces Proving Ground Command, Eglin Field, Florida, 'Final Report on Operational Suitability of the A-36 Type Airplane', 15 April 1943 (Quoted in Smith, P. C., *Straight Down!: The A-36A Dive Bomber in Action*, Crecy Publishing, Cheshire (2000) p. 27)

16. Mediterranean Allied Air Forces: Microfilmed Files. MEDITERRANEAN ALLIED TACTICAL AIR FORCE (MATAF). (North West Africa)

April–May 1943, ('Northwest African Air Forces Tactical Bulletin No. 23. The A-36 (Mustang Fighter-Bomber) in North Africa' July 1943), National Archives under AIR 51/4, 31 December 1943

17. Air Ministry: Fighter Command: Registered Files. Day Fighter aircraft requirements: Spring 1943. ('8B Minutes of conference 20 July 1942 Held at HQ 11 Group'), National Archives under AIR 16/329

18. Ministry of Supply, 'Aircraft Data Sheets and Photographs. United States of America types', Mustang I Card 3, National Archives under SUPP 9/2, 10 July 1943

19. Birch, David, *Rolls-Royce and the Mustang* (Rolls-Royce Heritage Trust Historical Series), Rolls-Royce Heritage Trust (1987), pp. 65–67

20. Air Ministry and Ministry of Defence, 'Royal Air Force Overseas Commands: Reports and Correspondence. A.O.C. in C. MIDDLE EAST. British Army co-operation tactical employment of Mustang aircraft: report' National Archives under AIR 23/7323, 31 December 1943

21. Air Ministry: Army Co-operation Command, Re-arming of Squadrons with Mustang aircraft, National Archives under AIR 39/111, May 1942–March 1943

22. Air Ministry, and Ministry of Defence: Papers accumulated by the Air Historical Branch. 'DIRECTORATE OF AIR TACTICS. Air Fighting Development Unit: report on Mustang I aircraft', (Addendum on P-51A based on information from a report of 8 June 1943 from USAAF School of Applied Tactics, Orlando, Florida), National Archives under AIR 20/3620, 5 May 1942

Chapter 5: Army Co-operation Command Rides On

1. Rohmer, Richard, *Generally speaking: the memoirs of Major-General Richard Rohmer*, Dundurn Press (2004) p. 66

2. Nesbit, R. C., *The Eyes of the RAF: A History of Photo-Reconnaissance*, Sutton (2003) p. 186

3. Air Ministry and Ministry of Defence, 'Royal Air Force Overseas Commands: Reports and Correspondence. A.O.C. in C. MIDDLE EAST. British Army co-operation tactical employment of Mustang aircraft: report' National archives under AIR 23/7323, 31 December 1943

4. War Cabinet and Cabinet: Chiefs of Staff Committee: Memoranda, 'THE ORGANISATION OF THE R.A.F. FOR CONTINENTAL OPERATIONS. Memorandum by the Chief of Air Staff', 29 April 1943, National Archives under CAB 80/69/24

5. Air Ministry and Ministry of Defence, 'Royal Air Force Overseas Commands: Reports and Correspondence. A.O.C. in C. MIDDLE EAST. British Army co-operation tactical employment of Mustang aircraft: report' National Archives under AIR 23/7323, 31 December 1943

6. '34 Wing: An Unofficial History' www.34wing.co.uk

7. Air Ministry: Allied Expeditionary Air Force, later Supreme Headquarters Allied Expeditionary Force (Air), and 2nd Tactical Air Force: Registered Files and Reports. '2ND TACTICAL AIR FORCE: Tactical Reconnaissance, 1944-1945: report', National Archives under AIR 37/54, 31 December 1945

Chapter 6: North Africa and the Mediterranean
1. Kalinowski, Francis S, II 'The History of the 154th (Observation, Tactical, Reconnaissance), Weather Reconnaissance Squadron (Medium) 1940–1945', 15th Air Force Website (www.15thaf.org) 2011, p.8
2. 111th Reconnaissance Squadron 'World War II Narrative History', Part VI www.texasmilitaryforcesmuseum.org
3. Ibid.
4. Air Ministry and Ministry of Defence, 'Royal Air Force Overseas Commands: Reports and Correspondence. A.O.C. in C. MIDDLE EAST. British Army co-operation tactical employment of Mustang aircraft: report' National Archives under AIR 23/7323, 31 December 1943
5. 525th Fighter Bomber Squadron, entries from 'The History of the 525th Fighter Squadron', extracted by the Air Force Historical Research Agency, published at www.86fighterbombergroup.com
6. Mediterranean Allied Air Forces: Microfilmed Files. MEDITERRANEAN ALLIED TACTICAL AIR FORCE (MATAF). (North West Africa) April-May 1943, ('Northwest African Air Forces Tactical Bulletin No. 23. The A-36 (Mustang Fighter-Bomber) in North Africa' July 1943), National Archives under AIR 51/4, 31 December 1943
7. Ibid.
8. 527th Fighter Bomber Squadron War Diary, published by the Air Force Historical Research Agency, reproduced at www.86fighterbombergroup.com

Chapter 7: The 'Underbelly of the Axis'
1. 526th Fighter Bomber Squadron War Diary, published by the Air Force Historical Research Agency, reproduced at www.86fighterbombergroup.com

Chapter 8: China-Burma-India
1. War Cabinet and Cabinet: Memoranda (GT, CP and G War Series). 'Memorandum. Former Reference: CP 316 (37). Defence Expenditure in Future Years. Author: Thomas W H Inskip', National Archives under CAB 24/273, December 1937
2. Weaver, Herbert and Bowen, Lee, 'China-Burma-India, from The Pacific: Guadalcanal to Saipan August 1942 to July 1944', in Craven, W. F. and Cate, J. L. *The Army Air Forces in WW2*, Vol.1, Office of Air Force History, Washington, D.C. (1949) p. 421

3. Torres, Major John J., 'Historical Analysis of the 1st Air Commando Group Operations in the CBI Theatre August 1943 to May 1944' (Research paper presented to the research department Air Command and Staff College), p. 2

4. Arnold, General H. H., 'The Aerial Invasion of Burma', *The National Geographic Magazine*, Vol. LXXXVI No. 2, August 1944, p. 129

5. Ibid. pp. 129–130

6. Van Wagner, R. D., '1st Air Commando Group: Any Time, Any Place, Any Where', Military History Series 86-1, USAF Air Command and Staff College, 1986, pp. 35–36

7. Smith, Peter C., *Straight Down!: The North American A-36 Dive Bomber In Action*, Crecy Publishing , Cheshire (2000) p. 139

8. Van Wagner, R.D., '1st Air Commando Group: Any Time, Any Place, Any Where', Military History Series 86-1, USAF Air Command and Staff College, 1986, p. 48

9. Weaver, Herbert and Bowen, Lee, 'China-Burma-India, from The Pacific: Guadalcanal to Saipan August 1942 to July 1944', in Craven, W. F. and Cate, J. L., *The Army Air Forces in WW2*, Vol. 1., Office of Air Force History, Washington, D.C. (1949) pp. 466–67

10. Ibid., p. 467

11. Ibid., p. 533

12. Ibid., p. 423

13. Ibid., p. 475

14. Ibid., p. 477

15. Ibid., pp. 481–2

16. Chindits Special Force Burma website '1st Air Commando', http://www.chindits.info/Thursday/AirCommando.htm

17. Michalke, J., '1st Special Operations Wing, Hurlburt Field, Florida – Commando Heritage', 1st Special Operations Wing, Office of History, p. 6

18. Arnold, General H. H., 'The Aerial Invasion of Burma', *The National Geographic Magazine*, Vol. LXXXVI No. 2, August 1944, p. 143

19. Van Wagner, R. D., '1st Air Commando Group: Any Time, Any Place, Any Where', Military History Series 86-1, USAF Air Command and Staff College, 1986, p. 76

20. Air Ministry and Ministry of Defence: Royal Air Force Overseas Commands: Reports and Correspondence. AIR COMMAND SOUTH-EAST ASIA. 'Employment of Air Commando Groups', (South-East Asia Command, Cypher Message from Mountbatten to Churchill, relevant extracts repeated JSM Washington 17 March 1944) National Archives under AIR 23/2267 31 December 1945

21. Weaver, Herbert and Bowen, Lee, 'China-Burma-India, from The Pacific: Guadalcanal to Saipan August 1942 to July 1944', in Craven, W. F. and Cate, J. L., *The Army Air Forces in WW2*, Vol. 1., Office of Air Force History, Washington, D.C. (1949) pp. 503–4

22. Van Wagner, R. D., '1st Air Commando Group: Any Time, Any Place, Any Where', Military History Series 86-1, USAF Air Command and Staff College, 1986, p. 64

23. Ibid., p. 84

24. Ibid.

25. Ibid., p. 87

26. Air Ministry and Ministry of Defence: Royal Air Force Overseas Commands: Reports and Correspondence. AIR COMMAND SOUTH-EAST ASIA. 'Employment of Air Commando Groups', (South-East Asia Command, Letter from Air Marshal G. Garrod to Air Vice Marshal J. W. Baker 12 July 1944), National Archives under AIR 23/2267

Chapter 9: 'Fortress Europe'

1. Air Ministry and successors: 'Operations Record Books, Squadrons. No 400 Squadron RCAF (Royal Canadian Air Force): Operations Record Book', Covering dates: February 1940–July 1945, National Archives under AIR 27/1770

2. Rohmer, Richard, *Generally speaking: the memoirs of Major-General Richard Rohmer*, Dundurn Press (2004) pp. 101–102

3. Rodgers, David P., 'The camera was their weapon', *Army*, Vol. 47, No.1, 1 April 1997, p. 53

4. Maurer, M., *Air Force Combat Units of WW2*, Office of Air Force History, Washington D.C. (1983) p. 133

5. Hill, Steven D., 'Invasion! Fortress Europe – Naval Aviation in France, Summer 1944', *Naval Aviation News* May–June 1994

6. Air Ministry and successors: 'Operations Record Books, Squadrons. Squadron Number: 414 RCAF (Royal Canadian Air Force) Records of Events: Y, June 1944. National Archives under AIR 27/1810/12

7. Rohmer, Richard, 'Generally speaking: the memoirs of Major-General Richard Rohmer', Dundurn Press 2004, p. 108

8. Ibid., pp. 11–12

9. Ibid., p. 12

10. Air Ministry: Allied Expeditionary Air Force, later Supreme Headquarters Allied Expeditionary Force (Air), and 2nd Tactical Air Force: Registered Files and Reports. '2ND TACTICAL AIR FORCE: Tactical Reconnaissance, 1944–1945: report', National Archives under AIR 37/54, 31 December 1945

11. Air Ministry and successors: 'Operations Record Books, Squadrons. No. 26 SQUADRON. Operations Record Books. No 26 Squadron: Operations Record Book. With appendices', Covering dates: January 1944–December 1945, National Archives under AIR 27/319

12. Simpson, Bill, *Spitfire Dive Bombers Versus the V2*, Pen and Sword (2007) pp. 136–7

Chapter 10: Loose Ends

1. Ministry of Supply: Establishment, Registered Files (Series 1). 'Type biographies and sources. Mustang aircraft', ('Fortnightly Mtgs between MAP and AM re Mustang with Merlin 61 engines: Production of new aircraft types'), National Archives under AVIA 46/132, 31 December 1944

2. Ministry of Supply and Ministry of Aircraft Production: 'North American Supply Missions, Second World War, Files. BRITISH AIR COMMISSION. Commodities. Packard-Merlin Mustang aircraft', National Archives under AVIA 38/882, 19 November 1942

3. Air Ministry and Ministry of Defence, 'Royal Air Force Overseas Commands: Reports and Correspondence. A.O.C. in C. MIDDLE EAST. British Army co-operation tactical employment of Mustang aircraft: report' National archives under AIR 23/7323, 31 December 1943

4. Air Ministry: Allied Expeditionary Air Force, later Supreme Headquarters Allied Expeditionary Force (Air), and 2nd Tactical Air Force: Registered Files and Reports. '2ND TACTICAL AIR FORCE: Tactical Reconnaissance, 1944-1945: report', National Archives under AIR 37/54, 31 December 1945

5. Whitney, Daniel D., *Vee's for Victory!: The Story of the Allison V-1710 Aircraft Engine, 1929-1948,* Schiffer Publishing Ltd, Atglen (1998) p. 188

6. Whitney, Daniel D. 'Supercharging the Allison: A Presentation to the Aircraft Engine Historical Society', 17 July 2009

7. www.airrace.com pages for 1947, 1948 and 1949

8. *The Official Guide to the Army Air Forces, the A-36A Preliminary Illustrated Parts Catalogue* (dated 15 March 1943) and *Standard List of Aircraft Names Approved by the Joint Aircraft Committee* (dated 1944).

Appendix 1: Technical Details

1. Secretary of the Air Force, 'Structural Repair Instructions for Airplanes Army Models A-36A, P-51, A, B, C, D, K and M, F-6B, C, D and K, and TF-51D, British Model Mustang', 30 June 1944 (revised 15 March 1952) p. 61

2. Air Ministry, 'Air Publication 2025A Pilot's Notes for Mustang MkI and MkIA Aeroplane' September 1941

3. Ibid.

4. Air Ministry, 'Air Publication 2025A&B Pilot's Notes for Mustang MkI Aircraft and Mustang MkIA Aircraft' 21 April 1944

5. Air Ministry, 'Aeroplane and Armament Experimental Establishment: Reports and Notes. Mustang aircraft: performance and handling trials', Weights, loading data and leading particulars, National Archives under AVIA 18/732, March 1942

6. Air Ministry, and Ministry of Defence: Papers accumulated by the Air Historical Branch. 'DIRECTORATE OF AIR TACTICS. Air Fighting Development Unit: report on Mustang I aircraft', National Archives under AIR 20/3620, 5 May 1942

7. Ministry of Supply, 'Aircraft Data Sheets and Photographs. United States of America types', Mustang I Card 3, National Archives under SUPP 9/2, 10 July 1943

8. Air Ministry and Ministry of Defence, 'Royal Air Force Overseas Commands: Reports and Correspondence. A.O.C. in C. MIDDLE EAST. British Army co-operation tactical employment of Mustang aircraft: report' National archives under AIR 23/7323, 31 December 1943

9. Air Ministry, 'Air Publication 2025A Volume 1: Service Instructions The Mustang I Aeroplane' (Preliminary Draft held by the RAF Museum, Hendon), 15 August 1941

10. Whitney, Daniel D., *Vee's for Victory!: The Story of the Allison V-1710 Aircraft Engine, 1929–1948*, Schiffer Publishing Ltd, Atglen (1998) p. 102

11. Air Ministry, 'Army Co-operation Command: Registered Files. Re-arming of Squadrons with Mustang aircraft', National Archives under AIR 39/111

12. Commanding General Army Air Forces, 'Erection and Maintenance Instructions for Army Model A-36A Airplane', 15 November 1943 (revised 25 October 1944), pp. 142–3